The Faber Book of
Comic Verse

also edited by Michael Roberts

THE FABER BOOK OF MODERN VERSE

The Faber Book of
COMIC
VERSE

Edited by
Michael Roberts

faber and faber

LONDON · BOSTON

First published in 1942
by Faber and Faber Limited
3 Queen Square London WC1N 3AU
Reprinted 1942, 1943, 1944 (twice), 1946, 1947,
1948, 1949, 1951, 1955, 1960 and 1968
This new and revised edition first published 1974
Reprinted 1980
Reissued 1989
Reprinted 1990

Printed in England by Clays Ltd, St Ives plc

ISBN 0–571–04833–1
ISBN 0–571–11263–3 Pbk

THE BEEHIVE INN, EAMONT BRIDGE

In this Hive we are all Alive
Good Liquor makes us Funny
If you be dry Step in and try
The Virtue of our Honey.

Preface

This collection of comic verse is intended to include nonsense, parody and comic satire, but not the more familiar comic songs and nursery rhymes. I have, in general, avoided 'light verse' or *vers de société*, and I have made no attempt to find suitable extracts from the longer poems of Chaucer, Skelton, Marvell, Dryden, Pope, Byron and Browning. Among long poems that are exclusively, continuously and irresistibly funny, Carroll's *Hunting of the Snark* is unique, and rather than chop it into mincemeat I have omitted it altogether.

Even with these arbitrary limitations, the field is ill-defined. The frontiers of comic verse are, at the best, shifting and uncertain. Light-hearted nonsense merges imperceptibly into fantastic and imaginative poetry; and comic poetry cannot be sharply distinguished from humorous ballads that depend for their effect more on the situation they describe than on their versification. It is not easy to distinguish between lyric poems that are intrinsically comic, and songs (such as *Father O'Flynn* and *Blaydon Races*) that go to a rollicking tune but are not outrageously funny in themselves; nor can any definite and final boundary be drawn between the satiric poem that ends in contemptuous or good-natured laughter and the more incisive satire that convicts its object (and sometimes its author) of culpable malice and stupidity. I can only say that I have chosen to draw my line somewhere between *Faradiddle Dyno* and *Hallo My Fancy*; between *If All the World were Paper* and

Tom O' Bedlam's Song; I have printed some of Gilbert's *Bab Ballads* but not the *Songs of a Savoyard*, *The Jackdaw of Rheims* but not *Get up and bar the Door*; I have included Mr Belloc's *Lines to a Don* but excluded his *Verses to a Lord*.

A collection ranging over three or four centuries of comic verse necessarily throws some light on the development of wit and humour—the subjects on which people find it necessary or possible to joke about vary from age to age—but, to use M. Bourget's distinction, I have preferred the actual to the historical. For that reason, some comic poems of considerable scholarly interest have been omitted—for example, Sir John Suckling's ingenious parody of Shakespeare, and Alexander Brome's *Palinode*, in which the poet offers to forsake the Muse for a business career (and foreshadows the light verse of a later age):

> *He that can buy and sell and cheat*
> *May quickly make a shift to get*
>   *His thousand pounds* per annum;
> *And purchase, without more ado*
> *The poems, and the poet too.*

In most of the poems I have followed the earliest available text, but once or twice I have preferred a later and improved reading to one earlier or more authentic. Thus I have printed the usual *Lines on Prince Frederick* though there is a much earlier version addressed to the family of Lord Chancellor Hyde, and I have printed the traditional version of Rochester's epigram on Charles II rather than the one beginning (in language that was even more insulting than it appears today): 'Here lies our mutton-eating King.'[1] In the lines describing Porson's visit to the Continent, I have preferred the reading that makes Professor Brunck occu-

[1] It may be worth mentioning that Charles, as usual, had the last word: 'My sayings are my own, my actions are my ministers'.'

pant of the Chair at Frankfort rather than the popular variant that places him at Strasbourg. The point is perhaps less important than it appears at first sight, for Porson never visited the Continent at all.

I have followed tradition in ascribing the lines on *An Austrian Army* to Alaric A. Watts, who, according to his son and biographer, contributed them to the *Literary Gazette* in 1820: there is, however, some evidence that they first appeared a few years earlier in *The Trifler*, a periodical written by the boys of Westminster School. The couplet on Cardinal Wolsey I have described as anonymous, though E. H. Barker (*Literary Anecdotes*, 1852) ascribes it to 'Mr Pitt, the translator of Virgil' (Christopher Pitt, 1699–1748). Southey's *March to Moscow* I have ruthlessly compressed. The well-known lines on Boston I have called anonymous in honour of the unknown Harvard man who drew their first rough draft; but they owe their present perfection to the protracted labours of Dr J. C. Bossidy (1860–1928), Dr S. C. Bushnell (1852–1930) and others. The lines on the amoeba, which appear anonymously in *Life*, by Sir Arthur Shipley, I have ascribed (on the authority of the Cambridge University Press) to Sir Arthur himself.

For permission to include copyright material, I offer my sincere thanks to the following authors, publishers, agents and authors' representatives:

For poems from *Balliol Rhymes*, to Basil Blackwell and Mott, Ltd.

For poems from *Sonnets and Verse* and from *Cautionary Verses*, by Hilaire Belloc, to the author and Gerald Duckworth and Co., Ltd.

For the Ballade by E. C. Bentley, to the author and Messrs A. P. Watt and Son. For poems from *Biography for Beginners*, to the same author and agents and to T. Werner Laurie, Ltd. For poems from *More Biography*, to the same author and agents and to Methuen and Co., Ltd.

11

For the quatrain by W. Bridges-Adams, to the author and Basil Blackwell and Mott, Ltd.

For the lines from the *Burgess Nonsense Book*, to Mr. Gelett Burgess and the Frederick A. Stokes Co.

For the poem from *Adamastor*, by Roy Campbell, to the author and to Faber and Faber, Ltd.

For poems from *The Collected Poems of G. K. Chesterton*, to the poet's executrix, to Messrs A. P. Watt and Son, and to Methuen and Co., Ltd. For *Anti-Christ*, by the same author, to the same executrix and agents, and to Burns Oates and Washbourne, Ltd.

For the poem by E. E. Cummings, to the author and to Harcourt Brace, and Co. Inc.

For the quatrain from *Thoughts without Words*, by Clarence Day, Jr, to the author and to Alfred A. Knopf, Inc.

For poems from *Old Possum's Book of Practical Cats*, by T. S. Eliot, to the author and Faber and Faber, Ltd.

For the poem from *The Gathering Storm*, by William Empson, to the author and to Chatto and Windus, Ltd.

For *Tony O*, by Colin Francis, to the author, to Walter de la Mare Esq., and to Constable and Co., Ltd.

For *Motor Bus* (from *Fifty Poems* by A. D. Godley) to the executors and the Oxford University Press.

For *Poetical Economy* (from *Deportmental Ditties* by Harry Graham) and for the poems from *Ruthless Rhymes* and *More Ruthless Rhymes*, to Mrs Graham, to Messrs A. P. Watt and Son, and to Edward Arnold and Co., Ltd.

For the poem by Robert Graves, to the author.

For the poem by Canon Gray, to the trustees and to Sheed and Ward, Ltd.

For two poems from *Premature Epitaphs*, by 'Kensal Green', to the author and Mr Cecil Palmer.

For the epigrams by G. R. Hamilton, to the author.

For the poem by Samuel Hoffenstein (from *Poems in Praise of Practically Nothing*), to the author and the Liveright Publishing Corporation.

12

For a poem from *Poems of Gerard Manley Hopkins*, to the poet's family and the Oxford University Press.

For *Infant Innocence*, by A. E. Housman, to the poet's executors and to Jonathan Cape, Ltd.

For the limerick by Professor Joad, to the author.

For the parodies from *The Table of Truth*, by Hugh Kingsmill, to the author, to Gilbert Wright, Ltd, and to Jarrolds (London) Ltd.

For the poem from *Departmental Ditties*, by Rudyard Kipling, to the poet's executrix, to Messrs A. P. Watt and Son, to Methuen and Co. Ltd., and to The Macmillan Co. of Canada.

For *Idealism*, by Mgr Ronald Knox, to the author and Messrs A. P. Watt and Son. For *Absolute and Abitofhell* (from *Essays in Satire*) to the same author and agents, and to Sheed and Ward, Ltd.

For *The Better Way* (from *Little Poems from the Greek* by Walter Leaf), to the author's executors and Mr Grant Richards.

For the parody by D. B. Wyndham Lewis (from *At the Green Goose*), to the author and to Hodder and Stoughton, Ltd.

For the quatrain by Hugh MacDiarmid, from *A Drunk Man Looks at the Thistle*, to the author and to William Blackwood and Sons, Ltd.

For the poems by Don Marquis, to Mrs Marquis and to Faber and Faber, Ltd.

For the poem by G. K. Menzies, to the author and the proprietors of *Punch*.

For the limerick by Ogden Nash (from *The Primrose Path*), to the author, to Curtis Brown, Ltd., and to John Lane, Ltd.

For a poem from *The Fivefold Screen*, by William Plomer, to the author and the Hogarth Press, Ltd.

For two poems from *Selected Poems* by Ezra Pound,

to the author, to Messrs Pearn, Pollinger and Higham, and to Faber and Faber, Ltd.

For the parody by Henry Reed, to the author and *The New Statesman and Nation*.

For the lines on the amoeba, from *Life* by Sir Arthur Shipley, to the Cambridge University Press.

For *The Horse*, by Naomi Royde Smith, to the author.

For an epigram by Sir John Squire, from *Poems in one Volume*, to the author, to Messrs A. P. Watt and Son, and to William Heinemann and Co., Ltd.

For *A Glass of Beer* (from *Collected Poems* by James Stephens), to the author and to Macmillan and Co., Ltd.

For *A Memory* (from *The Lowery Road* by L. A. G. Strong) and *The Brewer's Man* (from *Dublin Days* by the same author), to the author and to Basil Blackwell and Mott, Ltd.

For the poem from *The Lady is Cold*, by E. B. White, to the author and Harper and Brothers.

On the poems themselves, I have no comment to offer. This is neither the time nor the place for a serious discussion of the joke-evil and the dangers of using comedy in place of tragedy. I leave the reader to the simple pleasure of recognizing old acquaintances and of grudgingly admitting new, and to the more complex and perhaps greater pleasure of complaining that I have not, after all, unearthed his own private and unparalleled discovery.

1942   MICHAEL ROBERTS

14

Preface to the Second Edition

The first edition of *The Faber Book of Comic Verse* was
put together in a few months in the spring and summer
of 1941. Michael Roberts had just finished his *Recovery
of the West* (published by Faber in June of that year);
in the autumn he was to start work in the European
Services of the BBC. Meanwhile he was still Sixth
Form Master of the Royal Grammar School, Newcastle,
which since September 1939 had been in Penrith in
Cumberland. We were lucky to have our own books
with us in Penrith, and Michael was able to make an
occasional dash to Newcastle to tap the resources of
the Public Library and the Literary and Philosophical
Society; but he could not lay hands on several books
he wanted, including some early Ogden Nash. With
more books and more time available he could have
made a more thorough job of selection; but in the
summer of 1941 there were more things to worry about
than the thoroughness of an anthology of Comic Verse. It
was a lighthearted gesture in a not very lighthearted
time.

Indeed, much of the work involved looks a trifle
bizarre in the perspective of history. For instance, a
tremendous correspondence—about dates, and per-
mission to print—went on about Warham St Leger,
author of 'A False Gallop of Analogies', about whom
nothing was known except that in the 1880s he had
contributed to *Punch* and lived in Mortlake, then in
Kew. There was no racing at Doncaster in 1941 but the

hunt was up for St Leger. Ladies still in bombed London, and ladies bombed out of London, searched papers and pedigrees; a peer in Co. Cork sent family information across dangerous waters (letter opened by Censor): and this in August 1941 with the Germans nearing Moscow! They were even nearer when proofs came in October: I looked at Southey's 'March to Moscow': was this really the moment to give it a new run? Michael was more robust. If the Germans took Moscow, things would be so bad that nobody would care a damn about the anthology anyway; if they didn't, Southey's squib was all the more worth putting in.

One other poem certainly reflected the concerns of the time: Henry Reed's 'Chard Whitlow: Mr Eliot's Sunday Evening Postscript', for the Postscript—broadcast as far as I can remember on Sunday evenings after the 9 o'clock News—was as much a wartime institution as the playing of the National Anthems of the allies before the News. J. B. Priestley was the outstanding broadcaster; certainly Mr Eliot never delivered a Postscript except in Henry Reed's parody, which first appeared in a *New Statesman* competition, and won its original's accolade.

The years since publication have brought many corrections and alternative versions. Dunkeld, not Kilkell, has been claimed as the parish where they 'hangit the minister, droont the Precentor' ('Ech, sic a Pairish', p. 147); another version of the 'Beginning of an Undergraduate Poem' (p. 165) was found in a letter from Keats to Jane Reynolds; Sir Stephen Gaselee corrected the text of Canning's 'Political Despatch' (p. 98) from the original in the Foreign Office Library; Christopher Isherwood has been revealed as the author of 'The Common Cormorant or Shag' (p. 325). The anthologist's son Andrew, who later became an editor of *The Trifler* at Westminster School,

was able to confirm his father's statement that 'An
Austrian Army Awfully Arrayed' made its first appear-
ance in that periodical. Many readers offered discoveries
of their own; my favourite came from Monica Empson,
the work of an unknown poet discovered among her
grandfather's papers:

> 'Frank' said his angel
> 'March once more'.
> 'Yes' was the prompt reply.
> And then in far Somaliland
> He laid him down to die.

In this refurbished edition, some poems from the
later part have been dropped, to make room for new
material. I have now included a few that date back to
the 1920s, but which were not known to Michael
Roberts in 1941—Max Beerbohm's 'A Luncheon',
Thomas Hardy's 'A Refusal', which has a fresh irony
now that a Dean of Westminster *has* admitted Byron
to Poets' Corner—or, like some by Ogden Nash, not
then available. Otherwise, the additional poems are
post 1941. About their selection, I echo the remark in
the original introduction that 'the frontiers of comic
verse are, at the best, shifting and uncertain'. Like the
original selection, my additions are a highly personal
affair. I shall not pontificate on why I found them
comic; only admit to a fondness for the comic moments
of serious poets. New and topical themes are heard in
Peter Porter's 'Consumer's Report' and Edwin Morgan's
'The Computer's First Christmas Card', while Nash's
'Open Road' and Auden's 'Public Buildings' can surely
be called Poems of the Environment. But I was pleased
also to note, after I had made my selection, the return of
themes already stated: Lawrence Durrell celebrates the
Greek innkeeper Stavro in much the same spirits as
Burns celebrates John Dove, innkeeper of Mauchline;

Edwin Morgan plays with the place-names of Scotland
in 'Canedolia' as Robert Newell did with those of the
United States in 'The American Traveller'. Religion and
money continue to provide matter for comedy, in
poems by Nash, Betjeman, Frost and Dorothy Parker;
but the teaching of Eng. Lit.—see Amis, Burgess and
Ewart—seems rather to be replacing poets and poetry
as a favourite literary target. The last poem in the
refurbished anthology, as in the original one, was a
prize-winning entry in a *New Statesman* competition.
Leonard Cooper's 'Rhyming Prophecy' was for 1956;
it still seems all too topical. And the tail-piece, con-
cerned with sweetness and liquor, harks back to the
lines from the Beehive Inn, Eamont Bridge, which head
the whole collection.

For permission to include copyright material I thank
the following authors (or their representatives),
publishers and agents:

Kingsley Amis: 'Beowulf' from *A Case of Samples*,
Victor Gollancz Ltd.

W. H. Auden: 'Shorter Audens' from *Collected
Shorter Poems* 1966, *Homage to Clio* 1960 and *Academic
Graffiti* 1971, Faber and Faber Ltd.

Max Beerbohm: 'A Luncheon' from *Max in Verse* ed.
by J. G. Riewald, William Heinemann Ltd.

John Betjeman: 'In Westminster Abbey' from
Collected Poems, John Murray Ltd.

Anthony Burgess: 'Our Norman Betters', Deborah
Rogers Literary Agency Ltd. © Anthony Burgess.

Charles Causley: 'Betjeman 1984' from *Union
Street*, Rupert Hart-Davis Ltd. and David Higham
Associates.

Leonard Cooper: 'Rhyming Prophecy' from *Salome
Dear, Not in the Fridge* ed. Arthur Marshall, Allen &
Unwin.

Lawrence Durrell: 'Ballad of the Oedipus Complex',

19

Dorothy Parker: 'Partial Comfort' from *The Collected Dorothy Parker*, Duckworth, London, 1973; and from *The Portable Dorothy Parker*, Viking Press Inc. copyright 1928, © renewed 1956 by Dorothy Parker.

Peter Porter: 'A Consumer's Report' from *The Last of England* by Peter Porter © Oxford University Press 1970. Reprinted by permission of the publisher.

Stevie Smith: 'Person from Porlock' from *Selected Poems*, 'I Love the English Country Scene', 'Some are born to Peace and Joy' from *Frog Prince and Other Poems*, Longman Group Ltd.

Anne Tibble: 'Trials of a Tourist'.

John Updike: 'Apple' © 1958, 'Cog' © 1958 by John Updike; Jack' © 1957 by John Updike, and 'Mirror' © 1957 (both poems originally appeared in *The New Yorker*) by John Updike, 'Vacuum Cleaner' © 1958 by John Updike—all five from *Hoping for a Hoopoe*, Victor Gollancz Ltd. and Harper and Row Publishers Inc. 'Some Frenchmen' from *Midpoint*, Andre Deutsch Ltd. and Alfred A. Knopf Inc.

Douglas Young: 'Last Lauch' by permission of the literary executor of the late Douglas Young.

JANET ADAM SMITH

Index of Authors

(The authors of the Useful Couplets on p. 71, the Occasional Lapses on pp. 159–162, and the Potted Poems on p. 251, do not appear in this index)

21

Index of Authors

Index of Authors

Index of Authors

The Faber Book of
Comic Verse

BRING US IN GOOD ALE

Bring us in good ale, and bring us in good ale;
For our blessèd Lady sake bring us in good ale!

Bring us in no browne bred, for that is made of brane,
Nor bring us in no white bred, for therein is no gane,
   But bring us in good ale!

Bring us in no befe, for there is many bones,
But bring us in good ale, for that goth downe at ones,
   And bring us in good ale!

Bring us in no bacon, for that is passing fate,
But bring us in good ale, and gife us enought of that;
   And bring us in good ale!

Bring us in no mutton, for that is often lene,
Nor bring us in no tripes, for they be seldom clene,
   But bring us in good ale!

Bring us in no egges, for there are many schelles,
But bring us in good ale, and gife us nothing elles;
   And bring us in good ale!

Bring us in no butter, for therein are many heres,
Nor bring us in no pigges flesch, for that will make us
     bores,
   But bring us in good ale!

Bring us in no podinges, for therein is all Godes good,
Nor bring us in no venesen, for that is not for our blod;
   But bring us in good ale!

Bring us in no capons flesch, for that is ofte dere,
Nor bring us in no dokes flesch, for they slober in the
      mere,
   But bring us in good ale!

ANON

THESE WOMEN ALL

These women all,
Both great and small,
   Ar wavering to and fro,
Now her, now ther,
Now every wher:—
   But I will nott say so.

They love to range,
Ther myndes do chaunge;
   And maks ther frynd ther foe;
As lovers trewe
Eche daye they chewse new:—
   But I will nott say so.

They laughe, they smylle,
They do begyle,
   As dyce that men do throwe;
Who useth them mych
Shall never be ryche:—
   But I will nott say so.

Summe hot, sum cold,
Ther is no hold,

But as the wynd doth blowe;
When all is done,
They chaung lyke the moone:—
  But I will nott say so.

So thus one and other
Takith after ther mother,
  As cocke by kind doth crowe.
My song is ended,
The beste may be amended:—
  But I will nott say so.

HEATH

A WOMAN IS A WORTHY THING

I am as lighte as any roe
To preise womene where that I go.

To onpreise womene it were a shame,
For a woman was thy dame.
Our blessèd lady bereth the name
  Of all womene where that they go.

A women is a worthy thing;
They do the washe and do the wringe;
'Lullay, lullay!' she dothe thee singe;
  And yet she hath but care and wo.

A woman is a worthy wight;
She serveth a man both daye and night;
Thereto she putteth alle her might;
  And yet she hath but care and wo.

ANON

CAROL

My heart of gold as true as steel,
　As I me leanéd to a bough,
In faith but if ye love me well,
　Lord, so Robin lough!

My lady went to Canterbury,
　The saint to be her boot;
She met with Kate of Malmesbury:
　Why sleepest thou in an apple root?

Nine mile to Michaelmas,
　Our dame began to brew;
Michael set his mare to grass,
　Lord, so fast it snew!

For you, love, I brake my glass,
　Your gown is furred with blue;
The devil is dead, for there I was;
　Iwis it is full true.

And if ye sleep, the cock will crow,
　True heart, think what I say;
Jackanapes will make a mow,
　Look, who dare say him nay?

I pray you have me now in mind,
　I tell you of the matter;
He blew his horn against the wind;
　The crow goeth to the water.

Yet I tell you mickle more;
　The cat lieth in the cradle;
I pray you keep true heart in store;
　A penny for a ladle.

I swear by Saint Katherine of Kent,
　　The goose goeth to the green;
All our dogges tail is brent,
　　It is not as I ween

Tirlery lorpin, the laverock sang,
　　So merrily pipes the sparrow,
The cow brake loose, the rope ran home,
　　Sir, God give you good-morrow!

ANON

THE WIFE WHO WOULD A WANTON BE

All night I clatter upon my creed,
Prayand to God that I were dead;
　　Or else out of this world he were:
Then should I see for some remeid.
　　Wo worth marriage for evermair!

Ye should hear tell (an *he* were gane)
That I should be a wanton ane.
　　To learn the law of lovis layr
In our town like me should be nane.
　　Wo worth marriage for evermair!

I should put on my russet gown,
My red kirtill, my hose of brown,
　　And let them see my yellow hair
Under my kerchief hingand down.
　　Wo worth marriage for evermair!

Lovers both should hear and see,
I should love them that would love me;
　　Their hearts for me should ne'er be sair:
But aye unweddit should I be.
　　Wo worth marriage for evermair!

ANON

45

HOW THE FIRST HIELANDMAN WAS MADE

God and Saint Peter was gangand be the way
Heich up in Argyll where their gait lay.
Saint Peter said to God, in ane sport word—
'Can ye nocht mak a Hielandman of this horse turd?'
God turned owre the horse turd with his pykit staff,
And up start a Hielandman black as ony draff.
Quod God to the Hielandman, 'Where wilt thou now?'
'I will doun in the Lawland, Lord, and there steal a
    cow.'
'And thou steal a cow, carle, there they will hang thee.'
'What reck, Lord, of that, for anis mon I die.'
God then he leuch and owre the dyke lap,
And out of his sheath his gully outgat.
Saint Peter socht the gully fast up and doun,
Yet could not find it in all that braid roun.
'Now,' quod God, 'here a marvell, how can this be,
That I suld want my gully, and we here bot three.'
'Humf,' quod the Hielandman, and turned him about,
And at his plaid neuk the gully fell out.
'Fy,' quod Saint Peter, 'thou will never do weill;
And thou bot new made and sa soon gais to steal.'
'Humf,' quod the Hielandman, and sware be yon kirk,
'Sa lang as I may gear get to steal, I will never wirk.'

ANON

THE BEWTEIS OF THE FUTE-BALL

Brissit brawnis and broken banis,
Strife, discord, and waistis wanis,
Crookit in eild, syne halt withal—
Thir are the bewteis of the fute-ball.

ANON

46

FARA DIDDLE DYNO

Ha ha! Ha ha! This world doth pass
   Most merrily I'll be sworn,
For many an honest Indian ass
   Goes for a unicorn.
         Fara diddle dyno,
         This is idle fyno.

Tie hie! Tie hie! O sweet delight!
   He tickles this age that can
Call Tullia's ape a marmasyte
   And Leda's goose a swan.
         Fara diddle dyno,
         This is idle fyno.

So so! So so! Fine English days!
   For false play is no reproach,
For he that doth the coachman praise
   May safely use the coach.
         Fara diddle dyno,
         This is idle fyno.
               ANON

EPITAPH IN ST OLAVE'S, SOUTHWARK, ON MR MUNDAY

Hallowed be the Sabbaoth,
And farewell all worldly Pelfe;
The Weeke begins on Tuesday,
For Munday hath hang'd himselfe.

IN OBITUM PROMI

That Death should thus from hence our Butler catch,
Into my mind it cannot quickly sink;
Sure Death came thirsty to the Buttery Hatch
When he (that busy was) denied him drink.

Tut, 'twas not so; 'tis like he gave him liquor,
And Death, made drunk, took him away the quicker—
  Yet let not others grieve too much in mind,
  (The Butler gone) the keys are left behind.

HENRY PARROT

ON CARDINAL WOLSEY

Begot by Butchers, but by Bishops bred,
How high his honour holds his haughty head!

ANON

ON BOTCHING

God is no botcher, but when God wrought you two,
God wrought as like a botcher, as God might do.

JOHN HEYWOOD

TREASON

Treason doth never prosper—What's the reason?
If it doth prosper, none dare call it treason.

SIR JOHN HARINGTON

ALL THINGS HAVE SAVOUR

All things have savour, though some very small,
Nay, a box on the eare hath no smell at all.

ANON

ODD BUT TRUE

Oh that my Lungs could bleat like butter'd Pease;
But bleating of my lungs hath Caught the itch,
And are as mangy as the Irish seas
That doth ingender windmills on a Bitch.

I grant that Rainbowes being lull'd asleep,
Snort like a woodknife in a Lady's eyes;
Which makes her grieve to see a pudding creep,
For Creeping puddings only please the wise.

Not that a hard row'd herring should presume
To swing a tyth pig in a Cateskin purse;
For fear the hailstons which did fall at Rome,
By lesning of the fault should make it worse.

For 't is most certain Winter woolsacks grow
From geese to swans if men could keep them so,
Till that the sheep shorn Planets gave the hint
To pickle pancakes in Geneva print.

Some men there were that did suppose the skie
Was made of Carbonado'd Antidotes;
But my opinion is, a Whale's left eye,
Need not be coyned all King *Harry* groates.

The reason's plain, for Charon's Westerne barge
Running a tilt at the subjunctive mood,
Beckoned to Bednal Green, and gave him charge
To fasten padlockes with Antartic food.

The end will be the Mill ponds must be laded,
To fish for white pots in a Country dance;
So they that suffered wrong and were upbraded
Shall be made friends in a left handed Trance.

ANON

SONG

TO THE TUNE OF *CUCKOLDS ALL A-ROW*

Know then, my brethren, heaven is clear,
    And all the clouds are gone;
The righteous now shall flourish, and
    Good days are coming on:
Come then, my brethren, and be glad,
    And eke rejoice with me;
Lawn sleeves and rochets shall go down,
    And hey! then up go we!

We'll break the windows which the Whore
    Of Babylon hath painted,
And when the popish saints are down,
    Then Barrow shall be sainted.
There's neither cross nor crucifix
    Shall stand for men to see;
Rome's trash and trumperies shall go down,
    And hey! then up go we!

If once that Antichristian crew
    Be crush'd and overthrown,
We'll teach the nobles how to crouch,
    And keep the gentry down.
Good manners have an ill report,
    And turn to pride, we see;
We'll therefore cry good manners down,
    And hey! then up go we!

The name of lord shall be abhorr'd,
    For every man's a brother;
No reason why, in church or state,
    One man should rule another.

But when the change of government
    Shall set our fingers free,
We'll make the wanton sisters stoop,
    And hey! then up go we!

What though the King and Parliament
    Do not accord together,
We have more cause to be content,
    This is our sun-shine weather;
For if that reason should take place,
    And they should once agree,
Who would be in a Roundhead's case,
    For hey! then up go we!

What should we do then in this case,
    Let's put it to a venture,
If that we hold out seven years space,
    We'll sue out our indenture.
A time may come to make us rue,
    And time may set us free,
Except the gallows claim his due,
    For hey! then up go we!

ANON

THE DOWNFALL OF CHARING CROSS

Undone, undone the lawyers are,
    They wander about the towne,
Nor can find the way to Westminster,
    Now Charing-cross is downe:
At the end of the Strand, they make a stand,
    Swearing they are at a loss,
And chaffing say, that's not the way,
    They must go by Charing-cross.

51

The parliament to vote it down
    Conceived it very fitting,
For fear it should fall, and kill them all,
    In the house, as they were sitting.
They were told, god-wot, it had a plot,
    Which made them so hard-hearted,
To give command, it should not stand,
    But be taken down and carted.

But neither man, woman, nor child,
    Will say, I'm confident,
They ever heard it speak one word
    Against the parliament.
An informer swore, it letters bore,
    Or else it had been freed;
I'll take, in troth, my Bible oath,
    It could neither write, nor read.

The committee said, that verily
    To popery it was bent;
For ought I know, it might be so,
    For to church it never went.
What with excise, and such device,
    The kingdom doth begin
To think you'll leave them ne'er a cross,
    Without doors nor within.

Methinks the common-council should
    Of it have taken pity,
'Cause, good old cross, it always stood
    So firmly to the city.
Since crosses you so much disdain,
    Faith, if I were as you,
For fear the king should rule again,
    I'd pull down Tiburn too.

ANON

IF ALL THE WORLD WERE PAPER

If all the world were paper,
And all the sea were inke;
And all the trees were bread and cheese,
What should we do for drinke?

If all the world were sand 'o,
Oh, then what should we lack 'o:
If as they say there were no clay,
How should we make tobacco?

If all our vessels ran 'a,
If none but had a crack 'a;
If Spanish apes eat all the grapes,
What should we do for sack 'a?

If fryers had no bald pates,
Nor nuns had no dark cloysters,
If all the seas were beans and pease,
What should we do for oysters?

If there had been no projects,
Nor none that did great wrongs;
If fidlers shall turne players all,
What should we doe for songs?

If all things were eternall,
And nothing their end bringing;
If this should be, then how should we
Here make an end of singing?

ANON

HYE NONNY NONNY NOE

Downe lay the Shepherd Swaine
    so sober and demure
Wishing for his wench againe
    so bonny and so pure
With his head on hillock lowe
    and his arms akimboe,
And all was for the losse of his
    hye nonny nonny noe.

His Teares fell as thinne
    as water from the still,
His haire upon his chinne
    grew like Thyme upon a hill,
His cherry cheekes pale as snowe
    did testifye his mickle woe
And all was for the losse of his
    hye nonny nonny noe.

Sweet she was, as kind a love
    as ever fetter'd Swayne;
Never such a daynty one
    shall man enjoy again.
Sett a thousand on a rowe
    I forbid that any showe
Ever the like of her
    hye nonny nonny noe.

Face she had of Filberd hue
    and bosom'd like a Swan
Back she had of bended ewe,
    And wasted by a span.
Haire she had as black as Crowe
    from the head unto the toe
Downe downe all over her
    hye nonny nonny noe.

With her Mantle tuck't up high
   she foddered her flock
So bucksome and alluringly
   her knee upheld her smock
So nimbly did she use to goe,
   so smooth she danc't on tip-toe,
That all the men were fond of her
   hye nonny nonny noe.

She smiled like a Holy-day,
   and simpred like the Spring,
She pranck't it like a Popingaie,
   and like a Swallow sing:
She trip't it like a barren Doe,
   She strutted like a gor-crowe,
Which made the men so fond of her
   hye nonny nonny noe.

To sport it on the merry downe
   to daunce the Lively Haye,
To wrastle for a green gowne
   in heate of all the day.
Never would she say me no
   yet me thought I had tho
Never enough of her
   hye nonny nonny noe.

But gonne she is the prettiest lasse
   that ever trod on plaine.
What ever hath betide of her
   blame not the Shepherd Swayne
For why? she was her owne Foe,
   and gave herselfe the overthrowe
By being so franke of her
   hye nonny nonny noe.

ANON

THE COMMONS' PETITION
TO KING CHARLES II

In all humanity, we crave
Our Sovereign may be our slave;
And humbly beg, that he may be
Betrayed by us most loyally.

But if he please once to lay down
His Sceptre, Dignity, and Crown,
We'll make him, for the time to come,
The greatest Prince in Christendom.

THE KING'S ANSWER

Charles, at this time, having no need,
Thanks you as much as if he did.

JOHN WILMOT, EARL OF ROCHESTER

EPITAPH ON CHARLES II

Here lies our Sovereign Lord the King,
  Whose word no man relies on,
Who never said a foolish thing,
  Nor ever did a wise one.

JOHN WILMOT, EARL OF ROCHESTER

EPITAPH ON THE SECRETARY TO
THE MUSES

He's gone, and Fate admits of no return.
But whither is he gone? to's grave, no doubt;
Where, if there's any drink, he'll find it out.

JANE BARKER

SONG

Pious Selinda goes to prayers,
    If I but ask a favour;
And yet the tender fool's in tears,
    When she believes I'll leave her.

Would I were free from this restraint,
    Or else had hope to win her!
Would she could make of me a saint,
    Or I of her a sinner!

WILLIAM CONGREVE

SWEET SLUG-A-BED

Myrtilla, early on the lawn,
Steals roses from the blushing dawn,
But when Myrtilla sleeps till ten,
Aurora steals them back agen.

ANON

CLOË

Bright as the day, and like the morning fair,
Such Cloë is, and common as the air.

GEORGE GRANVILLE, LORD LANSDOWNE

DOCTOR FELL

I do not love thee, Doctor Fell,
The reason why I cannot tell,
But this one thing I know full well:
I do not love thee, Doctor Fell.

THOMAS BROWN

SIR HUDIBRAS, HIS PASSING WORTH

He was in *Logick* a great Critick,
Profoundly skill'd in Analytick.
He could distinguish, and divide
A Hair 'twixt *South* and *South-West* side:
On either which he would dispute,
Confute, change hands, and still confute.
He'd undertake to prove by force
Of Argument, a Man's no Horse.
He'd prove a Buzard is no Fowl,
And that a *Lord* may be an Owl;
A Calf an *Alderman*, a Goose a *Justice*,
And Rooks *Committee-men* and *Trustees*.
He'd run in Debt by Disputation,
And pay with Ratiocination,
All this by Syllogism, true
In Mood and Figure, he would do.

For *Rhetorick*, he could not ope
His mouth, but out there flew a Trope:
And when he hapned to break off
I'th middle of his speech, or cough,
H'had hard words, ready to shew why,
And tell what Rules he did it by.
Else when with greatest Art he spoke,
You'd think he talk'd like other folk.
For all a Rhetoricians Rules
Teach nothing but to name his Tools.
His ordinary Rate of Speech
In loftiness of sound was rich.
A *Babylonish* dialect,
Which learned Pedants much affect.
It was a parti-colour'd dress
Of patch'd and pyball'd Languages:

'Twas *English* cut on *Greek* and *Latin*,
Like Fustian heretofore on Sattin.
It had an odd promiscuous Tone,
As if h'had talk'd three parts in one.
Which made some think when he did gabble,
Th' had heard three Labourers of *Babel*;
Or *Cerberus* himself pronounce
A Leash of Languages at once.
This he as volubly would vent,
As if his stock would ne'r be spent.
And truly to support that charge
He had supplies as vast and large.
For he could coyn or counterfeit
New words with little or no wit:
Words so debas'd and hard, no stone
Was hard enough to touch them on.
And when with hasty noise he spoke 'em,
The Ignorant for currant took 'em,
That had the Orator who once
Did fill his Mouth with Pebble stones
When he harangu'd, but known his Phrase,
He would have us'd no other ways.

In *Mathematicks* he was greater
Then *Tycho Brahe*, or *Erra Pater*:
For he by *Geometrick* scale
Could take the size of *Pots of Ale*;
Resolve by Signes and Tangents straight,
If *Bread* or *Butter* wanted weight;
And wisely tell what hour o'th day
The Clock does strike, by *Algebra*.

Beside he was a shrewd *Philosopher*;
And had read every Text and gloss over:
What e'er the crabbed'st Author hath
He understood b'implicit Faith,

What ever *Sceptick* could inquere for;
For every *why* he had a *wherefore*:
Knew more then forty of them do,
As far as words and terms could go.
All which he understood by Rote,
And as occasion serv'd, would quote;
No matter whether right or wrong:
They might be either said or sung.
His Notions fitted things so well,
That which was which he could not tell;
But oftentimes mistook the one
For th'other, as Great Clerks have done.
He could reduce all things to Acts
And knew their Natures by Abstracts,
Where Entity and Quiddity
The Ghosts of defunct Bodies flie;
Where Truth in Person does appear,
Like words congeal'd in Northern Air.
He knew *what's what*, and that's as high
As *Metaphysick* wit can fly.
In *School Divinity* as able
As he that hight *Irrefragable*;
Profound in all the Nominal
And real ways beyond them all,
And with as delicate a Hand
Could twist as tough a Rope of Sand,
And weave fine Cobwebs, fit for skull
That's empty when the moon is full;
Such as take Lodgings in a Head
That's to be lett unfurnished.
He could raise Scruples dark and nice,
And after solve 'em in a trice:
As if Divinity had catch'd
The Itch, of purpose to be scratch'd;
Or, like a Mountebank, did wound
And stab her self with doubts profound,

Onely to shew with how small pain
The sores of faith are cur'd again;
Although by woful proof we find,
They always leave a Scar behind.
He knew the Seat of Paradise,
Could tell in what degree it lies:
And, as he was dispos'd, could prove it,
Below the Moon, or else above it:
What *Adam* dreamt of when his Bride
Came from her Closet in his side:
Whether the Devil tempted her
By a *High Dutch* Interpreter:
If either of them had a Navel;
Who first made Musick malleable:
Whether the Serpent at the fall
Had cloven Feet, or none at all,
All this without a Gloss or Comment,
He would unriddle in a moment
In proper terms, such as men smatter
When they throw out and miss the matter.

SAMUEL BUTLER

THE MAN IN THE WILDERNESS

The man in the wilderness asked of me,
How many strawberries grow in the sea?
I answered him as I thought good,
As many red herrings as grow in the wood.

ANON

THE MAN OF THESSALY

There was a Man of Thessaly,
    And he was wondrous wise:
He jumped into a briar hedge
    And scratched out both his eyes.
But when he saw his eyes were out,
    With all his might and main
He jumped into another hedge
    And scratched them in again.

ANON

GREAT BACCHUS: FROM THE GREEK

Great Bacchus, born in thunder and in fire,
By native heat asserts his dreadful sire.
Nourish'd near shady rills and cooling streams,
He to the nymphs avows his amorous flames.

To all the brethren at the Bell and Vine,
The moral says; mix water with your wine.

MATTHEW PRIOR

FATAL LOVE

Poor Hal caught his death standing under a spout,
Expecting till midnight when Nan would come out,
But fatal his patience, as cruel the dame,
And curs'd was the weather that quench'd the man's
    flame.

Whoe'er thou art, that read'st these moral lines,
Make love at home, and go to bed betimes.

MATTHEW PRIOR

A TRUE MAID

No, no; for my virginity,
    When I lose that, says Rose, I'll die:
Behind the elms, last night, cried Dick,
    Rose, were you not extremely sick?

MATTHEW PRIOR

EPIGRAM

To John I ow'd great obligation;
    But John unhappily thought fit
To publish it to all the nation:
    So John and I are more than quit.

MATTHEW PRIOR

ANOTHER

Yes, every poet is a fool;
    By demonstration Ned can show it:
Happy, could Ned's inverted rule
    Prove every fool to be a poet.

MATTHEW PRIOR

THE FIVE REASONS

If all be true that I do think,
There are *Five Reasons* we should drink;
Good Wine, a Friend, or being Dry,
Or lest we should be by and by;
Or any other Reason why.

HENRY ALDRICH

A NEW SONG OF NEW SIMILIES

My passion is as mustard strong;
  I sit all sober sad;
Drunk as a piper all day long,
  Or like a March-hare mad.

Round as a hoop the bumpers flow;
  I drink, yet can't forget her;
For, though as drunk as David's sow,
  I love her still the better.

Pert as a pear-monger I'd be,
  If Molly were but kind;
Cool as a cucumber could see
  The rest of womankind.

Like a stuck pig I gaping stare,
  And eye her o'er and o'er;
Lean as a rake with sighs and care;
  Sleek as a mouse before,

Plump as a partridge was I known,
  And soft as silk my skin,
My cheeks as fat as butter grown;
  But as a groat now thin!

I, melancholy as a cat,
  And kept awake to weep;
But she, insensible of that,
  Sound as a top can sleep.

Hard is her heart as flint or stone,
  She laughs to see me pale;
And merry as a grig is grown,
  And brisk as bottled ale.

The God of Love at her approach
    Is busy as a bee;
Hearts, sound as any bell or roach,
    Are smit and sigh like me.

Ay me! as thick as hops or hail,
    The fine men crowd about her;
But soon as dead as a door nail
    Shall I be, if without her.

Straight as my leg her shape appears,
    O were we join'd together!
My heart would be scot-free from cares,
    And lighter than a feather.

As fine as fivepence is her mien,
    No drum was ever tighter;
Her glance is as the razor keen,
    And not the sun is brighter.

As soft as pap her kisses are,
    Methinks I taste them yet;
Brown as a berry is her hair,
    Her eyes as black as jet:

As smooth as glass, as white as curds,
    Her pretty hand invites;
Sharp as a needle are her words;
    Her wit, like pepper, bites:

Brisk as a body-louse she trips,
    Clean as a penny drest;
Sweet as a rose her breath and lips,
    Round as the globe her breast.

Full as an egg was I with glee;
    And happy as a king.
Good Lord! how all men envy'd me!
    She lov'd like any thing.

But, false as hell! she, like the wind,
    Chang'd, as her sex must do;
Though seeming as the turtle kind,
    And like the gospel true.

If I and Molly could agree,
    Let who would take Peru!
Great as an emperor should I be,
    And richer than a Jew.

Till you grow tender as a chick,
    I'm dull as any post;
Let us, like burs, together stick,
    And warm as any toast.

You'll know me truer than a dye;
    And wish me better speed;
Flat as a flounder when I lie,
    And as a herring dead.

Sure as a gun, she'll drop a tear,
    And sigh, perhaps, and wish,
When I am rotten as a pear,
    And mute as any fish.

JOHN GAY

ON TWO MONOPOLISTS

Bone and Skin, two Millers thin,
    Would starve us all, or near it;
But be it known to Skin and Bone,
    That Flesh and Blood won't bear it.

JOHN BYROM

A JACOBITE TOAST

God bless the King!—I mean the Faith's Defender;
God bless (no harm in blessing) the Pretender!
But who Pretender is, or who is King,—
God bless us all! That's quite another thing.

JOHN BYROM

EPIGRAM IN 1715, AND A CAMBRIDGE REPLY

(In 1715, George I presented thirty thousand books to the University of Cambridge. About the same time a troop of horse was sent to Oxford to arrest Colonel Owen and some other Jacobites.)

I

King George, observing with judicious eyes
The state of both his Universities,
To Oxford sent a troop of horse; and why?
That learned body wanted loyalty.
To Cambridge books he sent, as well discerning
How much that loyal body wanted learning.

JOSEPH TRAPP

II

The king to Oxford sent a troop of horse,
For Tories know no argument but force;
With equal skill to Cambridge books he sent,
For Whigs admit no force but argument.

SIR WILLIAM BROWNE

A GENTLE ECHO ON WOMAN

(*In the Doric Manner*)

SHEPHERD: Echo, I ween, will in the wood reply,
And quaintly answer questions: shall I try?
        ECHO: Try.
What must we do our passion to express?
        Press.
How shall I please her, who ne'er loved before?
        Be Fore.
What most moves women when we them address?
        A dress.
Say, what can keep her chaste whom I adore?
        A door.
If music softens rocks, love tunes my lyre.
        Liar.
Then teach me, Echo, how shall I come by her?
        Buy her.
When bought, no question I shall be her dear?
        Her deer.
But deer have horns: how must I keep her under?
        Keep her under
But what can glad me when she's laid on bier?
        Beer.
What must I do when women will be kind?
        Be kind.
What must I do when women will be cross?
        Be cross.
Lord, what is she that can so turn and wind?
        Wind.
If she be wind, what stills her when she blows?
        Blows.
But if she bang again, still should I bang her?
        Bang her.

Is there no way to moderate her anger?

                             Hang her.

Thanks, gentle Echo! right thy answers tell
What woman is and how to guard her well.

                          Guard her well.

JONATHAN SWIFT

LINES ON SWIFT'S ANCESTORS

'Swift put up a plain monument to his grandfather, and also presented a cup to the church of Goodrich, or Gotheridge (Here-lordshire). He sent a pencilled elevation of the monument (a simple tablet) to Mrs Howard, who returned it with the following fines inscribed on the drawing by Pope.'—Scott's *Life of Swift*.

Jonathan Swift
Had the gift,
By fatherige, motherige,
And by brotherige,
To come from Gotherige,
But now is spoil'd clean
And an Irish dean:
In this church he has put
A stone of two foot,
With a cup and a can, sir,
In respect to his grandsire;
So, Ireland, change thy tone,
And cry, O hone! O hone!
For England hath its own.

ALEXANDER POPE

EPIGRAM

ENGRAVED ON THE COLLAR OF A DOG GIVEN TO HIS ROYAL HIGHNESS, FREDERICK, PRINCE OF WALES

I am his Highness' dog at Kew;
Pray tell me, sir, whose dog are you?

ALEXANDER POPE

ON CERTAIN LADIES

When other fair ones to the shades go down,
Still Chloe, Flavia, Delia, stay in town:
Those ghosts of beauty wandering here reside,
And haunt the places where their honour died.

ALEXANDER POPE

ON THE NEW LAUREATE

In merry old England, it once was a rule,
The king had his poet, as well as his fool;
And now we're so frugal, I'd have you to know it,
That Cibber may serve both for fool and for poet.

ANON

ON SIR JOHN VANBRUGH, ARCHITECT

Under this stone, reader, survey
Dead Sir John Vanbrugh's house of clay
Lie heavy on him, earth! for he
Laid many heavy loads on thee.

ABEL EVANS

TADLOW

When Tadlow walks the streets the paviours cry,
'God bless you, sir!' and lay their rammers by.

ABEL EVANS

USEFUL COUPLETS

O what a tricksie lerned nicking straine
Is this applauded, sencles, modern vaine!
JOHN MARSTON: *A Toy to Mocke an Ape* (1598)

All other joyes to this are folly
None so sweete as Melancholy.
ROBERT BURTON: *Abstract of Melancholy* (1621)

What frenzy has of late possess'd the brain!
Though few can write, yet fewer can refrain.
SAMUEL GARTH: *Claremont* (1715)

Like cats in air-pumps, to subsist we strive
On joys too thin to keep the soul alive.
EDWARD YOUNG: *Satire V* (1728)

With skill she vibrates her eternal tongue
For ever most divinely in the wrong.
EDWARD YOUNG: *Satire VI* (1728)

Another writes because his father writ,
And proves himself a bastard by his wit.
EDWARD YOUNG: *First Epistle to Mr Pope* (1730)

Undisciplined in dull Discretion's rules,
Untaught and undebauch'd by boarding-schools.
CHARLES CHURCHILL: *The Times* (1764)

Caress'd and courted, Faber seems to stand
A mighty pillar in a guilty land.
CHARLES CHURCHILL: *The Times* (1764)

THE MAN OF TASTE

Huge commentators grace my learned shelves,
Notes upon books out-do the books themselves.
Critics indeed are valuable men,
But hyper-critics are as good again.
Though Blackmore's works my soul with rapture fill,
With notes by Bentley they'd be better still.
The Boghouse-Miscellany's well design'd
To ease the body, and improve the mind.
Swift's whims and jokes for my resentment call,
For he displeases me that pleases all.

Verse without rhyme I never could endure,
Uncouth in numbers, and in sense obscure.
To him as nature, when he ceased to see,
Milton's an universal blank to me.
Confirm'd and settled by the nation's voice,
Rhyme is the poet's pride, and people's choice.
Always upheld by national support,
Of market, university, and court;
Thomson, write blank! but know that for that reason
These lines shall live when thine are out of season.
Rhyme binds and beautifies the poet's lays,
As London ladies owe their shape to stays.

T'improve in morals Mandevil I read,
And Tyndal's scruples are my settled creed.
I travell'd early, and I soon saw through
Religion all, ere I was twenty-two.
Shame, pain, or poverty shall I endure,
When ropes or opium can my ease procure?
When money's gone, and I no debts can pay,
Self-murder is an honourable way.
As Pasaran directs, I'd end my life,
And kill myself, my daughter, and my wife.

Burn but that Bible which the parson quotes,
And men of spirit all shall cut their throats.

But not to writings I confine my pen,
I have a taste for buildings, music, men.
Young travell'd coxcombs mighty knowledge boast,
With superficial smattering at most.
Not so my mind, unsatisfied with hints,
Knows more than Budgell writes, or Roberts prints.
I know the town, all houses I have seen,
From Hyde-Park corner down to Bednal-Green.
Sure wretched Wren was taught by bungling Jones,
To murder mortar, and disfigure stones!
Who in Whitehall can symmetry discern?
I reckon Covent-Garden church a barn.
Nor hate I less thy vile cathedral, Paul!
The choir's too big, the cupola's too small:
Substantial walls and heavy roofs I like,
'Tis Vanbrugh's structures that my fancy strike:
Such noble ruins every pile would make,
I wish they'd tumble for the prospect's sake.

In curious paintings I'm exceeding nice,
And know their several beauties by their price
Auctions and sales I constantly attend,
But choose my pictures by a skilful friend.
Originals and copies much the same,
The picture's value is the painter's name.

My taste in sculpture from my choice is seen,
I buy no statues that are not obscene.
In spite of Addison and ancient Rome,
Sir Cloudesley Shovel's is my favourite tomb.
How oft have I with admiration stood,
To view some city-magistrate in wood!
I gaze with pleasure on a lord-mayor's head,
Cast with propriety in gilded lead.

Oh could I view, through London as I pass,
Some broad Sir Balaam in Corinthian brass:
High on a pedestal, ye freemen, place
His magisterial paunch and griping face;
Letter'd and gilt, let him adorn Cheapside,
And grant the tradesman what a king's denied.

Without Italian, or without an ear,
To Bononcini's music I adhere;
Music has charms to sooth a savage breast,
And therefore proper at a sheriff's feast
My soul has oft a secret pleasure found
In the harmonious bagpipe's lofty sound.
Bagpipes for men, shrill German-flutes for boys,
I'm English born, and love a grumbling noise.

Oh, could a British barony be sold!
I would bright honour buy with dazzling gold.
Could I the privilege of peer procure,
The rich I'd bully, and oppress the poor.
To give is wrong, but it is wronger still
On any terms to pay a tradesman's bill.
I'd make the insolent mechanics stay,
And keep my ready money all for play.
I'd try if any pleasure could be found
In tossing up for twenty thousand pound:
Had I whole counties, I to White's would go,
And set land, woods, and rivers, at a throw.
But should I meet with an unlucky run,
And at a throw be gloriously undone;
My debts of honour I'd discharge the first;
Let all my lawful creditors be cursed:
My title would preserve me from arrest,
And seizing hired horses is a jest.

To boon companions I my time would give;
With players, pimps, and parasites, I'd live.

I would with jockeys from Newmarket dine,
And to rough-riders give my choicest wine;
I would caress some stableman of note,
And imitate his language and his coat.
My evenings all I would with sharpers spend,
And make the thief-catcher my bosom friend;
In Fig the prize-fighter by day delight,
And sup with Colley Cibber every night.

I am a politician too, and hate,
Of any party, ministers of state;
I'm for an act, that he, who sev'n whole years
Has served his king and country, lose his ears.

Thus from my birth I'm qualified, you find,
To give the laws of taste to human kind.
Mine are the gallant schemes of politesse,
For books and buildings, politics and dress.
This is true taste, and whoso likes it not,
Is blockhead, coxcomb, puppy, fool, and sot.

JAMES BRAMSTON

THE WRITER

Titus reads neither prose nor rhyme;
He writes himself; he has no time.

HILDEBRAND JACOB

RONDEAU

By two black eyes my heart was won,
Sure never wretch was more undone.
To Celia with my suit I came,
    But she, regardless of her prize,
Thought proper to reward my flame
    With two black eyes!   ANON

75

HAMLET'S SOLILOQUY IMITATED

To print, or not to print—that is the question.
Whether 'tis better in a trunk to bury
The quirks and crotchets of outrageous fancy,
Or send a well-wrote copy to the press,
And by disclosing, end them? To print, to doubt
No more; and by one act to say we end
The head-ach, and a thousand natural shocks
Of scribbling frenzy—'tis a consummation
Devoutly to be wish'd. To print—to beam
From the same shelf with Pope, in calf well bound!
To sleep, perchance, with Quarles—Ay there's the rub—
For to what class a writer may be doom'd,
When he hath shuffled off some paltry stuff,
Must give us pause.—There's the respect that makes
Th' unwilling poet keep his piece nine years.
For who would bear th' impatient thirst of fame,
The pride of conscious merit, and 'bove all,
The tedious importunity of friends,
When as himself might his quietus make
With a bare inkhorn? Who would fardles bear?
To groan and sweat under a load of wit?
But that the tread of steep Parnassus' hill,
That undiscover'd country, with whose bays
Few travellers return, puzzles the will,
And makes us rather bear to live unknown,
Than run the hazard to be known, and damn'd.
Thus critics do make cowards of us all.
And thus the healthful face of many a poem
Is sickly'd o'er with a pale manuscript;
And enterprisers of great fire, and spirit,
With this regard from Dodsley turn away,
And lose the name of authors.

RICHARD JAGO

THE PAINS OF EDUCATION

Accursed the man, whom fate ordains, in spite,
And cruel parents teach, to read and write!
What need of letters? wherefore should we spell?
Why write our names? a mark will do as well.
Much are the precious hours of youth misspent
In climbing learning's rugged, steep ascent;
When to the top the bold adventurer's got,
He reigns, vain monarch o'er a barren spot,
Whilst in the vale of ignorance below
Folly and vice to rank luxuriance grow;
Honours and wealth pour in on every side,
And proud preferment rolls her golden tide.
O'er crabbèd authors life's gay prime to waste,
To cramp wild genius in the chains of taste,
To bear the slavish drudgery of schools,
And tamely stoop to every pedant's rules;
For seven long years debarr'd of liberal ease,
To plod in college trammels to degrees;
Beneath the weight of solemn toys to groan,
Sleep over books, and leave mankind unknown;
To praise each senior blockhead's threadbare tale,
And laugh till reason blush, and spirits fail:
Manhood with vile submission to disgrace,
And cap the fool, whose merit is his place,
Vice-Chancellors, whose knowledge is but small,
And Chancellors who nothing know at all.

CHARLES CHURCHILL

EPIGRAM ON VOLTAIRE

You are so witty, profligate, and thin,
At once we think you Milton, Death, and Sin.

EDWARD YOUNG

77

SATIRE UPON THE HEADS; OR, NEVER A BARREL THE BETTER HERRING

O Cambridge, attend
To the Satire I've pen'd
On the Heads of thy Houses,
Thou Seat of the Muses!

Know the Master of Jesus
Does hugely displease us;
The Master of Maudlin
In the same dirt is dawdling;
The Master of Sidney
Is of the same kidney;
The Master of Trinity
To him bears affinity;
As the Master of Keys
Is as like as two pease,
So the Master of Queen's
Is as like as two beans;
The Master of King's
Copies them in all things;
The Master of Catherine
Takes them all for his pattern;
The Master of Clare
Hits them all to a hair;
The Master of Christ
By the rest is enticed;
But the Master of Emmanuel
Follows them like a spaniel;
The Master of Benet
Is of the like tenet;
The Master of Pembroke
Has from them his system took;
The Master of Peter's
Has all the same features;

The Master of St John's
Like the rest of the Dons.

P.S.—As to Trinity Hall
We say nothing at all.

THOMAS GRAY

ON A FAVOURITE CAT DROWNED IN
A TUB OF GOLDFISHES

'Twas on a lofty vase's side,
Where China's gayest art had dy'd
   The azure flowers that blow;
Demurest of the tabby kind,
The pensive Selima reclin'd,
   Gazed on the lake below.

Her conscious tail her joy declar'd;
The fair round face, the snowy beard,
   The velvet of her paws,
Her coat, that with the tortoise vies,
Her ears of jet, and emerald eyes,
   She saw; and purr'd applause.

Still had she gaz'd, but 'midst the tide
Two angel forms were seen to glide,
   The Genii of the stream:
Their scaly armour's Tyrian hue
Thro' richest purple to the view
   Betray'd a golden gleam.

The hapless Nymph with wonder saw:
A whisker first and then a claw,
   With many an ardent wish,
She stretch'd in vain to reach the prize.
What female heart can gold despise?
   What Cat's averse to fish?

Presumptuous maid! with looks intent
Again she stretch'd, again she bent,
  Nor knew the gulf between.
(Malignant Fate sat by, and smil'd)
The slipp'ry verge her feet beguil'd;
  She tumbled headlong in.

Eight times emerging from the flood
She mew'd to ev'ry watry god
  Some speedy aid to send.
No Dolphin came, no Nereid stirr'd,
Nor cruel *Tom* nor *Susan* heard.
  A fav'rite has no friend!

From hence, ye Beauties, undeceiv'd,
Know one false step is ne'er retriev'd,
  And be with caution bold.
Not all that tempts your wand'ring eyes
And heedless hearts, is lawful prize;
  Nor all, that glisters, gold.

THOMAS GRAY

IN THE DUMPS

We're all in the dumps,
  For diamonds are trumps;
The kittens are gone to St Paul's!
  The babies are bit,
  The Moon's in a fit,
And the houses are built without walls.

ANON

MRS MARY BLAIZE

Good people all, with one accord,
    Lament for Madam Blaize,
Who never wanted a good word—
    From those who spoke her praise.

The needy seldom pass'd her door,
    And always found her kind;
She freely lent to all the poor—
    Who left a pledge behind.

She strove the neighbourhood to please
    With manners wondrous winning;
And never followed wicked ways—
    Unless when she was sinning.

At church, in silks and satins new
    With hoop of monstrous size,
She never slumbered in her pew—
    But when she shut her eyes.

Her love was sought, I do aver,
    By twenty beaux and more;
The King himself has followed her—
    When she has walk'd before.

But now, her wealth and finery fled,
    Her hangers-on cut short-all:
The doctors found, when she was dead,—
    Her last disorder mortal.

Let us lament, in sorrow sore,
    For Kent Street well may say,
That had she lived a twelvemonth more,—
    She had not died to-day.

OLIVER GOLDSMITH

ELEGY ON THE DEATH OF A MAD DOG

Good people all, of every sort,
    Give ear unto my song;
And if you find it wond'rous short,
    It cannot hold you long.

In Islington there was a man,
    Of whom the world might say,
That still a godly race he ran,
    Whene'er he went to pray.

A kind and gentle heart he had,
    To comfort friends and foes;
The naked every day he clad,
    When he put on his clothes.

And in that town a dog was found,
    As many dogs there be,
Both mongrel, puppy, whelp, and hound,
    And curs of low degree.

This dog and man at first were friends;
    But when a pique began,
The dog, to gain some private ends,
    Went mad and bit the man.

Around from all the neighbouring streets
    The wond'ring neighbours ran,
And swore the dog had lost its wits,
    To bite so good a man.

The wound it seem'd both sore and sad
    To every Christian eye;
And while they swore the dog was mad,
    They swore the man would die.

But soon a wonder came to light,
　That showed the rogues they lied:
The man recover'd of the bite,
　The dog it was that died.

OLIVER GOLDSMITH

THE AULD SECEDER CAT

There was a Presbyterian cat
Went forth to catch her prey;
She brought a mouse intill the house,
Upon the Sabbath day.
The minister, offended
With such an act profane,
Laid down his book, the cat he took,
And bound her with a chain.

Thou vile malicious creature,
Thou murderer, said he,
Oh do you think to bring to Hell
My holy wife and me?
But be thou well assured,
That blood for blood shall pay,
For taking of the mouse's life
Upon the Sabbath Day.

Then he took doun his Bible,
And fervently he prayed,
That the great sin the cat had done
Might not on him be laid.
Then forth to exe-cu-ti-on,
Poor Baudrons she was drawn,
And on a tree they hanged her hie,
And then they sung a psalm.

ANON

ON SIR JOHN HILL, M.D., PLAYWRIGHT

For physic and farces his equal there scarce is;
His farces are physic; his physic a farce is.

DAVID GARRICK

THE GREAT PANJANDRUM

So she went into the garden
to cut a cabbage-leaf
to make an apple-pie;
and at the same time
a great she-bear, coming down the street,
pops its head into the shop.
What! no soap?
      So he died,
and she very imprudently married the Barber:
and there were present
the Picninnies,
     and the Joblillies,
       and the Garyulies,
and the great Panjandrum himself,
with the little round button at top;
and they all fell to playing the game of catch-as-
    catch-can,
till the gunpowder ran out at the heels of their boots.

SAMUEL FOOTE

BURLESQUE OF LOPE DE VEGA

If the man who turnips cries,
Cry not when his father dies,
'Tis a proof that he had rather
Have a turnip than his father.

SAMUEL JOHNSON

LINES IN RIDICULE OF CERTAIN POEMS PUBLISHED IN 1777

Wheresoe'er I turn my view,
All is strange, yet nothing new;
Endless labour all along,
Endless labour to be wrong;
Phrase that time hath flung away,
Uncouth words in disarray,
Trick'd in antique ruff and bonnet,
Ode and elegy and sonnet.

SAMUEL JOHNSON

IMITATION OF THE STYLE OF * * * *

Hermit hoar, in solemn cell
    Wearing out life's evening grey;
Strike thy bosom, Sage, and tell
    What is bliss, and which the way.

Thus I spoke, and speaking sigh'd,
    Scarce repress'd the starting tear,
When the hoary sage, reply'd,
    Come, my lad, and drink some beer.

SAMUEL JOHNSON

AN EXPOSTULATION

When late I attempted your pity to move,
    What made you so deaf to my prayers?
Perhaps it was right to dissemble your love,
    But—why did you kick me downstairs?

ISAAC BICKERSTAFF

ON DR SAMUEL OGDEN

When Ogden his prosaic verse
    In Latin numbers drest,
The Roman language proved too weak
    To stand the critic's test.

To English Rhime he next essay'd
    To shew he'd some pretence;
But ah! Rhime only would not do;
    They still expected sense.

Enraged the Doctor swore he'd place
    On critics no reliance;
So wrapt his thoughts in Arabic
    And bid 'em all defiance.

                R. P. ARDEN

THE QUESTION

Yes, yes, I grant the sons of earth
Are doom'd to trouble from their birth.
We all of sorrow have our share;
But say, is yours without compare?

                JAMES BEATTIE

ON THE AUTHOR OF THE *TREATISE OF HUMAN NATURE*

David Hume ate a swinging great dinner,
    And grew every day fatter and fatter;
And yet the huge bulk of a sinner
    Said there was neither spirit or matter.

                J. H. BEATTIE

EPITAPHS

ON RICHARD HIND

Here lies the body of Richard Hind,
Who was neither ingenious, sober, nor kind.

ON WILL SMITH

Here lies Will Smith—and, what's something rarish,
He was born, bred, and hanged, all in the same parish

AT GREAT TORRINGTON, DEVON

Here lies a man who was killed by lightning;
He died when his prospects seemed to be brightening
He might have cut a flash in this world of trouble,
But the flash cut him, and he lies in the stubble.

AT ABERDEEN

Here lie I, Martin Elginbrodde:
Have mercy o' my soul, Lord God,
As I wad do, were I Lord God,
And ye were Martin Elginbrodde.

AT HADLEIGH, SUFFOLK

To free me from domestic strife
Death called at my house, but he spake with my wife,
Susan, wife of David Pattison, lies here,
Stop, Reader, and if not in a hurry, shed a tear.

AT POTTERNE, WILTSHIRE

Here lies Mary, the wife of John Ford,
We hope her soul is gone to the Lord;
But if for Hell she has chang'd this life
She had better be there than be John Ford's wife.

AT UPTON-ON-SEVERN

Beneath this stone in hopes of Zion
Doth lie the landlord of the Lion;
His son keeps on the business still,
Resigned unto the heavenly will.

AT LEEDS

Here lies my wife,
   Here lies she;
Hallelujah!
   Hallelujee!

EPIGRAMS: ANONYMOUS

ON LORD CHESTERFIELD AND HIS SON

Vile Stanhope, demons blush to tell,
   In twice two hundred places
Has shown his son the road to Hell,
   Escorted by the Graces.

But little did th' ungenerous lad
   Concern himself about 'em;
For, base, degenerate, meanly bad,
   He sneak'd to Hell without 'em.

ON PRINCE FREDERICK

Here lies Fred,
Who was alive and is dead.
Had it been his father,
I had much rather;
Had it been his brother,
Still better than another;
Had it been his sister,
No one would have miss'd her;
Had it been the whole generation,
Still better for the nation;
But since 'tis only Fred,
Who was alive and is dead,
There's no more to be said.

ON INCLOSURES

'Tis bad enough in man or woman
To steal a goose from off a common;
But surely he's without excuse
Who steals the common from the goose.

ON A CLERGYMAN'S HORSE BITING HIM

The steed bit his master;
How came this to pass?
He heard the good pastor
Cry, 'All flesh is grass.'

ON DR ISAAC LETSOME

When people's ill they comes to I,
I physics, bleeds, and sweats 'em,
Sometimes they live, sometimes they die;
What's that to I? I Letsome.

EPITAPH ON JOHN DOVE

Innkeeper, Mauchline

Here lies Johnny Pidgeon;
What was his religion?
    Wha e'er desires to ken,
To some other warl'
Maun follow the carl,
    For here Johnny Pidgeon had nane!
Strong ale was ablution,
Small beer persecution,
    A dram was memento mori;
But a full flowing bowl
Was the saving his soul,
    And port was celestial glory.

ROBERT BURNS

EPITAPH ON A SCHOOLMASTER

In Cleish Parish, Kinross-shire

Here lie Willie Michie's banes;
    O Satan, when ye tak him,
Gie him the schoolin' of your weans,
    For clever deils he'll mak them!

ROBERT BURNS

ON ELPHINSTON'S TRANSLATION OF MARTIAL

O thou whom Poetry abhors,
Whom Prose has turned out of doors,
Heard'st thou that groan?—proceed no further,
'Twas laurel'd Martial roaring murther.

ROBERT BURNS

SIR JOSHUA REYNOLDS

When Sir Joshua Reynolds died
  All Nature was degraded;
The King dropp'd a tear into the Queen's Ear,
  And all his Pictures Faded.

WILLIAM BLAKE

ON CROMEK

A Petty Sneaking Knave I knew—
O Mr Cromek, how do ye do?

WILLIAM BLAKE

TO WILLIAM HAYLEY

Thy Friendship oft has made my heart to ache:
Do be my enemy, for Friendship's sake.

WILLIAM BLAKE

ON PETER ROBINSON

Here lies the preacher, judge and poet, Peter,
Who broke the laws of God, and man, and metre.

FRANCIS JEFFREY

PORSON ON HIS MAJESTY'S GOVERNMENT

Your foe in war to overrate
A maxim is of ancient date;
Then sure 'tis right, in time of trouble,
That our good rulers should see double.

RICHARD PORSON

PORSON ON GERMAN SCHOLARSHIP

The Germans in Greek
Are sadly to seek;
Not five in five score,
But ninety-five more;
All, save only HERMAN,
And HERMAN's a German.

RICHARD PORSON

A NOTE ON THE LATIN GERUNDS

When Dido found Aeneas would not come,
She mourned in silence, and was Di-Do-Dum.

RICHARD PORSON

TO DR KIPLING

(*Editor of the Codex Bezæ*)

Orthodoxy's staunch adherent,
Bishop Watson's great vice-gerent,
Sub-Professor Dr Kipling,
Leave off your Yorkshire trick of tippling:
For while thy Beza is in hand
Man's salvation's at a stand.

RICHARD PORSON

ON A DOCTOR OF DIVINITY

Here lies a Doctor of Divinity,
He was a fellow of Trinity;
He knew as much about Divinity
As other fellows do of Trinity.

RICHARD PORSON

92

PORSON'S VISIT TO THE CONTINENT

I went to Frankfort and got drunk
With that most learn'd professor, Brunck;
I went to Wortz and got more drunken
With that more learn'd professor, Ruhnken.

RICHARD PORSON

ON MY JOYFUL DEPARTURE

FROM THE CITY OF COLOGNE

As I am a Rhymer,
And now at least a merry one,
Mr Mum's Rudesheimer
And the church of St Geryon
Are the two things alone
That deserve to be known
In the body-and-soul-stinking town of Cologne.

S. T. COLERIDGE

ON A LORD

Here lies the Devil—ask no other name.
Well—but you mean Lord—? Hush! we mean the same.

S. T. COLERIDGE

SWANS SING BEFORE THEY DIE

Swans sing before they die—'twere no bad thing
Should certain persons die before they sing.

S. T. COLERIDGE

THE DEVIL'S THOUGHTS

From his brimstone bed at break of day
A-walking the Devil is gone,
To visit his snug little farm the earth,
And see how his stock goes on.

Over the hill and over the dale,
And he went over the plain,
And backward and forward he switched his long tail
As a gentleman switches his cane.

And how then was the Devil dressed?
Oh! he was in his Sunday's best:
His jacket was red and his breeches were blue,
And there was a hole where the tail came through.

He saw a Lawyer killing a Viper
On a dunghill hard by his own stable;
And the Devil smiled, for it put him in mind
Of Cain and his brother, Abel.

He saw an Apothecary on a white horse
Ride by on his vocations,
And the Devil thought of his old Friend
Death in the Revelations.

He saw a cottage with a double coach-house,
A cottage of gentility;
And the Devil did grin, for his darling sin
Is pride that apes humility.

He peep'd into a rich bookseller's shop,
Quoth he! we are both of one college!
For I sate myself, like a cormorant, once
Hard by the tree of knowledge.

94

Down the river did glide, with wind and tide,
A pig, with vast celerity;
And the Devil look'd wise as he saw how the while,
It cut its own throat. 'There!' quoth he with a smile,
'Goes 'England's commercial prosperity'.'

As he went through Cold-Bath fields he saw
A solitary cell;
And the Devil was pleased, for it gave him a hint
For improving his prisons in Hell.

General Gascoigne's burning face
He saw with consternation,
And back to hell his way did he take,
For the Devil thought by a slight mistake
It was general conflagration.

S. T. COLERIDGE AND ROBERT SOUTHEY

THE FRIEND OF HUMANITY

(*In imitation of Southey*)

FRIEND OF HUMANITY:

'Needy Knife-grinder! whither are you going?
Rough is the road, your wheel is out of order—
Bleak blows the blast; your hat has got a hole in 't,
              So have your breeches!

'Weary Knife-grinder! little think the proud ones,
Who in their coaches roll along the turnpike-
road, what hard work 'tis crying all day "Knives and
              Scissors to grind O!"

'Tell me, Knife-grinder, how you came to grind knives?
Did some rich man tyrannically use you?
Was it the squire, or parson of the parish?
              Or the attorney?

95

'Was it the squire, for killing of his game? or
Covetous parson, for his tithes distraining?
Or roguish lawyer, made you lose your little
    All in a lawsuit?

'(Have you not read the Rights of Man, by Tom
    Paine?)
Drops of compassion tremble on my eyelids,
Ready to fall, as soon as you have told your
    Pitiful story.'

KNIFE-GRINDER:

'Story! God bless you! I have none to tell, sir,
Only last night a-drinking at the Chequers,
This poor old hat and breeches, as you see, were
    Torn in a scuffle.

'Constables came up for to take me into
Custody; they took me before the justice;
Justice Oldmixon put me in the parish
    Stocks for a vagrant.

'I should be glad to drink your Honour's health in
A pot of beer, if you will give me sixpence;
But for my part, I never love to meddle
    With politics, sir.'

FRIEND OF HUMANITY:

'I give thee sixpence! I will see thee damn'd first—
Wretch! whom no sense of wrongs can rouse to
    vengeance;
Sordid, unfeeling, reprobate, degraded,
    Spiritless outcast!'

(*Kicks the Knife-grinder, overturns his wheel, and
    exit in a transport of Republican enthusiasm
    and universal philanthropy.*)

GEORGE CANNING AND J. H. FRERE

BALLYNAHINCH

*A New Song said to be in great vogue among the Loyal
Troops in the North of Ireland. It is attributed (as our
Correspondent informs us) to a Fifer in the Drumbally-
roney Volunteers.*

A certain great statesman, whom all of us know,
In a certain assembly, no long while ago,
Declared from this maxim he never would flinch,
'That no town was so *Loyal* as Ballynahinch.'

The great Statesman, it seems had perus'd all their
    faces
And been mightily struck with their loyal grimaces;
While each townsman had sung, like a throstle or finch,
'We are all of us loyal at Ballynahinch.'

The great Statesman return'd to his speeches and
    readings,
And the Ballynahinchers resum'd their proceedings;
They had most of them sworn '*We'll be true to the Frinch,*'
So *Loyal* a town was this Ballynahinch!

Determin'd their landlord's fine words to make good,
They hid Pikes in his haggard, cut Staves in his wood;
And attack'd the King's troops—the assertion to clinch
That no town was so *Loyal* as Ballynahinch.

O! had we but trusted the *Rebel's* professions,
Met their cannon with smiles, and their pikes with
    concessions:
Tho' they still took an *ell*, when we gave them an *inch*,
They would all have been *Loyal*—like Ballynahinch.

                    GEORGE CANNING

INSCRIPTION

(*In imitation of Southey*)

FOR THE DOOR OF THE CELL IN NEWGATE
WHERE MRS BROWNRIGG, THE 'PRENTICE-CIDE,
WAS CONFINED PREVIOUS TO HER EXECUTION

For one long term, or e'er her trial came,
Here BROWNRIGG linger'd. Often have these cells
Echoed her blasphemies, as with shrill voice
She scream'd for fresh Geneva. Not to her
Did the blithe fields of Tothill, or thy street,
St. Giles, its fair varieties expand;
Till at the last, in slow-drawn cart she went
To execution. Dost thou ask her crime?
SHE WHIPP'D TWO FEMALE 'PRENTICES TO DEATH,
AND HID THEM IN THE COAL-HOLE. For her mind
Shap'd strictest plans of discipline. Sage schemes!
Such as Lycurgus taught, when at the shrine
Of the Orthyan Goddess he bade flog
The little Spartans; such as erst chastised
Our MILTON, when at college. For this act
Did BROWNRIGG swing. Harsh laws! But time shall come
When France shall reign, and laws be all repealed!

GEORGE CANNING AND J. H. FRERE

A POLITICAL DESPATCH

In matters of commerce the fault of the Dutch
Is offering too little and asking too much.
The French are with equal advantage content,
So we clap on Dutch bottoms just 20 per cent.
    20 per cent — 20 per cent,
Vous frapperez Falck avec 20 per cent.

GEORGE CANNING

THE SAILOR'S CONSOLATION

One night came on a hurricane,
  The sea was mountains rolling,
When Barney Buntline slewed his quid
  And said to Billy Bowline:
'A strong nor'-wester's blowing, Bill:
  Hark: don't ye hear it roar now?
Lord help 'em, how I pities them
  Unhappy folks on shore now.

'Foolhardy chaps as live in towns,
  What danger they are all in,
And now lie quaking in their beds.
  For fear the roof should fall in!
Poor creatures, how they envies us
  And wishes, I've a notion,
For our good luck in such a storm
  To be upon the ocean!

'And as for them that's out all day
  On business from their houses,
And late at night returning home
  To cheer their babes and spouses;
While you and I, Bill, on the deck
  Are comfortably lying,
My eyes! what tiles and chimney-pots
  About their heads are flying!

'Both you and I have oft-times heard
  How men are killed and undone
By overturns from carriages,
  By thieves and fires, in London.
We know what risks these landsmen run,
  From noblemen to tailors;
Then, Bill, let us thank Providence
  That you and I are sailors.'

CHARLES DIBDIN

THE MARCH TO MOSCOW

The Emperor Nap he would set off
On a summer excursion to Moscow;
The fields were green and the sky was blue,
    Morbleu! Parbleu!
What a splendid excursion to Moscow!

The Emperor Nap he talk'd so big
    That he frighten'd Mr Roscoe.
And Counsellor Brougham was all in a fume
    At the thought of the march to Moscow:
The Russians, he said, they were undone,
    And the great Fee-Faw-Fum
    Would presently come,
With a hop, step, and jump, unto London,
    For, as for his conquering Russia,
    However some persons might scoff it,
    Do it he could, do it he would,
And from doing it nothing would come but good,
    And nothing would call him off it.

But the Russians stoutly they turned to
    Upon the road to Moscow.
Nap had to fight his way all through;
They could fight, though they could not parlez-vous;
But the fields were green, and the sky was blue,
    Morbleu! Parbleu!
    And so he got to Moscow.

He found the place too warm for him,
    For they set fire to Moscow.
To get there had cost him much ado,
And then no better course he knew
While the fields were green, and the sky was blue,
    Morbleu! Parbleu!
    But to march back again from Moscow.

The Russians they stuck close to him
    All on the road from Moscow—
And Shouvaloff he shovell'd them off,
And Markoff he mark'd them off,
And Krosnoff he cross'd them off,
And Touchkoff he touch'd them off,
And Boroskoff he bored them off,
And Kutousoff he cut them off,
And Parenzoff he pared them off,
And Worronzoff he worried them off,
And Doctoroff he doctor'd them off,
And Rodinoff he flogg'd them off.
And, last of all, an Admiral came,
A terrible man with a terrible name,
A name which you all know by sight very well,
But which no one can speak, and no one can spell.

And then came on the frost and snow
    All on the road from Moscow.
Worse and worse every day the elements grew,
The fields were so white and the sky was so blue,
    Sacrebleu! Ventrebleu!
What a horrible journey from Moscow.

Too cold upon the road was he;
    Too hot he had been at Moscow;
But colder and hotter he may be,
    For the grave is colder than Muscovy;
And a place there is to be kept in view,
Where the fire is red, and the brimstone blue,
    Morbleu! Parbleu!
But there he must stay for a very long day,
For from thence there is no stealing away,
    As there was on the road from Moscow.

ROBERT SOUTHEY

A TALE OF DRURY LANE

(*After Sir Walter Scott*)

'Thus he went on, stringing one extravagance upon another, in the style his books of chivalry had taught him, and imitating, as near as he could, their very phrase.'—*Don Quixote.*

(*To be spoken by Mr Kemble, in a suit of the Black Prince's Armour, borrowed from the Tower.*)

THE NIGHT

On fair Augusta's towers and trees
Flitted the silent midnight breeze,
Curling the foliage as it past,
Which from the moon-tipp'd plumage cast
A spangled light, like dancing spray,
Then re-assumed its still array;
When, as night's lamp unclouded hung,
And down its full effulgence flung,
It shed such soft and balmy power
That cot and castle, hall and bower,
And spire and dome, and turret height,
Appeared to slumber in the light.
From Henry's chapel, Rufus' hall,
To Savoy, Temple, and St Paul;
From Knightsbridge, Pancras, Camden Town,
To Redriffe, Shadwell, Horsleydown,
No voice was heard, no eye unclosed,
But all in deepest sleep reposed.
They might have thought, who gazed around,
Amid a silence so profound,
   It made the senses thrill,
That 'twas no place inhabited,
But some vast city of the dead,
   All was so hushed and still.

THE BURNING

As Chaos, which, by heavenly doom,
Had slept in everlasting gloom,
Started with terror and surprise
When light first flash'd upon her eyes:
So London's sons in nightcap woke,
    In bedgown woke her dames;
For shouts were heard 'mid fire and smoke,
And twice ten hundred voices spoke,
    'The playhouse is in flames!'

And lo! where Catherine Street extends,
A fiery tail its lustre lends
    To every window-pane;
Blushes each spout in Martlet Court,
And Barbican, moth-eaten fort,
And Covent Garden kennels sport
    A bright ensanguin'd drain;

Meux's new brewhouse shows the light,
Rowland Hill's chapel, and the height
    Where patent shot they sell;
The Tennis Court, so fair and tall,
Partakes the ray, with Surgeons' Hall,
The Ticket Porters' House of Call,
Old Bedlam, close by London Wall,
Wright's shrimp and oyster shop withal,
    And Richardson's Hotel.

Nor these alone, but far and wide,
Across red Thames's gleaming tide,
To distant fields, the blaze was borne,
And daisy white and hoary thorn
In borrow'd lustre seem to sham
The rose or red sweet Wil-li-am.
To those who on the hills around
Beheld the flames from Drury's mound,

As from a lofty altar rise,
It seemed that nations did conspire,
To offer to the god of fire
  Some vast stupendous sacrifice!

The summon'd firemen woke at call,
And hied them to their stations all:
Starting from short and broken snooze,
Each sought his pond'rous hobnailed shoes.
But first his worsted hosen plied,
Plush breeches next, in crimson dyed,
  His nether bulk embraced;
Then jacket thick of red or blue,
Whose massy shoulders gave to view
The badge of each respective crew
  In tin or copper traced.
The engines thunder'd through the street,
Fire-hook, pipe, bucket, all complete,
And torches glared, and clattering feet
  Along the pavement paced.

And one, the leader of the band,
From Charing Cross along the Strand,
Like stag by beagles hunted hard,
Ran till he stopp'd at Vin'gar Yard.
The burning badge his shoulder bore,
The belt and oil-skin hat he wore,
The cane he had, his men to bang,
Show'd Foreman of the British gang.
His name was Higginbottom; now
'Tis meet that I should tell you how
  The others came in view:
The Sun, the London, and the Rock,
The Pelican, which nought can shock,
Th' Exchange, where old insurers flock,
  The Eagle, where the new;

With these came Rumford, Bumford, Cole,
Robins from Hockley in the Hole,
Lawson and Dawson, cheek by jowl,
    Crump from St Giles's Pound:
Whitford and Mitford join'd the train,
Huggins and Muggins from Chick Lane,
And Clutterbuck, who got a sprain
    Before the plug was found.
Scroggins and Jobson did not sleep,
But ah! no trophy could they reap,
For both were in the Donjon Keep
    Of Bridewell's gloomy mound.

E'en Higginbottom now was posed,
For sadder scene was ne'er disclosed;
Without, within, in hideous show,
Devouring flames resistless glow,
And blazing rafters downward go,
And never halloo 'Heads below?'
    Nor notice give at all:
The firemen, terrified, are slow
To bid the pumping torrent flow,
    For fear the roof should fall.
Back, Robins, back, Crumps, stand aloof!
Whitford, keep near the walls!
Huggins, regard your own behoof,
For lo! the blazing, rocking roof
Down, down, in thunder falls!

An awful pause succeeds the stroke,
And o'er the ruins volumed smoke,
Rolling around in pitchy shroud,
Conceal'd them from the astonish'd crowd.
At length the mist awhile was clear'd,
When lo! amid the wreck uprear'd,
Gradual a moving head appear'd,

And Eagle fireman knew
'Twas Joseph Muggins, name rever'd,
    The foreman of their crew.
Loud shouted all in sign of woe,
'A Muggins! to the rescue ho!'
    And poured the hissing tide;
Meanwhile the Muggins fought amain,
And strove and struggled all in vain
For, rallying but to fall again
    He totter'd, sunk, and died!

Did none attempt, before he fell,
To succour one they loved so well?
Yes, Higginbottom did aspire
(His fireman's soul was all on fire),
    His brother chief to save;
But ah! his reckless generous ire
    Served but to share his grave!
'Mid blazing beams and scalding streams,
Through fire and smoke he dauntless broke,
    Where Muggins broke before.
But sulphry stench and boiling drench
Destroying sight o'erwhelmed him quite,
    He sunk to rise no more.
Still o'er his head, while fate he braved,
His whizzing water-pipe he waved!
'Whitford and Mitford, ply your pumps,
You, Clutterbuck, come, stir your stumps,
Why are you in such doleful dumps?
A fireman, and afraid of bumps!—
What are they fear'd on? fools! 'od rot 'em!'
Were the last words of Higginbottom.

                              HORACE SMITH

CONVERSATION IN CRAVEN STREET, STRAND

JAMES SMITH:

At the top of my street the attorneys abound,
    And down at the bottom the barges are found:
Fly, Honesty, fly to some safer retreat,
    For there's craft in the river, and craft in the street.

SIR GEORGE ROSE:

Why should Honesty fly to a safer retreat,
    From attorneys and barges, 'od rot 'em?
For the lawyers are *just* at the top of the street,
    And the barges are *just* at the bottom.

JAMES SMITH AND SIR GEORGE ROSE

A CHANCERY SUIT

Mr Leach made a speech,
    Angry, neat, and wrong;
Mr Hart, on the other part,
    Was right, dull, and long.

Mr Bell spoke very well,
    Though nobody knew about what;
Mr Trower talked for an hour,
    Sat down, fatigued and hot.

Mr Parker made that darker,
    Which was dark enough without;
Mr Cooke quoted his book,
    And the Chancellor said, *I doubt*.

SIR GEORGE ROSE

107

ON SCOTT'S *THE FIELD OF WATERLOO*

On Waterloo's ensanguined plain
Lie tens of thousands of the slain;
But none, by sabre or by shot,
Fell half so flat as Walter Scott.

THOMAS, LORD ERSKINE

THE VILLAGE OF BALMAQUHAPPLE

D'ye ken the big village of Balmaquhapple,
The great muckle village of Balmaquhapple?
'Tis steep'd in iniquity up to the thrapple,
An' what's to become o' poor Balmaquhapple?
Fling a' aff your bannets, an' kneel for your life, fo'ks,
And pray to St Andrew, the god o' the Fife fo'ks;
Gar a' the hills yout wi' sheer vociferation,
And thus you may cry on sic needfu' occasion:

'O, blessed St Andrew, if e'er ye could pıty fo'k,
Men fo'k or women fo'k, country or city fo'k,
Come for this aince wi' the auld thief to grapple,
An' save the great village of Balmaquhapple
Frae drinking an' leeing, an' flyting an' swearing,
An' sins that ye wad be affrontit at hearing,
An' cheating an' stealing; O, grant them redemption,
All save an' except the few after to mention:

'There's Johnny the elder, wha hopes ne'er to need ye,
Sae pawkie, sae holy, sae gruff, an' sae greedy;
Wha prays every hour as the wayfarer passes,
But aye at a hole where he watches the lasses;

He's cheated a thousand, an' e'en to this day yet,
Can cheat a young lass, or they're leears that say it
Then gie him his gate; he's sae slee an' sae civil,
Perhaps in the end he may wheedle the devil.

'There's Cappie the cobbler, an' Tammie the tinman,
An' Dickie the brewer, an' Peter the skinman,
An' Geordie our deacon, for want of a better,
An' Bess, wha delights in the sins that beset her.
O, worthy St Andrew, we canna compel ye,
But ye ken as well as a body can tell ye,
If these gang to heaven, we'll a' be sae shockit,
Your garret o' blue will but thinly be stockit.

'But for a' the rest, for the women's sake, save them,
Their bodies at least, an' their sauls, if they have them;
But it puzzles Jock Lesly, an' sma' it avails,
If they dwell in their stamocks, their heads, or their
    tails;
An' save, without word of confession auricular,
The clerk's bonny daughters, an' Bell in particular;
For ye ken that their beauty's the pride an' the staple
Of the great wicked village of Balmaquhapple!'

JAMES HOGG

A RIDDLE

Q. Why is a Pump like V-sc--nt C--stl-r-gh?
A. Because it is a slender thing of wood,
    That up and down its awkward arm doth sway,
    And coolly spout and spout and spout away,
    In one weak, washy, everlasting flood!

THOMAS MOORE

EPITAPH ON ROBERT SOUTHEY

Beneath these poppies buried deep,
　　The bones of Bob the bard lie hid;
Peace to his manes; and may he sleep
　　As soundly as his readers did!

Through every sort of verse meandering,
　　Bob went without a hitch or fall,
Through epic, Sapphic, Alexandrine,
　　To verse that was no verse at all;

Till fiction having done enough,
　　To make a bard at least absurd,
And give his readers *quantum suff.*,
　　He took to praising George the Third.

And now, in virtue of his crown,
　　Dooms us, poor whigs, at once to slaughter;
Like Donellan of bad renown,
　　Poisoning us all with laurel-water.

And yet at times some awful qualms he
　　Felt about leaving honour's track;
And though he's got a butt of Malmsey,
　　It may not save him from a sack.

Death, weary of so dull a writer,
　　Put to his books a *finis* thus.
Oh! may the earth on him lie lighter
　　Than did his quartos upon us!

THOMAS MOORE

EPITAPH ON A TUFT-HUNTER

Lament, lament, Sir Isaac Heard,
  Put mourning round thy page, Debrett,
For here lies one, who ne'er preferr'd
  A Viscount to a Marquis yet.

Beside him place the God of Wit,
  Before him Beauty's rosiest girls,
Apollo for a *star* he'd quit,
  And Love's own sister for an Earl's.

Did niggard fate no peers afford,
  He took, of course, to peers' relations;
And, rather than not sport a Lord,
  Put up with even the last creations.

Even Irish names, could he but tag 'em
  With 'Lord' and 'Duke', were sweet to call;
And, at a pinch, Lord Ballyraggum
  Was better than no Lord at all.

Heaven grant him now some noble nook,
  For, rest his soul! he'd rather be
Genteelly damn'd beside a Duke,
  Than sav'd in vulgar company.

THOMAS MOORE

A JOKE VERSIFIED

'Come, come,' said Tom's father, 'at your time of life,
There's no longer excuse for thus playing the rake—
It is time you should think, boy, of taking a wife.'—
'Why so it is, father,—whose wife shall I take?'

THOMAS MOORE

111

TORY PLEDGES

I pledge myself through thick and thin,
  To labour still, with zeal devout,
To get the Outs, poor devils, in,
  And turn the Inns, the wretches, out.

I pledge myself, though much bereft
  Of ways and means of ruling ill,
To make the most of what are left,
  And stick to all that's rotten still.

Though gone the days of place and pelf,
  And drones no more take all the honey,
I pledge myself to cram myself
  With all I can of public money;

To quarter on that social purse
  My nephews, nieces, sisters, brothers,
Nor, so *we* prosper, care a curse
  How much 'tis at th' expense of others.

I pledge myself, whenever Right
  And Might on any point divide,
Not to ask which is black or white,
  But take, at once, the strongest side.

For instance, in all Tithe discussions,
  I'm *for* the Reverend encroachers:—
I loathe the Poles, applaud the Russians,—
  Am *for* the Squires *against* the Poachers.

Betwixt the Corn-Lords and the Poor
  I've not the slightest hesitation,—
The people *must* be starv'd to insure
  The Land its due remuneration.

I pledge myself to be no more
    With Ireland's wrongs bepros'd or shamm'd,—
I vote her grievances a *bore*,
    So she may suffer, and be d——d.

Or if she kick, let it console us,
    We still have plenty of red coats,
To cram the Church, that general bolus,
    Down any giv'n amount of throats.

I dearly love the Frankfort Diet,—
    Think newspapers the worst of crimes;
And would, to give some chance of quiet,
    Hang all the writers of *The Times*;

Break all their correspondents' bones,
    All authors of 'Reply', 'Rejoinder',
From the Anti-Tory, Colonel J——es,
    To the Anti-Suttee, Mr P-ynd-r.

Such are the Pledges I propose;
    And though I can't now offer gold,
There's many a way of buying those
    Who've but the taste for being sold.

So here's, with three times three hurrahs,
    A toast, of which you'll not complain,—
'Long life to jobbing; may the days
    Of Peculation shine again!'

THOMAS MOORE

ON A SQUINTING POETESS

To no one Muse does she her glance confine,
But has an eye, at once, to all the Nine.

THOMAS MOORE

113

FRAGMENT OF A CHARACTER

Here lies Factotum Ned at last;
   Long as he breath'd the vital air,
Nothing throughout all Europe pass'd,
   In which Ned hadn't some small share.

Whoe'er was in, whoe'er was out,
   Whatever statesmen did or said,
If not exactly brought about,
   'Twas all, at least, contriv'd by Ned.

With Nap, if Russia went to war,
   'Twas owing, under Providence,
To certain hints Ned gave the Czar—
   (Vide his pamphlet—price, sixpence.)

If France was beat at Waterloo—
   As all but Frenchmen think she was—
To Ned, as Wellington well knew,
   Was owing half that day's applause.

Then for his news—no envoy's bag
   E'er pass'd so many secrets through it;
Scarcely a telegraph could wag
   Its wooden finger, but Ned knew it.

Such tales he had of foreign plots,
   With foreign names, one's ear to buzz in!
From Russia, *chefs* and *ofs* in lots,
   From Poland, *owskis* by the dozen.

When George, alarm'd for England's creed,
   Turn'd out the last Whig ministry,
And men ask'd—who advis'd the deed?
   Ned modestly confess'd 'twas he.

For though, by some unlucky miss,
　　He had not downright *seen* the King,
He sent such hints through Viscount *This*,
　　To Marquis *That*, as clench'd the thing.

The same it was in science, arts,
　　The Drama, Books, MS. and printed—
Kean learn'd from Ned his cleverest parts,
　　And Scott's last work by him was hinted.

Childe Harold in the proofs he read,
　　And, here and there, infus'd some soul in't—
Nay, Davy's Lamp, till seen by Ned,
　　Had—odd enough—an awkward hole in't.

'Twas thus, all-doing and all-knowing,
　　Wit, statesman, boxer, chymist, singer,
Whatever was the best pye going,
　　In *that* Ned—trust him—had his finger.

THOMAS MOORE

A WYKEHAMIST'S ADDRESS TO LEARNING

Oh, make me, Sphere-descended Queen,
A Bishop or at least a Dean.

P. N. SHUTTLEWORTH (*afterwards Warden of New College and Bishop of Chichester*)

A SONNET

O lovely O most charming pug
Thy gracefull air and heavenly mug
The beauties of his mind do shine
And every bit is shaped so fine
Your very tail is most devine
Your teeth is whiter than the snow
You are a great buck and a bow
Your eyes are of so fine a shape
More like a christains then an ape
His cheeks is like the roses blume
Your hair is like the ravens plume
His noses cast is of the roman
He is a very pretty weomen
I could not get a rhyme for roman
And was oblidged to call it weoman.

MARJORY FLEMING

ON T. MOORE'S POEMS

Lalla Rookh
Is a naughty book
By Tommy Moore,
Who has written four;
Each warmer
Than the former,
So the most recent
Is the least decent.

ANON

THERE WAS A NAUGHTY BOY

(*From a letter to Fanny Keats*)

There was a naughty Boy,
   And a naughty Boy was he,
He ran away to Scotland
   The people for to see—

      Then he found
      That the ground
      Was as hard,
      That a yard
      Was as long,
      That a song
      Was as merry,
      That a cherry
      Was as red—
      That lead
      Was as weighty,
      That fourscore
      Was as eighty,
      That a door
      Was as wooden
      As in England —

So he stood in his shoes
   And he wonder'd,
   He wonder'd,
He stood in his shoes
   And he wonder'd.

JOHN KEATS

HE LIVED AMIDST TH' UNTRODDEN WAYS

He lived amidst th' untrodden ways
    To Rydal Lake that lead;
A bard whom there were none to praise,
    And very few to read.

Behind a cloud his mystic sense,
    Deep hidden, who can spy?
Bright as the night when not a star
    Is shining in the sky.

Unread his works—his 'Milk White Doe'
    With dust is dark and dim;
It's still in Longman's shop, and oh!
    The difference to him!

HARTLEY COLERIDGE

ON A PAINTED WOMAN

To youths, who hurry thus away,
    How silly your desire is
At such an early hour to pay
    Your compliments to Iris.

Stop, prithee, stop, ye hasty beaux,
    No longer urge this race on;
Though Iris has put on her clothes,
    She has not put her face on.

P. B. SHELLEY

THE BELLE OF THE BALL ROOM

Years—years ago—ere yet my dreams
　　Had been of being wise or witty,—
Ere I had done with writing themes,
　　Or yawn'd o'er this infernal Chitty;—
Years—years ago,—while all my joy
　　Was in my fowling piece and filly,—
In short, while I was yet a boy,
　　I fell in love with Laura Lily.

I saw her at the County Ball:
　　There, when the sounds of flute and fiddle
Gave signal sweet in that old hall
　　Of hands across and down the middle,
Hers was the subtlest spell by far
　　Of all that set young hearts romancing;
She was our queen, our rose, our star;
　　And then she danced—O Heaven, her dancing!

Dark was her hair, her hand was white;
　　Her voice was exquisitely tender;
Her eyes were full of liquid light;
　　I never saw a waist so slender!
Her every look, her every smile,
　　Shot right and left a score of arrows;
I thought 'twas Venus from her isle,
　　And wonder'd where she'd left her sparrows.

She talk'd,—of politics or prayers,—
　　Or Southey's prose, or Wordsworth's sonnets,—
Of danglers—or of dancing bears,
　　Of battles—or the last new bonnets,
By candlelight, at twelve o'clock,
　　To me it mattered not a tittle;
If those bright lips had quoted Locke,
　　I might have thought they murmur'd Little.

Through sunny May, through sultry June,
    I loved her with a love eternal;
I spoke her praises to the moon,
    I wrote them to the Sunday Journal:
My mother laugh'd; I soon found out
    That ancient ladies have no feeling:
My father frown'd; but how should gout
    See any happiness in kneeling?

She was the daughter of a Dean,
    Rich, fat, and rather apoplectic;
She had one brother, just thirteen,
    Whose colour was extremely hectic;
Her grandmother for many a year
    Had fed the parish with her bounty;
Her second cousin was a peer,
    And Lord Lieutenant of the County.

But titles and the three per cents.,
    And mortgages, and great relations,
And India bonds, and tithes, and rents,
    Oh what are they to love's sensations?
Black eyes, fair forehead, clustering locks—
    Such wealth, such honours, Cupid chooses;
He cares as little for the Stocks
    As Baron Rothschild for the Muses.

She sketch'd; the vale, the wood, the beech,
    Grew lovelier from her pencil's shading:
She botanized; I envied each
    Young blossom in her boudoir fading:
She warbled Handel; it was grand;
    She made the Catalani jealous:
She touch'd the organ; I could stand
    For hours and hours to blow the bellows.

She kept an album, too, at home,
  Well fill'd with all an album's glories;
Paintings of butterflies, and Rome,
  Patterns for trimmings, Persian stories;
Soft songs to Julia's cockatoo,
  Fierce odes to Famine and to Slaughter,
And autographs of Prince Leboo,
  And recipes for elder-water.

And she was flatter'd, worshipp'd, bored;
  Her steps were watch'd, her dress was noted;
Her poodle dog was quite adored,
  Her sayings were extremely quoted;
She laugh'd and every heart was glad,
  As if the taxes were abolish'd;
She frown'd, and every look was sad,
  As if the Opera were demolish'd.

She smiled on many, just for fun,—
  I knew that there was nothing in it;
I was the first—the only one
  Her heart had thought of for a minute.—
I knew it, for she told me so,
  In phrase which was divinely moulded;
She wrote a charming hand,—and oh!
  How sweetly all her notes were folded!

Our love was like most other loves;—
  A little glow, a little shiver,
A rose-bud, and a pair of gloves,
  And 'Fly not yet'—upon the river;
Some jealousy of some-one's heir,
  Some hopes of dying broken hearted,
A miniature, a lock of hair,
  The usual vows,—and then we parted.

We parted; months and years roll'd by;
    We met again four summers after:
Our parting was all sob and sigh;
    Our meeting was all mirth and laughter:
For in my heart's most secret cell
    There had been many other lodgers;
And she was not the ball-room's Belle,
    But only—Mrs Something Rogers!

W. M. PRAED

A FRIEND

Who borrows all your ready cash,
And with it cuts a mighty dash,
Proving the lender weak and rash?—
               Your friend!

Who finds out every secret fault,
Misjudges every word and thought,
And makes you pass for worse than nought?—
               Your friend!

Who wins your money at deep play,
Then tells you that the world doth say,
' 'Twere wise from clubs you kept away?'—
               Your friend!

Who sells you, for the longest price,
Horses, a dealer, in a trice,
Would find unsound and full of vice?—
               Your friend!

Who eats your dinners, then looks shrewd;
Wishes you had a cook like Ude,
For then much oftener would intrude?—
               Your friend!

Who tells you that you've shocking wine,
And owns that, though he sports not fine,
Crockford's the only place to dine?—
                    Your friend!

Who wheedles you with words most fond
To sign for him a heavy bond,
'Or else, by Jove, must quick abscond?'—
                    Your friend!

Who makes you all the interest pay,
With principal, some future day,
And laughs at what you then may say?—
                    Your friend!

Who makes deep love unto your wife,
Knowing you prize her more than life,
And breeds between you hate and strife?—
                    Your friend!

Who, when you've got into a brawl,
Insists that out your man you call,
Then gets you shot, which ends it all?—
                    Your friend!!!

                    MARGUERITE POWER,
                    COUNTESS OF BLESSINGTON

ON THOMAS, SECOND EARL OF ONSLOW

What can Tommy Onslow do?
Drive a phaeton and two.
Can Tommy Onslow do no more?
Yes; drive a phaeton and four.

                    ANON

FREE THOUGHTS ON SEVERAL
EMINENT COMPOSERS

Some cry up Haydn, some Mozart,
Just as the whim bites; for my part,
I do not care a farthing candle
For either of them, or for Handel.—
Cannot a man live free and easy,
Without admiring Pergolesi?
Or thro' the world with comfort go,
That never heard of Doctor Blow?
So help me God, I hardly have;
And yet I eat, and drink, and shave,
Like other people, if you watch it,
And know no more of Stave or Crotchet,
Than did the primitive Peruvians;
Or those old ante-queer-Diluvians
That lived in the unwash'd world with Tubal,
Before that dirty blacksmith Jubal
By stroke on anvil, or by summ'at,
Found out, to his great surprise, the gamut
I care no more for Cimarosa,
Than he did for Salvator Rosa,
Being no painter; and bad luck
Be mine, if I can bear that Gluck!
Old Tycho Brahe, and modern Herschel,
Had something in 'em; but who's Purcel?
The devil, with his foot so cloven,
For aught I care, may take Beethoven;
And, if the bargain does not suit,
I'll throw him Weber in to boot.
There's not the splitting of a splinter
To choose 'twixt him last named, and Winter
Of Doctor Pepusch old queen Dido
Knew just as much, God knows, as I do.

I would not go four miles to visit
Sebastian Bach (or Batch, which is it?);
No more I would for Bononcini.
As for Novello, or Rossini,
I shall not say a word to grieve 'em,
Because they're living; so I leave 'em.

CHARLES LAMB

A FABLE

(*In imitation of Dryden*)

A dingy donkey, formal and unchanged,
Browsed in the lane and o'er the common ranged.
Proud of his ancient asinine possessions,
Free from the panniers of the grave professions,
He lived at ease; and chancing once to find
A lion's skin, the fancy took his mind
To personate the monarch of the wood;
And for a time the stratagem held good.
He moved with so majestical a pace
That bears and wolves and all the savage race
Gazed in admiring awe, ranging aloof,
Not over-anxious for a clearer proof—
Longer he might have triumph'd—but alas!
In an unguarded hour it came to pass
He bray'd aloud; and show'd himself an ass!

The moral of this tale I could not guess
Till Mr Landor sent his works to press.

J. H. FRERE

LITTLE BILLEE

There were three sailors of Bristol city
Who took a boat and went to sea,
But first with beef and captain's biscuits
And pickled pork they loaded she.

There was gorging Jack and guzzling Jimmy
And the youngest he was little Billee.
Now when they had got as far as the Equator
They'd nothing left but one split pea.

Says gorging Jack to guzzling Jimmy,
'I am extremely hungaree.'
To gorging Jack says guzzling Jimmy,
'We've nothing left, us must eat we.'

Says gorging Jack to guzzling Jimmy,
'With one another we shouldn't agree!
There's little Bill, he's young and tender,
We're old and tough, so let's eat he.'

'Oh! Billee, we're going to kill and eat you
So undo the button of your chemie.'
When Bill received this information
He used his pocket handkerchie.

'First let me say my catechism,
Which my poor mammy taught to me.'
'Make haste, make haste,' says guzzling Jimmy,
While Jack pulled out his snickersnee.

So Billee went up to the main top gallant mast,
And down he fell on his bended knee.
He scarce had come to the twelfth commandment
When up he jumps, 'There's land I see:

'Jerusalem and Madagascar,
And North and South Amerikee:
There's a British flag a-riding at anchor,
With Admiral Napier, K.C.B.'

So when they got aboard of the Admiral's,
He hanged fat Jack and flogged Jimmee:
But as for little Bill he made him
The Captain of a Seventy-three.

W. M. THACKERAY

THE SORROWS OF WERTHER

Werther had a love for Charlotte
    Such as words could never utter;
Would you know how first he met her?
    She was cutting bread and butter.

Charlotte was a married lady,
    And a moral man was Werther,
And for all the wealth of Indies,
    Would do nothing for to hurt her.

So he sigh'd and pined and ogled,
    And his passion boil'd and bubbled,
Till he blew his silly brains out,
    And no more was by it troubled.

Charlotte, having seen his body
    Borne before her on a shutter,
Like a well-conducted person,
    Went on cutting bread and butter.

W. M. THACKERAY

FAITHLESS NELLIE GRAY

Ben Battle was a soldier bold,
    And used to war's alarms;
But a cannon-ball took off his legs,
    So he laid down his arms.

Now as they bore him off the field,
    Said he, 'Let others shoot,
For here I leave my second leg,
    And the Forty-second Foot!'

The army-surgeons made him limbs:
    Said he:—'They're only pegs:
But there's as wooden members quite
    As represent my legs!'

Now Ben he loved a pretty maid,
    Her name was Nellie Gray:
So he went to pay her his devours
    When he'd devoured his pay!

But when he called on Nellie Gray,
    She made him quite a scoff;
And when she saw his wooden legs
    Began to take them off!

'O, Nellie Gray! O, Nellie Gray!
    Is this your love so warm?
The love that loves a scarlet coat
    Should be more uniform!'

She said, 'I loved a soldier once,
    For he was blythe and brave;
But I will never have a man
    With both legs in the grave!
128

'Before you had those timber toes,
    Your love I did allow,
But then, you know, you stand upon
    Another footing now!'

'O, Nellie Gray! O, Nellie Gray!
    For all your jeering speeches,
At duty's call, I left my legs
    In Badajos's *breaches!*'

'Why, then,' she said, 'you've lost the feet
    Of legs in war's alarms,
And now you cannot wear your shoes
    Upon your feats of arms!'

'Oh, false and fickle Nellie Gray;
    I know why you refuse:—
Though I've no feet—some other man
    Is standing in my shoes!

'I wish I ne'er had seen your face;
    But now, a long farewell!
For you will be my death, alas!
    You will not be my *Nell!*'

Now when he went from Nellie Gray,
    His heart so heavy got—
And life was such a burthen grown,
    It made him take a knot!

So round his melancholy neck,
    A rope he did entwine,
And, for his second time in life,
    Enlisted in the Line!

One end he tied around a beam,
    And then removed his pegs,
And as his legs were off,—of course,
    He soon was off his legs!

And there he hung, till he was dead
    As any nail in town,—
For though distress had cut him up,
    It could not cut him down!

A dozen men sat on his corpse,
    To find out why he died—
And they buried Ben in four cross-roads,
    With a *stake* in his inside!

THOMAS HOOD

SALLY BROWN

Young Ben he was a nice young man,
    A carpenter by trade;
And he fell in love with Sally Brown,
    That was a lady's maid.

But as they fetch'd a walk one day,
    They met a press-gang crew;
And Sally she did faint away,
    Whilst Ben he was brought to.

The Boatswain swore with wicked words,
    Enough to shock a saint,
But though she did seem in a fit,
    'Twas nothing but a feint.

'Come, girl,' said he, 'hold up your head,
    He'll be as good as me;
For when your swain is in our boat,
    A boatswain he will be.'

So when they'd made their game of her
    And taken off her elf,
She roused, and found she only was
    A-coming to herself.

'And is he gone, and is he gone?'
  She cried, and wept outright:
'Then I will to the water side
  And see him out of sight.'

A waterman came up to her,—
  'Now, young woman,' said he,
'If you weep on so, you will make
  Eye-water in the sea.'

'Alas! they've taken my beau Ben,
  To sail with old Benbow;'
And her woe began to run afresh,
  As if she'd said Gee woe!

Says he, 'They've only taken him
  To the Tender ship, you see;'
'The Tender-ship,' cried Sally Brown,
  'What a hard-ship that must be!'

'O! would I were a mermaid now,
  For then I'd follow him;
But, Oh!—I'm not a fish-woman,
  And so I cannot swim.

'Alas! I was not born beneath
  "The virgin and the scales,"
So I must curse my cruel stars,
  And walk about in Wales.'

Now Ben had sail'd to many a place
  That's underneath the world;
But in two years the ship came home,
  And all the sails were furl'd.

But when he call'd on Sally Brown,
  To see how she went on,
He found she'd got another Ben,
  Whose Christian name was John.

'O Sally Brown, O Sally Brown,
   How could you serve me so,
I've met with many a breeze before,
   But never such a blow!'

Then reading on his 'bacco box,
   He heaved a heavy sigh,
And then began to eye his pipe,
   And then to pipe his eye.

And then he tried to sing 'All's Well,'
   But could not, though he tried;
His head was turn'd, and so he chew'd
   His pigtail till he died.

His death, which happen'd in his berth,
   At forty-odd befell:
They went and told the sexton, and
   The sexton toll'd the bell.

THOMAS HOOD

A NOCTURNAL SKETCH

Even is come; and from the dark Park, hark,
The signal of the setting sun—one gun!
And six is sounding from the chime, prime time
To go and see the Drury-Lane Dane slain,—
Or hear Othello's jealous doubt spout out,—
Or Macbeth raving at that shade-made blade,
Denying to his frantic clutch much touch;—
Or else to see Ducrow with wide stride ride
Four horses as no other man can span;
Or in the small Olympic Pit, sit split
Laughing at Liston, while you quiz his phiz.

Anon Night comes, and with her wings brings things
Such as, with his poetic tongue, Young sung;
The gas up-blazes with its bright white light,
And paralytic watchmen prowl, howl, growl,
About the streets and take up Pall-Mall Sal,
Who, hasting to her nightly jobs, robs fobs.

Now thieves to enter for your cash, smash, crash,
Past drowsy Charley, in a deep sleep, creep,
But frightened by Policeman B3, flee,
And while they're going, whisper low, 'No go!'

Now puss, while folks are in their beds, treads leads,
And sleepers waking grumble, 'Drat that cat!'
Who in the gutter caterwauls, squalls, mauls
Some feline foe, and screams in shrill ill-will.

Now Bulls of Bashan, of a prize size, rise
In childish dreams and with a roar gore poor
Georgy, or Charley, or Billy, willy-nilly;—
But Nursemaid, in a nightmare rest, chest-press'd,
Dreameth of one of her old flames, James Games,
And that she hears—what faith is man's!—Ann's banns
And his, from Reverend Mr Rice, twice, thrice:
White ribbons flourish, and a stout shout out,
That upward goes, shows Rose knows those bows' woes!

THOMAS HOOD

ATHOL BROSE

Charm'd with a drink which Highlanders compose,
    A German traveller exclaim'd with glee,—
'Potztausend! sare, if dis is Athol Brose,
    How goot dere Athol Boetry must be!'

THOMAS HOOD

TO MINERVA

My temples throb, my pulses boil,
   I'm sick of Song, and Ode, and Ballad—
So, Thyrsis, take the Midnight Oil,
   And pour it on a lobster salad.

My brain is dull, my sight is foul,
   I cannot write a verse, or read—
Then, Pallas, take away thine Owl,
   And let us have a lark instead.

                   THOMAS HOOD

TO MR MURRAY

I

Strahan, Tonson, Lintot of the times,
Patron and publisher of rhymes,
For thee the bard up Pindus climbs,
        My Murray.

To thee, with hope and terror dumb,
The unfledged MS. authors come;
Thou printest all—and sellest some—
        My Murray.

Upon thy table's baize so green
The last new Quarterly is seen,—
But where is thy new Magazine,
        My Murray?

Along thy sprucest bookshelves shine
The works thou deemest most divine—
The 'Art of Cookery,' and mine,
        My Murray.

134

Tours, Travels, Essays, too, I wist,
And Sermons, to thy mill bring grist;
And then thou hast the 'Navy List,'
   My Murray.

And Heaven forbid I should conclude
Without 'the Board of Longitude,'
Although this narrow paper would,
   My Murray.

II

For Orford and for Waldegrave
You give much more than me you gave;
Which is not fairly to behave,
   My Murray.

Because if a live dog, 'tis said,
Be worth a lion fairly sped,
A *live lord* must be worth *two* dead,
   My Murray.

And if, as the opinion goes,
Verse hath a better sale than prose,—
Certes, I should have more than those,
   My Murray.

But now this sheet is nearly cramm'd,
So, if *you will*, *I* sha'n't be shamm'd,
And if you *won't*, *you* may be damn'd,
   My Murray.

     GEORGE GORDON, LORD BYRON

EPIGRAM ON JOHN BULL

The world is a bundle of hay,
　　Mankind are the asses who pull;
Each tugs it a different way,
　　And the greatest of all is John Bull.

　　　　　GEORGE GORDON, LORD BYRON

IRELAND NEVER WAS CONTENTED

　　　Ireland never was contented.
　　　Say you so? You are demented.
　　　Ireland was contented when
　　　All could use the sword and pen,
　　　And when Tara rose so high
　　　That her turrets split the sky,
　　　And about her courts were seen
　　　Liveried angels robed in green,
　　　Wearing, by St Patrick's bounty,
　　　Emeralds big as half the county.

　　　　　　　W. S. LANDOR

ON THE FOUR GEORGES

George the First was always reckon'd
Vile—but viler George the Second;
And what mortal ever heard
Any good of George the Third?
When from earth the Fourth descended,
God be praised, the Georges ended.

　　　　　　　W. S. LANDOR

RICH AND POOR; OR, SAINT AND SINNER

The poor man's sins are glaring;
In the face of ghostly warning
    He is caught in the fact
    Of an overt act—
Buying greens on Sunday morning.

The rich man's sins are hidden
In the pomp of wealth and station;
    And escape the sight
    Of the children of light,
Who are wise in their generation.

The rich man has a kitchen,
And cooks to dress his dinner;
    The poor who would roast
    To the baker's must post,
And thus becomes a sinner.

The rich man has a cellar,
And a ready butler by him;
    The poor must steer
    For his pint of beer
Where the Saint can't choose but spy him.

The rich man's painted windows
Hide the concerts of the quality;
    The poor can but share
    A crack'd fiddle in the air,
Which offends all sound morality.

The rich man is invisible
In the crowd of his gay society;
    But the poor man's delight
    Is a sore in the sight,
And a stench in the nose of piety.

T. L. PEACOCK

137

THE JACKDAW OF RHEIMS

The Jackdaw sat on the Cardinal's chair!
Bishop, and abbot, and prior were there;
  Many a monk and many a friar,
  Many a knight and many a squire,
With a great many more of lesser degree,—
In sooth a goodly company;
And they served the Lord Primate on bended knee.
  Never, I ween,
  Was a prouder seen,
Read of in books, or dreamt of in dreams,
Than the Cardinal Lord Archbishop of Rheims!

  In and out
  Through the motley rout,
That little Jackdaw kept hopping about;
  Here and there
  Like a dog in a fair,
  Over comfits and cates,
  And dishes and plates,
Cowl and cope, and rochet and pall,
Mitre and crosier! he hopped upon all!
  With saucy air,
  He perched on the chair
Where, in state, the great Lord Cardinal sat
In the great Lord Cardinal's great red hat;
  And he peered in the face
  Of his Lordship's Grace,
With a satisfied look, as if he would say,
'We two are the greatest folks here to-day!'
  And the priests with awe,
  As such freaks they saw,
Said, 'The Devil must be in that little Jackdaw!'

The feast was over, the board was cleared,
The flawns and the custards had all disappeared,
And six little Singing-boys,—dear little souls!
In nice clean faces, and nice white stoles,
    Came in order due,
    Two by two,
Marching that grand refectory through!
A nice little boy held a golden ewer,
Embossed and filled with water, as pure
As any that flows between Rheims and Namur,
Which a nice little boy stood ready to catch
In a fine golden hand-basin made to match.
Two nice little boys, rather more grown,
Carried lavender-water, and eau de Cologne;
And a nice little boy had a nice cake of soap,
Worthy of washing the hands of the Pope.
    One little boy more
    A napkin bore,
Of the best white diaper, fringed with pink,
And a Cardinal's Hat marked in 'permanent ink'.

The great Lord Cardinal turns at the sight
Of these nice little boys dressed all in white:
    From his finger he draws
    His costly turquoise;
And, not thinking at all about little Jackdaws,
    Deposits it straight
    By the side of his plate,
While the nice little boys on his Eminence wait;
Till, when nobody's dreaming of any such thing,
That little Jackdaw hops off with the ring!

    There's a cry and a shout,
    And a deuce of a rout,
And nobody seems to know what they're about,
But the Monks have their pockets all turned inside out.

    The Friars are kneeling,
    And hunting and feeling
The carpet, the floor, and the walls, and the ceiling.
    The Cardinal drew
    Off each plum-coloured shoe,
And left his red stockings exposed to the view;
    He peeps, and he feels
    In the toes and the heels;
They turn up the dishes,—they turn up the plates,—
They take up the poker and poke out the grates,
    They turn up the rugs,
    They examine the mugs:—
    But, no!—no such thing;—
    They can't find THE RING!
And the Abbot declared that, 'when nobody twigged it,
Some rascal or other had popped in, and prigged it!'

The Cardinal rose with a dignified look,
He called for his candle, his bell, and his book!
    In holy anger, and pious grief
    He solemnly cursed that rascally thief!
    He cursed him at board, he cursed him in bed;
    From the sole of his foot to the crown of his head;
    He cursed him in sleeping, that every night
    He should dream of the devil, and wake in a fright;
    He cursed him in eating, he cursed him in drinking,
    He cursed him in coughing, in sneezing, in winking;
    He cursed him in sitting, in standing, in lying;
    He cursed him in walking, in riding, in flying,
    He cursed him in living, he cursed him in dying!—
Never was heard such a terrible curse!!
    But what gave rise
    To no little surprise,
Nobody seemed one penny the worse!

    The day was gone,
    The night came on

The Monks and the Friars they searched till dawn;
    When the Sacristan saw,
    On crumpled claw,
Come limping a poor little lame Jackdaw!
    No longer gay,
    As on yesterday;
His feathers all seemed to be turned the wrong way;—
His pinions drooped—he could hardly stand,—
His head was as bald as the palm of your hand;
    His eye so dim,
    So wasted each limb,
That, heedless of grammar, they all cried, 'THAT'S HIM—
That's the scamp that has done this scandalous thing!
That's the thief that has got my Lord Cardinal's Ring!'
    The poor little Jackdaw,
    When the Monks he saw,
Feebly gave vent to the ghost of a caw;
And turned his bald head, as much as to say,
'Pray, be so good as to walk this way!'
    Slower and slower
    He limped on before,
Till they came to the back of the belfry door,
    Where the first thing they saw,
    Midst the sticks and the straw,
Was the RING in the nest of that little Jackdaw!

Then the great Lord Cardinal called for his book,
And off that terrible curse he took;
    The mute expression
    Served in lieu of confession,
And, being thus coupled with full restitution,
The Jackdaw got plenary absolution!
    —When these words were heard,
    That poor little bird
Was so changed in a moment, 'twas really absurd.

He grew sleek, and fat;
    In addition to that,
A fresh crop of feathers came thick as a mat!
    His tail waggled more
    Even than before,
But no longer it wagged with an impudent air,
No longer he perched on the Cardinal's chair.
    He hopped now about
    With a gait devout;
At Matins, at Vespers, he never was out;
And, so far from any more pilfering deeds,
He always seemed telling the Confessor's beads.
If any one lied,—or if any one swore,—
Or slumbered in prayer-time and happened to snore,
    That good Jackdaw
    Would give a great 'Caw!'
As much as to say, 'Don't do so any more!'
While many remarked, as his manners they saw,
That they 'never had known such a pious Jackdaw.'
    He long lived the pride
    Of that country side,
And at last in the odour of sanctity died;
    When, as words were too faint
    His merits to paint,
The Conclave determined to make him a Saint;
And on newly-made Saints and Popes, as you know,
It's the custom, at Rome, new names to bestow,
So they canonized him by the name of Jim Crow! ·

R. H. BARHAM

142

NOT A SOUS HAD HE GOT

Not a *sous* had he got,—not a guinea or note,
  And he look'd confoundedly flurried,
As he bolted away without paying his shot,
  And the Landlady after him hurried.

We saw him again at dead of night,
  When home from the Club returning;
We twigg'd the Doctor beneath the light
  Of the gas-lamp brilliantly burning.

All bare, and exposed to the midnight dews,
  Reclined in the gutter we found him;
And he look'd like a gentleman taking a snooze,
  With his *Marshall* cloak around him.

'The Doctor's as drunk as the d——,' we said,
  And we managed a shutter to borrow;
We raised him, and sigh'd at the thought that his head
  Would 'consumedly ache' on the morrow.

We bore him home, and we put him to bed,
  And we told his wife and his daughter
To give him, next morning, a couple of red
      Herrings, with soda-water.

Loudly they talk'd of his money that's gone,
  And his Lady began to upbraid him;
But little he reck'd, so they let him snore on
  'Neath the counterpane just as we laid him.

We tuck'd him in, and had hardly done
  When, beneath the window calling,
We heard the rough voice of a son of a gun
  Of a watchman 'One o'clock!' bawling.

Slowly and sadly we all walk'd down
   From his room in the uppermost story;
A rushlight we placed on the cold hearth-stone,
   And we left him alone in his glory.

R. H. BARHAM

MORE EPITAPHS

ANDREW GEAR OF SUNDERLAND

Here lies the body of Andrew Gear,
Whose mouth did stretch from ear to ear;
Stranger, step lightly o'er his head,
For if he gapes, by Josh, you're dead

JOHN BUN

Here lies John Bun,
He was killed by a gun,
His name was not Bun, but Wood,
But Wood would not rhyme with gun, but Bun would.

MARY ANN

Mary Ann has gone to rest,
Safe at last on Abraham's breast,
Which may be nuts for Mary Ann,
But is certainly rough on Abraham.

JOHNNY DOW

Wha lies here?
I, Johnny Dow.
Hoo! Johnny, is that you?
Ay, man, but a'm dead now.

A BREWER

Here lies poor Burton,
He was both hale and stout;
Death laid him on his bitter bier,
Now in another world he hops about.

A DENTIST

Stranger! Approach this spot with gravity!
John Brown is filling his last cavity.

A 'PRIZE' POEM

Full many a gem of purest ray serene,
That to be hated needs but to be seen,
Invites my lays; be present sylvan maids,
And graceful deer reposing in the shades.

I am the Morning and the Evening Star,
Drag the slow barge, or wheel the rapid car
While wrapped in fire the realms of ether glow,
Or private dirt in public virtue throw.

How small of all that human hearts endure
The short and simple annals of the poor!
I would commend their bodies to the rack;
At least we'll die with harness on our back!

Remote, unfriended, melancholy, slow,
Virtue alone is happiness below!
As vipers sting, though dead, by some review;
And now thou seest my soul's angelic hue.

SHIRLEY BROOKS

FOR A' THAT AND A' THAT

(In imitation of Burns)

More luck to honest poverty,
    It claims respect, and a' that;
But honest wealth's a better thing,
    We dare be rich for a' that.
      For a' that, and a' that,
        And spooney cant and a' that,
      A man may have a ten-pun note,
      And be a brick for a' that.

What though on soup and fish we dine,
    Wear evening togs and a' that,
A man may like good meat and wine,
    Nor be a knave for a' that.
      For a' that, and a' that,
        Their fustian talk and a' that,
      A gentleman, however clean,
      May have a heart for a' that.

You see yon prater called a Beales,
    Who bawls and brays and a' that,
Tho' hundreds cheer his blatant bosh,
    He's but a goose for a' that.
      For a' that, and a' that,
        His Bubblyjocks, and a' that,
      A man with twenty grains of sense,
      He looks and laughs at a' that.

A prince can make a belted knight,
    A marquis, duke, and a' that,
And if the title's earned, all right,
    Old England's fond of a' that.

For a' that, and a' that,
    Beales' balderdash, and a' that,
A name that tells of service done
    Is worth the wear, for a' that.

Then let us pray that come it may
    And come it will for a' that,
That common sense may take the place
    Of common cant and a' that.
    For a' that, and a' that,
    Who cackles trash and a' that,
    Or be he lord, or be he low,
      The man's an ass for a' that.

SHIRLEY BROOKS

EIGHTEEN-FORTY-THREE

The Free Kirk,
The wee kirk,
The Kirk without the steeple;
The Auld Kirk,
The cauld Kirk,
The Kirk without the people.

ANON

ECH, SIC A PAIRISH

Ech, sic a pairish, a pairish, a pairish,
  Ech, sic a pairish was little Kilkell:
They hae hangit the minister, droont the Precentor,
  They Pu'd down the steeple, and drunkit the bell.

ANON

LET US ALL BE UNHAPPY ON SUNDAY

We zealots, made up of stiff clay,
  The sour-looking children of sorrow,
While not over jolly today,
  Resolve to be wretched tomorrow.
We can't for a certainty tell
  What mirth may molest us on Monday;
But, at least, to begin the week well,
  Let us all be unhappy on Sunday.

What though a good precept we strain
  Till hateful and hurtful we make it!
While though, in thus pulling the rein,
  We may draw it so tight as to break it!
Abroad we forbid folks to roam,
  For fear they get social or frisky;
But of course they can sit still at home,
  And get dismally drunk upon whisky.

LORD NEAVES

STRICTURES ON THE ECONOMY OF NATURE

A' things created have their uses,
  This truth will bear nae doots,
As far as hauds to fleas and louses
  An' ither bitin' brutes.
I ken the use o' crawlin' clocks
  An' bugs upon you creepin';
But what's the use o' Barbara Fox?
  By jingo, that's a deep ane!

GEORGE OUTRAM

148

SONNET FOUND IN A DESERTED
MAD-HOUSE

Oh that my soul a marrow-bone might seize!
For the old egg of my desire is broken,
Spilled is the pearly white and spilled the yolk, and
As the mild melancholy contents grease
My path the shorn lamb baas like bumblebees.
Time's trashy purse is as a taken token
Or like a thrilling recitation, spoken
By mournful mouths filled full of mirth and cheese.

And yet, why should I clasp the earthful urn?
Or find the frittered fig that felt the fast?
Or choose to chase the cheese around the churn?
Or swallow any pill from out the past?
Ah, no Love, not while your hot kisses burn
Like a potato riding on the blast.

ANON

SONNET TO BRITAIN
BY THE D—— OF W——

Halt! Shoulder arms! Recover! As you were!
  Right wheel! Eyes left! Attention! Stand at ease!
  O Britain! O My country! Words like these
Have made thy name a terror and a fear
To all the nations. Witness Ebro's banks,
  Assaye, Toulouse, Nivelle, and Waterloo,
  Where the grim despot muttered—*Sauve qui peut!*
And Ney fled darkling.—Silence in the ranks!
Inspired by these, amidst the iron crash
  Of armies, in the centre of his troop
The soldier stands—unmovable, not rash—
  Until the forces of the foeman droop;
Then knocks the Frenchmen to eternal smash,
  Pounding them into mummy. Shoulder, hoop!

W. E. AYTOUN

149

THE MASSACRE OF THE MACPHERSON

Fhairshon swore a feud
    Against the clan M'Tavish;
Marched into their land
    To murder and to rafish;
For he did resolve
    To extirpate the vipers,
With four-and-twenty men
    And five-and-thirty pipers.

But when he had gone
    Half-way down Strath Canaan,
Of his fighting tail
    Just three were remainin'.
They were all he had,
    To back him in ta battle;
All the rest had gone
    Off, to drive ta cattle.

'Fery coot!' cried Fhairshon,
    'So my clan disgraced is;
Lads, we'll need to fight
    Pefore we touch the peasties.
Here's Mhic-Mac-Methusaleh
    Coming wi' his fassals,
Gillies seventy-three,
    And sixty Dhuinewassails!'

'Coot tay to you, sir;
    Are you not ta Fhairshon?
Was you coming here
    To fisit any person?
You are a plackguard, sir!
    It is now six hundred
Coot long years, and more,
    Since my glen was plunder'd.'

'Fat is tat you say?
   Dare you cock your peaver?
I will teach you, sir,
   Fat is coot pehaviour!
You shall not exist
   For another day more;
I will shoot you, sir,
   Or stap you with my claymore!'

'I am fery glad,
   To learn what you mention,
Since I can prevent
   Any such intention.'
So Mhic-Mac-Methusaleh
   Gave some warlike howls,
Trew his skhian-dhu,
   An' stuck it in his powels.

In this fery way
   Tied ta faliant Fhairshon,
Who was always thought
   A superior person.
Fhairshon had a son,
   Who married Noah's daughter,
And nearly spoil'd ta Flood,
   By trinking up ta water:

Which he would have done,
   I at least pelieve it,
Had ta mixture peen
   Only half Glenlivet.
This is all my tale:
   Sirs, I hope 'tis new t'ye!
Here's your fery good healths,
   And tamn ta whusky duty!

W. E. AYTOUN

THE LAY OF THE LOVELORN

(In imitation of Tennyson)

Comrades, you may pass the rosy. With permission of
    the chair,
I shall leave you for a little, for I'd like to take the
    air.

Whether 'twas the sauce at dinner, or that glass of
    ginger-beer,
Or these strong cheroots, I know not, but I feel a little
    queer.

Let me go. Nay, Chuckster, blow me, 'pon my soul, this
    is too bad!
When you want me, ask the waiter; he knows where I'm
    to be had.

Whew! This is a great relief now! Let me but undo my
    stock;
Resting here beneath the porch, my nerves will steady
    like a rock.

In my ears I hear the singing of a lot of favourite
    tunes—
Bless my heart, how very odd! Why, surely there's a
    brace of moons!

See! the stars! how bright they twinkle, winking with a
    frosty glare,
Like my faithless cousin Amy when she drove me to
    despair.

Oh, my cousin, spider-hearted! Oh, my Amy! No, con-
    found it!
I must wear the mournful willow,—all around my heart
    I've bound it.

Falser than the bank of fancy, frailer than a shilling
 glove,
Puppet to a father's anger, minion to a nabob's love!

Is it well to wish thee happy? Having known me, could
 you ever
Stoop to marry half a heart, and little more than half
 a liver?

Happy! Damme! Thou shalt lower to his level day by
 day,
Changing from the best of china to the commonest of
 clay.

As the husband is, the wife is,—he is stomach-plagued
 and old;
And his curry soups will make thy cheek the colour of
 his gold.

When his feeble love is sated, he will hold thee surely
 then
Something lower than his hookah,—something less than
 his cayenne.

What is this? His eyes are pinky. Was't the claret?
 Oh, no, no,—
Bless your soul! it was the salmon,—salmon always
 makes him so.

Take him to thy dainty chamber—soothe him with thy
 lightest fancies;
He will understand thee, won't he?—pay thee with a
 lover's glances?

Louder than the loudest trumpet, harsh as harshest
 ophicleide,
Nasal respirations answer the endearments of his bride.

Sweet response, delightful music! Gaze upon thy noble
 charge,
Till the spirit fill thy bosom that inspired the meek
 Laffarge.

Better thou wert dead before me,—better, better that
 I stood,
Looking on thy murdered body, like the injured Daniel
 Good!

Better thou and I were lying, cold and timber-stiff and
 dead,
With a pan of burning charcoal underneath our nuptial
 bed!

Cursed be the Bank of England's notes, that tempt the
 soul to sin!
Cursed be the want of acres,—doubly cursed the want
 of tin!

Cursed be the marriage-contract, that enslaved thy soul
 to greed!
Cursed be the sallow lawyer, that prepared and drew the
 deed!

Cursed be his foul apprentice, who the loathsome fees
 did earn!
Cursed be the clerk and parson,—cursed be the whole
 concern!

Oh, 'tis well that I should bluster,—much I'm like to
 make of that;
Better comfort have I found in singing 'All Around my
 Hat.'

But that song, so wildly plaintive, palls upon my Bri-
 tish ears.
'Twill not do to pine for ever,—I am getting up in years.

154

Can't I turn the honest penny, scribbling for the weekly
    press,
And in writing Sunday libels drown my private wretch-
    edness?

Oh, to feel the wild pulsation that in manhood's dawn
    I knew,
When my days were all before me, and my years were
    twenty-two!

When I smoked my independent pipe along the Quad-
    rant wide,
With the many larks of London flaring up on every
    side;

When I went the pace so wildly, caring little what
    might come;
Coffee-milling care and sorrow, with a nose-adapted
    thumb;

Felt the exquisite enjoyment, tossing nightly off, oh
    heavens!
Brandies at the Cider Cellars, kidneys smoking-hot at
    Evans'!

Or in the Adelphi sitting, half in rapture, half in tears,
Saw the glorious melodrama conjure up the shades of
    years!

Saw Jack Sheppard, noble stripling, act his wondrous
    feats again,
Snapping Newgate's bars of iron, like an infant's daisy
    chain.

Might was right, and all the terrors, which had held the
    world in awe,
Were despised, and prigging prospered, spite of Laurie,
    spite of law,

In such scenes as these I triumphed, ere my passion's
    edge was rusted,
And my cousin's cold refusal left me very much dis-
    gusted!

Since, my heart is sere and withered, and I do not care
    a curse,
Whether worse shall be the better, or the better be the
    worse.

Hark! my merry comrades call me, bawling for another
    jorum;
They would mock me in derision, should I thus appear
    before 'em.

Womankind no more shall vex me, such at least as go
    arrayed
In the most expensive satins and the newest silk
    brocade.

I'll to Afric, lion-haunted, where the giant forest
    yields
Rarer robes and finer tissue than are sold at Spital-
    fields.

Or to burst all chains of habit, flinging habit's self
    aside,
I shall walk the tangled jungle in mankind's primeval
    pride;

Feeding on the luscious berries and the rich cassava
    root,
Lots of dates and lots of guavas, clusters of forbidden
    fruit.

Never comes the trader thither, never o'er the purple
    main
Sounds the oath of British commerce, or the accent of
    Cockaigne.

There, methinks, would be enjoyment, where no envious
    rule prevents;
Sink the steamboats! cuss the railways! rot, O rot the
    Three per Cents!

There the passions, cramped no longer, shall have space
    to breathe, my cousin!
I will wed some savage woman—nay, I'll wed at least a
    dozen.

There I'll rear my young mulattoes, as no Bond Street
    brats are reared:
They shall dive for alligators, catch the wild goats by
    the beard—

Whistle to the cockatoos, and mock the hairy faced
    baboon,
Worship mighty Mumbo Jumbo in the mountains of
    the Moon.

I myself, in far Timbuctoo, leopard's blood will daily
    quaff,
Ride a tiger-hunting, mounted on a thorough-bred
    giraffe.

Fiercely shall I shout the war-whoop, as some sullen
    stream he crosses,
Startling from their noonday slumbers iron-bound
    rhinoceroses.

Fool! again the dream, the fancy! But I know my words
    are mad,
For I hold the grey barbarian lower than the Christian
    cad.

I the swell—the city dandy! I to seek such horrid
    places,—
I to haunt with squalid negroes, blubber-lips, and
    monkey-faces!

I to wed with Coromantees! I, who managed—very
   near—
To secure the heart and fortune of the widow Shilli-
   beer!

Stuff and nonsense! let me never fling a single chance
   away;
Maids ere now, I know, have loved me, and another
   maiden may.

'Morning Post' ('The Times' won't trust me) help me,
   as I know you can;
I will pen an advertisement,—that's a never-failing
   plan.

'WANTED—By a bard, in wedlock, some young interest-
   ing woman:
Looks are not so much an object, if the shiners be forth-
   coming!

'Hymen's chains the advertiser vows shall be but silken
   fetters;
Please address to A. T., Chelsea. N.B.—You must pay
   the letters.'

That's the sort of thing to do it. Now I'll go and taste
   the balmy,—
Rest thee with thy yellow nabob, spider-hearted Cousin
   Amy!

SIR THEODORE MARTIN

OCCASIONAL LAPSES

And now where're he strayes,
Among the Galilean mountaines,
Or more unwellcome wayes,
He's followed by two faithfull fountaines;
Two walking baths; two weeping motions;
Portable, & compendious oceans.
    RICHARD CRASHAW: *Saint Mary Magdalene*

Weeping o'er the sacred urn,
Ever shall the Muses mourn;
Ever shall their numbers flow,
Ever elegant in woe.
AMBROSE PHILIPS: *To the Memory of Lord Halifax*

The Furies sink upon their iron beds,
And snakes uncurl'd hang listening round their heads.
    ALEXANDER POPE: *Ode on St Cecilia's Day*

Since Brunswick's smile has authoris'd my muse,
Chaste be her conduct, and sublime her views.
    EDWARD YOUNG: *The Instalment*

Does nature bear a tyrant's breast?
Is she the friend of stern control?
Wears she the despot's purple vest?
Or fetters she the free-born soul?
    JOHN LANGHORNE: *Owen of Carron*

159

And thou, Dalhousie, the Great God of War,
Lieutena.1t-Colonel to the Earl of Mar.

ANON

The beetle loves his unpretending track,
The snail the house he carries on his back;
The far-fetched worm with pleasure would disown
The bed we give him, though of softest down.

WILLIAM WORDSWORTH: *Liberty*

Dash back that ocean with a pier,
   Strow yonder mountain flat,
A railway here, a tunnel there,
   Mix me this zone with that.

ALFRED, LORD TENNYSON: *Mechanophilus*

Winter is gone, and spring is over,
The cuckoo-flowers grow mauver and mauver.

ALFRED AUSTIN

When with staid mothers' milk and sunshine warmed
The pasture's frisky innocents bucked up.

ALFRED AUSTIN: *The Human Tragedy*

Poor South! Her books get fewer and fewer,
She was never much given to literature.

J. GORDON COOGLER

Napoleon hoped that all the world would fall beneath
      his sway;
He failed in his ambition; and where is he today?
Neither the Nations of the East nor the Nations of the West
Have thought the thing Napoleon thought was to their
      interest.

AN UNKNOWN LIEUTENANT-COLONEL

No more will I endure love's pleasing pain
Nor round my heart's leg tie his galling chain.

> A YOUNG TRADESMAN (quoted by Coleridge:
> *Biographia Literaria*)

Long live our dear and noble Queen
Victoria; who at Aberdeen,
Today, amidst her people's seen
Unveilèd to her country's gaze
A lov'd one's statue, ne'er t'erase
'T from memory. With fortitude
The ceremony she withstood.

> EDWARD EDWIN FOOT: *On the Inauguration
> of the memorial statue of His Late Royal
> Highness the Prince Consort*

How beautiful their feet, who follow in that train.

> MARTIN TUPPER: *The Train of Religion*

Her lips they are redder than coral
    That under the ocean grows;
She is sweet, she is fair, she is moral,
    My beautiful Georgian rose!

> ANON

And have we lost another friend?
    How sad the news to tell!
Alas! Poor Mr Yarker's gone—
    Hark to the tolling bell!
Alas! how many now drop off—
    What numbers are unwell;
Another mortal borne away—
    Hark to the tolling bell!

> JOHN CLOSE OF KIRKBY STEPHEN ('Poet Close')
> *In Respectful Memory of Mr Yarker*

161

Entrapped inside a submarine,
With death approaching on the scene,
The crew compose their minds to dice,
More for the Pleasure than the Vice.

CONGRESSMAN H. C. CANFIELD: *On the Loss of
U.S. Submarine S*4

And now, kind friends, what I have wrote,
    I hope you will pass o'er,
And not criticize as some have done
    Hitherto herebefore.

JULIA MOORE: *The Sweet Singer of Michigan*

CHECK TO SONG

I dream'd that I walk'd in Italy
    When the day was going down,
By a water that silently wander'd by
    Thro' an old dim-lighted town,

Till I came to a palace fair to see.
    Wide open the windows were
My love at a window sat; and she
    Beckon'd me up the stair. . . .

When I came to the little rose-colour'd room,
    From the curtains out flew a bat.
The window was open: and in the gloom
    My love at the window sat.

She sat with her guitar on her knee,
    But she was not singing a note,
For someone had drawn (ah, who could it be?)
    A knife across her throat.

OWEN MEREDITH

162

THE FEMALE FRIEND

In this imperfect, gloomy scene
   Of complicated ill,
How rarely is a day serene,
   The throbbing bosom still!
Will not a beauteous landscape bright
   Or music's soothing sound,
Console the heart, afford delight,
   And throw sweet peace around?
They may; but never comfort lend
Like an accomplish'd female friend!

With such a friend the social hour
   In sweetest pleasure glides;
There is in female charms a power
   Which lastingly abides;
The fragrance of the blushing rose,
   Its tints and splendid hue,
Will with the season decompose,
   And pass as flitting dew;
On firmer ties his joys depend
Who has a faithful female friend!

As orbs revolve, and years recede
   And seasons onward roll,
The fancy may on beauties feed
   With discontented soul;
A thousand objects bright and fair
   May for a moment shine,
Yet many a sigh and many a tear
   But mark their swift decline;
While lasting joys the man attend
Who has a polish'd female friend!

                  REV. CORNELIUS WHUR

SHE WAS POOR BUT SHE WAS HONEST

She was poor, but she was honest,
    Victim of the squire's whim:
First he loved her, then he left her,
    And she lost her honest name.

Then she ran away to London,
    For to hide her grief and shame;
There she met another squire,
    And she lost her name again.

See her riding in her carriage,
    In the Park and all so gay:
All the nibs and nobby persons
    Come to pass the time of day.

See the little old-world village
    Where her aged parents live,
Drinking the champagne she sends them;
    But they never can forgive.

In the rich man's arms she flutters,
    Like a bird with broken wing:
First he loved her, then he left her,
    And she hasn't got a ring.

See him in the splendid mansion,
    Entertaining with the best,
While the girl that he has ruined,
    Entertains a sordid guest.

See him in the House of Commons,
    Making laws to put down crime,
While the victim of his passions
    Trails her way through mud and slime.

164

Standing on the bridge at midnight,
    She says: 'Farewell, blighted Love.'
There's a scream, a splash—Good Heavens!
    What is she a-doing of?

Then they drag her from the river,
    Water from her clothes they wrang,
For they thought that she was drownded;
    But the corpse got up and sang:

'It's the same the whole world over;
    It's the poor that gets the blame,
It's the rich that gets the pleasure.
    Isn't it a blooming shame?'

ANON

THE FLEAS

Great fleas have little fleas upon their backs to bite 'em,
And little fleas have lesser fleas and so ad infinitum.
And the great fleas themselves, in turn, have greater
    fleas to go on;
While these again have greater still, and greater still,
    and so on.

A. DE MORGAN

BEGINNING OF AN UNDERGRADUATE POEM

(Completed by Dr Mansel)

When the sun's perpendicular rays
Illumine the depths of the sea—
The fishes, beginning to sweat,
Cry, *Damn it, how hot we shall be!*

ANON

AN AUSTRIAN ARMY

An Austrian army awfully array'd,
Boldly by battery besieged Belgrade.
Cossack commanders cannonading come
Dealing destruction's devastating doom:
Every endeavour,engineers essay,
For fame, for fortune fighting-furious fray!
Generals 'gainst generals grapple, gracious God!
How Heaven honours heroic hardihood!
Infuriate—indiscriminate in ill—
Kinsmen kill kindred—kindred kinsmen kill:
Labour low levels loftiest, longest lines,
Men march 'mid mounds, 'mid moles, 'mid murd'rous
    mines:
Now noisy noxious numbers notice nought
Of outward obstacles, opposing ought—
Poor patriots—partly purchased—partly press'd,
Quite quaking, quickly 'Quarter! quarter!' quest:
Reason returns, religious right redounds,
Suwarrow stops such sanguinary sounds.
Truce to thee, Turkey, triumph to thy train,
Unwise, unjust, unmerciful Ukraine!
Vanish, vain victory! Vanish, victory vain!
Why wish we warfare? Wherefore welcome were
Xerxes, Ximenes, Xanthus, Xavier?
Yield, yield, ye youths, ye yeomen, yield your yell:
Zeno's, Zimmermann's, Zoroaster's zeal,
Again attract ; arts against arms appeal !

                                    ALARIC A. WATTS

SOLILOQUY OF THE SPANISH CLOISTER

Gr-r-r—there go, my heart's abhorrence!
   Water your damned flower-pots, do!
If hate killed men, Brother Lawrence,
   God's blood, would not mine kill you!
What? your myrtle-bush wants trimming
   Oh, that rose has prior claims—
Needs its leaden vase filled brimming?
   Hell dry you up with its flames!

At the meal we sit together:
   Salve tibi! I must hear
Wise talk of the kind of weather,
   Sort of season, time of year:
Not a plenteous cork-crop: scarcely
   Dare we hope oak-galls, I doubt:
What's the Latin name for 'parsley'?
   What's the Greek name for Swine's Snout

Whew! We'll have our platter burnished,
   Laid with care on our own shelf!
With a fire-new spoon we're furnished,
   And a goblet for ourself,
Rinsed like something sacrificial
   Ere 'tis fit to touch our chaps—
Marked with L. for our initial!
   (He, he! There his lily snaps!)

Saint, forsooth! While brown Dolores
   Squats outside the Convent bank,
With Sanchicha, telling stories,
   Steeping tresses in the tank,
Blue-black, lustrous, thick like horsehairs
   —Can't I see his dead eye glow
Bright, as 'twere a Barbary corsair's?
   (That is, if he'd let it show!)

When he finishes refection,
  Knife and fork he never lays
Cross-wise, to my recollection,
  As do I, in Jesu's praise,
I, the Trinity illustrate,
  Drinking watered orange-pulp—
In three sips the Arian frustrate;
  While he drains his at one gulp!

Oh, those melons! If he's able
  We're to have a feast; so nice!
One goes to the Abbot's table,
  All of us get each a slice.
How go on your flowers? None double?
  Not one fruit-sort can you spy?
Strange!—And I, too, at such trouble,
  Keep 'em close-nipped on the sly!

There's a great text in Galatians,
  Once you trip on it, entails
Twenty-nine distinct damnations,
  One sure, if another fails.
If I trip him just a-dying,
  Sure of Heaven as sure can be,
Spin him round and send him flying
  Off to Hell, a Manichee?

Or, my scrofulous French novel,
  On grey paper with blunt type!
Simply glance at it, you grovel
  Hand and foot in Belial's gripe:
If I double down its pages
  At the woeful sixteenth print,
When he gathers his greengages,
  Ope a sieve and slip it in't?

Or, there's Satan!—one might venture
   Pledge one's soul to him, yet leave
Such a flaw in the indenture
   As he'd miss till, past retrieve,
Blasted lay that rose-acacia
   We're so proud of! *Hy, Zy, Hine* . . .
'St, there's Vespers! *Plena gratiâ*
   Ave, Virgo! Gr-r-r—you swine!

ROBERT BROWNING

THE LATEST DECALOGUE

Thou shalt have one God only; who
Would be at the expense of two?
No graven images may be
Worshipped, except the currency:
Swear not at all; for, for thy curse
Thine enemy is none the worse:
At church on Sunday to attend
Will serve to keep the world thy friend:
Honour thy parents; that is, all
From whom advancement may befall:
Thou shalt not kill; but need'st not strive
Officiously to keep alive:
Do not adultery commit;
Advantage rarely comes of it:
Thou shalt not steal; an empty feat,
When it's so lucrative to cheat:
Bear not false witness; let the lie
Have time on its own wings to fly:
Thou shalt not covet, but tradition
Approves all forms of competition.

A. H. CLOUGH

SPECTATOR AB EXTRA

I

As I sat at the Café I said to myself,
They may talk as they please about what they call pelf,
They may sneer as they like about eating and drinking,
But help it I cannot, I cannot help thinking
    How pleasant it is to have money, heigh-ho!
    How pleasant it is to have money.

I sit at my table *en grand seigneur*,
And when I have done, throw a crust to the poor;
Not only the pleasure itself of good living,
But also the pleasure of now and then giving:
    So pleasant it is to have money, heigh-ho!
    So pleasant it is to have money.

They may talk as they please about what they call pelf,
And how one ought never to think of one's self,
How pleasures of thought surpass eating and drinking—
My pleasure of thought is the pleasure of thinking
    How pleasant it is to have money, heigh-ho!
    How pleasant it is to have money.

II

Le Dîner

Come along, 'tis the time, ten or more minutes past,
And he who came first had to wait for the last;
The oysters ere this had been in and been out;
Whilst I have been sitting and thinking about
    How pleasant it is to have money, heigh-ho!
    How pleasant it is to have money.

170

A clear soup with eggs; *voilà tout*; of the fish
The *filets de sole* are a moderate dish
A la Orly, but you're for red mullet, you say:
By the gods of good fare, who can question to-day
   How pleasant it is to have money, heigh-ho!
   How pleasant it is to have money.

After oysters, sauterne; then sherry; champagne,
Ere one bottle goes, comes another again;
Fly up, thou bold cork, to the ceiling above,
And tell to our ears in the sound that they love
   How pleasant it is to have money, heigh-ho!
   How pleasant it is to have money.

I've the simplest of palates; absurd it may be,
But I almost could dine on a *poulet-au-riz*,
Fish and soup and omelette and that—but the deuce—
There were to be woodcocks, and not *Charlotte Russe!*
   So pleasant it is to have money, heigh-ho!
   So pleasant it is to have money.

Your Chablis is acid, away with the Hock,
Give me the pure juice of the purple Médoc:
St Peray is exquisite; but, if you please,
Some Burgundy just before tasting the cheese.
   So pleasant it is to have money, heigh-ho!
   So pleasant it is to have money.

As for that, pass the bottle, and d——n the expense,
I've seen it observed by a writer of sense,
That the labouring classes could scarce live a day,
If people like us didn't eat, drink, and pay.
   So useful it is to have money, heigh-ho!
   So useful it is to have money.

One ought to be grateful, I quite apprehend,
Having dinner and supper and plenty to spend,

And so suppose now, while the things go away,
By way of a grace we all stand up and say
   How pleasant it is to have money, heigh-ho!
   How pleasant it is to have money.

III

Parvenant

I cannot but ask, in the park and the streets
When I look at the number of persons one meets,
What e'er in the world the poor devils can do
Whose fathers and mothers can't give them a *sou*.
   So needful it is to have money, heigh-ho!
   So needful it is to have money.

I ride, and I drive, and I care not a d——n,
The people look up and they ask who I am;
And if I should chance to run over a cad,
I can pay for the damage, if ever so bad.
   So useful it is to have money, heigh-ho!
   So useful it is to have money.

It was but this winter I came up to town,
And already I'm gaining a sort of renown;
Find my way to good houses without much ado,
Am beginning to see the nobility too.
   So useful it is to have money, heigh-ho!
   So useful it is to have money.

O dear what a pity they ever should lose it,
Since they are the people that know how to use it;
So easy, so stately, such manners, such dinners,
And yet, after all, it is we are the winners.
   So needful it is to have money, heigh-ho!
   So needful it is to have money.

It's all very well to be handsome and tall,
Which certainly makes you look well at a ball;
It's all very well to be clever and witty,
But if you are poor, why it's only a pity.
  So needful it is to have money, heigh-ho!
  So needful it is to have money.

There's something undoubtedly in a fine air,
To know how to smile and be able to stare.
High breeding is something, but well-bred or not,
In the end the one question is, what have you got.
  So needful it is to have money, heigh-ho!
  So needful it is to have money.

And the angels in pink and the angels in blue,
In muslins and moires so lovely and new,
What is it they want, and so wish you to guess,
But if you have money, the answer is Yes.
  So needful, they tell you, is money, heigh-ho!
  So needful it is to have money.

A. H. CLOUGH

EPIGRAM

ON SIR ROGER PHILLIMORE (1810-1885) AND HIS BROTHER, GEORGE PHILLIMORE

When Nature dreamt of making bores,
She formed a brace of Phillimores;
Sooner than make a Phillimost,
Nature herself would yield the ghost.

ANON

173

REPLY TO DIPSYCHUS

This world is very odd we see,
    We do not comprehend it;
But in one fact we all agree,
    God won't, and we can't mend it.

Being common sense, it can't be sin
    To take it as I find it;
The pleasure to take pleasure in;
    The pain, try not to mind it.

These juicy meats, this flashing wine,
    May be an unreal mere appearance;
Only—for my inside, in fine,
    They have a singular coherence.

Oh yes, my pensive youth, abstain;
    And any empty sick sensation,
Remember, anything like pain
    Is only your imagination.

Trust me, I've read your German sage
    To far more purpose than e'er you did;
You find it in his wisest page,
    Whom God deludes is well deluded.

                                   A. H. CLOUGH

ON CHRISTOPHER WORDSWORTH,
MASTER OF TRINITY

Who wrote *Who wrote Icon Basilike?*
I, said the Master of Trinity,
With my small ability,
I wrote *Who wrote Icon Basilike?*

                                   B. H. KENNEDY

174

HENDECASYLLABICS

O you chorus of indolent reviewers,
Irresponsible, indolent reviewers,
Look, I come to the test, a tiny poem
All composed in a metre of Catullus,
All in quantity, careful of my motion,
Like the skater on ice that hardly bears him,
Lest I fall unawares before the people,
Waking laughter in indolent reviewers.
Should I flounder awhile without a tumble
Thro' this metrification of Catullus,
They should speak to me not without a welcome,
All that chorus of indolent reviewers.
Hard, hard, hard is it, only not to tumble,
So fantastical is the dainty metre.
Wherefore slight me not wholly, nor believe me
Too presumptuous, indolent reviewers.
O blatant Magazines, regard me rather—
Since I blush to belaud myself a moment—
As some rare little rose, a piece of inmost
Horticultural art, or half coquette-like
Maiden, not to be greeted unbenignly.

ALFRED, LORD TENNYSON

THE DOLGELLEY HOTEL

If ever you go to Dolgelley,
    Don't stay at the —— HOTEL;
There's nothing to put in your belly,
    And no-one to answer the bell.

THOMAS HUGHES

HOW PLEASANT TO KNOW MR LEAR

'How pleasant to know Mr Lear!'
  Who has written such volumes of stuff!
Some think him ill-tempered and queer,
  But a few think him pleasant enough.

His mind is concrete and fastidious,
  His nose is remarkably big;
His visage is more or less hideous,
  His beard it resembles a wig.

He has ears, and two eyes, and ten fingers,
  Leastways if you reckon two thumbs;
Long ago he was one of the singers,
  But now he is one of the dumbs.

He sits in a beautiful parlour,
  With hundreds of books on the wall;
He drinks a great deal of Marsala,
  But never gets tipsy at all.

He has many friends, laymen and clerical,
  Old Foss is the name of his cat:
His body is perfectly spherical,
  He weareth a runcible hat.

When he walks in a waterproof white,
  The children run after him so!
Calling out, 'He's come out in his night-
  gown, that crazy old Englishman, oh!'

He weeps by the side of the ocean,
  He weeps on the top of the hill;
He purchases pancakes and lotion,
  And chocolate shrimps from the mill.

176

He reads but he cannot speak Spanish,
   He cannot abide ginger-beer:
Ere the days of his pilgrimage vanish.
   How pleasant to know Mr Lear!

EDWARD LEAR

LIMERICKS

I

There was an Old Man with a beard,
Who said, 'It is just as I feared!—
   Two Owls and a Hen,
   Four Larks and a Wren,
Have all built their nests in my beard!'

II

There was an Old Man who said, 'Hush!
I perceive a young bird in this bush!'
   When they said, 'Is it small?'
   He replied, 'Not at all!
It is four times as big as the bush!'

III

There was an Old Man of Hong Kong,
Who never did anything wrong;
   He lay on his back,
   With his head in a sack,
That innocuous Old Man of Hong Kong.

IV

There was an Old Person of Anerley,
Whose conduct was strange and unmannerly:
   He rushed down the Strand,
   With a Pig in each hand,
But returned in the evening to Anerley.

EDWARD LEAR

THE DONG WITH A LUMINOUS NOSE

When awful darkness and silence reign
Over the great Gromboolian plain,
   Through the long, long wintry nights;—
When the angry breakers roar
As they beat on the rocky shore;—
   When Storm-clouds brood on the towering heights
Of the Hills of the Chankly Bore:—

Then, through the vast and gloomy dark,
There moves what seems a fiery spark,
   A lonely spark with silvery rays
     Piercing the coal-black night,—
     A meteor strange and bright:—
   Hither and thither the vision strays,
     A single lurid light.

Slowly it wanders,—pauses,—creeps,—
Anon it sparkles,—flashes and leaps;
And ever as onward it gleaming goes
A light on the Bong-tree stems it throws.
And those who watch at that midnight hour
From Hall or Terrace, or lofty Tower,
Cry, as the wild light passes along,—
     'The Dong!—the Dong!
   'The wandering Dong through the forest goes!
     'The Dong! the Dong!
   'The Dong with a luminous Nose!'

     Long years ago
    The Dong was happy and gay,
Till he fell in love with a Jumbly Girl
    Who came to those shores one day
For the Jumblies came in a Sieve, they did,—
Landing at eve near the Zemmery Fidd

Where the Oblong Oysters grow,
And the rocks are smooth and gray.

And all the woods and the valleys rang
With the Chorus they daily and nightly sang,—
  'Far and few, far and few,
  Are the lands where the Jumblies live;
  Their heads are green, and their hands are blue,
  And they went to sea in a sieve.'

Happily, happily passed those days!
 While the cheerful Jumblies staid;
 They danced in circlets all night long,
 To the plaintive pipe of the lively Dong,
  In moonlight, shine, or shade.
For day and night he was always there
By the side of the Jumbly Girl so fair,
With her sky-blue hands, and her sea-green hair.
Till the morning came of that hateful day
When the Jumblies sailed in their sieve away,
And the Dong was left on the cruel shore
Gazing—gazing for evermore,—
Ever keeping his weary eyes on
That pea-green sail on the far horizon,—
Singing the Jumbly Chorus still
As he sate all day on the grassy hill,—
  'Far and few, far and few,
  Are the lands where the Jumblies live;
  Their heads are green, and their hands are blue,
  And they went to sea in a sieve.'

 But when the sun was low in the West,
  The Dong arose and said,—
 'What little sense I once possessed
  Has quite gone out of my head!'
179

And since that day he wanders still
By lake and forest, marsh and hill,
Singing—'O somewhere, in valley or plain
'Might I find my Jumbly Girl again!
'For ever I'll seek by lake and shore
'Till I find my Jumbly Girl once more!'
    Playing a pipe with silvery squeaks,
    Since then his Jumbly Girl he seeks,
    And because by night he could not see,
    He gathered the bark of the Twangum Tree
        On the flowery plain that grows.
        And he wove him a wondrous Nose,—
    A Nose as strange as a Nose could be!
Of vast proportions and painted red,
And tied with cords to the back of his head.
        —In a hollow rounded space it ended
        With a luminous lamp within suspended,
            All fenced about
            With a bandage stout
            To prevent the wind from blowing it out;—
        And with holes all round to send the light,
        In gleaming rays on the dismal night.

And now each night, and all night long,
Over those plains still roams the Dong;
And above the wail of the Chimp and Snipe
You may hear the squeak of his plaintive pipe
While ever he seeks, but seeks in vain
To meet with his Jumbly Girl again;
Lonely and wild—all night he goes,—
The Dong with a luminous Nose!
And all who watch at the midnight hour,
From Hall or Terrace, or lofty Tower,
Cry, as they trace the Meteor bright,
Moving along through the dreary night,—

'This is the hour when forth he goes,
'The Dong with a luminous Nose!
'Yonder—over the plain he goes;
　'He goes:
　'He goes;
'The Dong with a luminous Nose!'

EDWARD LEAR

THE POBBLE WHO HAS NO TOES

I

The Pobble who has no toes
　Had once as many as we;
When they said, 'Some day you may lose them all';—
　He replied,—'Fish fiddle de-dee!'
And his Aunt Jobiska made him drink,
Lavender water tinged with pink,
For she said, 'The World in general knows
There's nothing so good for a Pobble's toes!'

II

The Pobble who has no toes,
　Swam across the Bristol Channel;
But before he set out he wrapped his nose,
　In a piece of scarlet flannel.
For his Aunt Jobiska said, 'No harm
'Can come to his toes if his nose is warm;
'And it's perfectly known that a Pobble's toes
'Are safe,—provided he minds his nose.'

III

The Pobble swam fast and well,
　And when boats or ships came near him
He tinkledy-binkledy-winkled a bell,
　So that all the world could hear him.

181

And all the Sailors and Admirals cried,
When they saw him nearing the further side,—
'He has gone to fish, for his Aunt Jobiska's
'Runcible Cat with crimson whiskers!'

IV

But before he touched the shore,
    The shore of the Bristol Channel,
A sea-green Porpoise carried away
    His wrapper of scarlet flannel.
And when he came to observe his feet,
Formerly garnished with toes so neat,
His face at once became forlorn
On perceiving that all his toes were gone!

V

And nobody ever knew
From that dark day to the present,
Whoso had taken the Pobble's toes,
    In a manner so far from pleasant.
Whether the shrimps or crawfish gray,
Or crafty Mermaids stole them away—
Nobody knew; and nobody knows
How the Pobble was robbed of his twice five toes!

VI

The Pobble who has no toes
    Was placed in a friendly Bark,
And they rowed him back, and carried him up,
    To his Aunt Jobiska's Park.
And she made him a feast at his earnest wish
Of eggs and buttercups fried with fish;—
And she said,—'It's a fact the whole world knows,
'That Pobbles are happier without their toes.'

EDWARD LEAR

182

THE AKOND OF SWAT

Who or why, or which, or *what*,
                    Is the Akond of SWAT?

Is he tall or short, or dark or fair?
Does he sit on a stool or a sofa or chair,   or SQUAT,
                    The Akond of Swat?

Is he wise or foolish, young or old?
Does he drink his soup and his coffee cold,   or HOT,
                    The Akond of Swat?

Does he sing or whistle, jabber or talk,
And when riding abroad does he gallop or walk,   or TROT,
                    The Akond of Swat?

Does he wear a turban, a fez, or a hat?
Does he sleep on a mattress, a bed, or a mat,   or a COT,
                    The Akond of Swat?

When he writes a copy in round-hand size,
Does he cross his T's and finish his I's   with a DOT,
                    The Akond of Swat?

Can he write a letter concisely clear
Without a speck or a smudge or smear   or BLOT,
                    The Akond of Swat?

Do his people like him extremely well?
Or do they, whenever they can, rebel,   or PLOT,
                    At the Akond of Swat?

If he catches them then, either old or young,
Does he have them chopped in pieces or hung,   or SHOT,
                    The Akond of Swat?

Do his people prig in the lanes or park?
Or even at times, when days are dark,   GAROTTE?
                    O the Akond of Swat?

Does he study the wants of his own dominion?
Or doesn't he care for public opinion   a JOT,
                    The Akond of Swat?

To amuse his mind do his people show him
Pictures, or any one's last new poem,   or WHAT,
                    For the Akond of Swat?

At night if he suddenly screams and wakes,
Do they bring him only a few small cakes,   or a LOT,
                    For the Akond of Swat?

Does he live on turnips, tea, or tripe?
Does he like his shawl to be marked with a stripe, or a DOT,
                    The Akond of Swat?

Does he like to lie on his back in a boat
Like the lady who lived in that isle remote,   SHALLOTT,
                    The Akond of Swat?

Is he quiet, or always making a fuss?
Is his steward a Swiss or a Swede or a Russ,   or a SCOT,
                    The Akond of Swat?

Does he like to sit by the calm blue wave?
Or to sleep and snore in a dark green cave,   or a GROT,
                    The Akond of Swat?

Does he drink small beer from a silver jug?
Or a bowl? or a glass? or a cup? or a mug?   or a POT,
                    The Akond of Swat?

Does he beat his wife with a gold-topped pipe,
When she lets the gooseberries grow too ripe,   or ROT,
               The Akond of Swat?

Does he wear a white tie when he dines with friends,
And tie it neat in a bow with ends,   or a KNOT,
               The Akond of Swat?

Does he like new cream, and hate mince-pies?
When he looks at the sun does he wink his eyes,   or NOT,
               The Akond of Swat?

Does he teach his subjects to roast and bake?
Does he sail about on an inland lake,   in a YACHT,
               The Akond of Swat?

Some one, or nobody, knows I wot
Who or which or why or what
               Is the Akond of Swat!

                   EDWARD LEAR

YOU ARE OLD, FATHER WILLIAM

'You are old, Father William,' the young man said,
  'And your hair has become very white;
And yet you incessantly stand on your head—
  Do you think, at your age, it is right?'

'In my youth,' Father William replied to his son,
  'I feared it might injure the brain;
But, now that I'm perfectly sure I have none,
  Why, I do it again and again.'

'You are old,' said the youth, 'as I mentioned before,
  And have grown most uncommonly fat;
Yet you turned a back-somersault in at the door—
  Pray, what is the reason of that?'

'In my youth,' said the sage, as he shook his grey locks,
  'I kept all my limbs very supple
By the use of this ointment—one shilling the box—
  Allow me to sell you a couple?'

'You are old,' said the youth, 'and your jaws are too
    weak
  For anything tougher than suet;
Yet you finished the goose, with the bones and the
    beak—
  Pray, how did you manage to do it?'

'In my youth,' said his father, 'I took to the law,
  And argued each case with my wife;
And the muscular strength, which it gave to my jaw,
  Has lasted the rest of my life.'

'You are old,' said the youth, 'one would hardly suppose
  That your eye was as steady as ever;
Yet you balance an eel on the end of your nose—
  What made you so awfully clever?'

'I have answered three questions, and that is enough,'
  Said his father; 'don't give yourself airs!
Do you think I can listen all day to such stuff?
  Be off, or I'll kick you downstairs!'

LEWIS CARROLL

SPEAK ROUGHLY TO YOUR LITTLE BOY

Speak roughly to your little boy,
  And beat him when he sneezes;
He only does it to annoy,
  Because he knows it teases.
            Chorus: Wow! Wow! Wow!

I speak severely to my boy,
  I beat him when he sneezes;
For he can thoroughly enjoy
  The pepper when he pleases!
            Chorus: Wow! Wow! Wow!

LEWIS CARROLL

HOW DOTH THE LITTLE CROCODILE

How doth the little crocodile
  Improve his shining tail,
And pour the waters of the Nile
  On every golden scale!

How cheerfully he seems to grin,
  How neatly spreads his claws,
And welcomes little fishes in,
  With gently smiling jaws!

LEWIS CARROLL

SILENCE IN COURT

They told me you had been to her,
    And mentioned me to him:
She gave me a good character,
    But said I could not swim.

He sent them word I had not gone,
    (We know it to be true):
If she should push the matter on,
    What would become of you?

I gave her one, they gave him two,
    You gave us three or more;
They all returned from him to you,
    Though they were mine before.

If I or she should chance to be
    Involved in this affair,
He trusts to you to set them free,
    Exactly as we were.

My notion was that you had been
    (Before she had this fit)
An obstacle that came between
    Him, and ourselves, and it.

Don't let him know she liked them best,
    For this must ever be
A secret kept from all the rest,
    Between yourself and me.

LEWIS CARROLL

'TIS THE VOICE OF THE LOBSTER

'Tis the voice of the Lobster; I heard him declare,
'You have baked me too brown, I must sugar my hair.'
As a duck with its eyelids, so he with his nose
Trims his belt and his buttons, and turns out his toes.

When the sands are all dry, he is gay as a lark,
And will talk in contemptuous tones of the Shark:
But, when the tide rises and sharks are around,
His voice has a timid and tremulous sound.

LEWIS CARROLL

THE WALRUS AND THE CARPENTER

The sun was shining on the sea,
    Shining with all his might:
He did his very best to make
    The billows smooth and bright—
And this was odd, because it was
    The middle of the night.

The moon was shining sulkily,
    Because she thought the sun
Had got no business to be there
    After the day was done—
'It's very rude of him,' she said,
    'To come and spoil the fun!'

The sea was wet as wet could be,
    The sands were dry as dry.
You could not see a cloud, because
    No cloud was in the sky:
No birds were flying overhead—
    There were no birds to fly.

189

The Walrus and the Carpenter
    Were walking close at hand:
They wept like anything to see
    Such quantities of sand:
'If this were only cleared away,'
    They said, 'it *would* be grand!'

'If seven maids with seven mops
    Swept it for half a year,
Do you suppose,' the Walrus said,
    'That they could get it clear?'
'I doubt it,' said the Carpenter,
    And shed a bitter tear.

'O Oysters, come and walk with us!'
    The Walrus did beseech.
'A pleasant walk, a pleasant talk,
    Along the briny beach:
We cannot do with more than four,
    To give a hand to each.'

The eldest Oyster looked at him,
    But not a word he said:
The eldest Oyster winked his eye,
    And shook his heavy head—
Meaning to say he did not choose
    To leave the oyster-bed.

But four young Oysters hurried up,
    All eager for the treat:
Their coats were brushed, their faces washed
    Their shoes were clean and neat—
And this was odd, because, you know,
    They hadn't any feet.

Four other Oysters followed them,
    And yet another four;
And thick and fast they came at last,
    And more, and more, and more—
All hopping through the frothy waves,
    And scrambling to the shore.

The Walrus and the Carpenter
    Walked on a mile or so,
And then they rested on a rock
    Conveniently low:
And all the little Oysters stood
    And waited in a row.

'The time has come,' the Walrus said,
    'To talk of many things:
Of shoes—and ships—and sealing wax—
    Of cabbages—and kings—
And why the sea is boiling hot—
    And whether pigs have wings.'

'But wait a bit,' the Oysters cried,
    'Before we have our chat;
For some of us are out of breath,
    And all of us are fat!'
'No hurry!' said the Carpenter.
    They thanked him much for that.

'A loaf of bread,' the Walrus said,
    'Is what we chiefly need:
Pepper and vinegar besides
    Are very good indeed—
Now, if you're ready, Oysters dear,
    We can begin to feed.'

'But not on us!' the Oysters cried,
    Turning a little blue.
'After such kindness that would be
    A dismal thing to do!'
'The night is fine,' the Walrus said,
    'Do you admire the view?

'It was so kind of you to come,
    And you are very nice!'
The Carpenter said nothing but
    'Cut us another slice.
I wish you were not quite so deaf—
    I've had to ask you twice!'

'It seems a shame,' the Walrus said,
    'To play them such a trick.
After we've brought them out so far,
    And made them trot so quick!'
The Carpenter said nothing but
    'The butter's spread too thick!'

'I weep for you,' the Walrus said:
    'I deeply sympathize.'
With sobs and tears he sorted out
    Those of the largest size,
Holding his pocket-handkerchief
    Before his streaming eyes.

'O Oysters,' said the Carpenter,
    'You've had a pleasant run!
Shall we be trotting home again?'
    But answer came there none—
And this was scarcely odd, because
    They'd eaten every one.

                                    LEWIS CARROLL

JABBERWOCKY

'Twas brillig, and the slithy toves
  Did gyre and gimble in the wabe;
All mimsy were the borogoves,
    And the mome raths outgrabe.

'Beware the Jabberwock, my son!
  The jaws that bite, the claws that catch!
Beware the Jubjub bird and shun
    The frumious Bandersnatch!'

He took his vorpal sword in hand:
  Long time the manxome foe he sought—
So rested he by the Tumtum tree,
    And stood awhile in thought.

And as in uffish thought he stood,
  The Jabberwock, with eyes of flame,
Came whiffling through the tulgey wood,
    And burbled as it came!

One, two! One, two! And through and through
  The vorpal blade went snicker-snack!
He left it dead, and with its head
    He went galumphing back.

'And hast thou slain the Jabberwock!
  Come to my arms, my beamish boy!
O frabjous day! Callooh! Callay!'
    He chortled in his joy.

'Twas brillig, and the slithy toves
  Did gyre and gimble in the wabe;
All mimsy were the borogoves,
    And the mome raths outgrabe.

LEWIS CARROLL

193

THE WHITE KNIGHT'S SONG

I'll tell thee everything I can;
  There's little to relate.
I saw an aged aged man,
  A-sitting on a gate.
'Who are you, aged man?' I said.
  'And how is it you live?'
And his answer trickled through my head
  Like water through a sieve.

He said 'I look for butterflies
  That sleep among the wheat:
I make them into mutton-pies,
  And sell them in the street.
I sell them unto men,' he said,
  'Who sail on stormy seas;
And that's the way I get my bread—
  A trifle, if you please.'

But I was thinking of a plan
  To dye one's whiskers green,
And always use so large a fan
  That they could not be seen.
So, having no reply to give
  To what the old man said,
I cried 'Come, tell me how you live!'
  And thumped him on the head.

His accents mild took up the tale:
  He said 'I go my ways,
And when I find a mountain-rill,
  I set it in a blaze;
And thence they make a stuff they call
  Rowland's Macassar-Oil—
Yet twopence-halfpenny is all
  They give me for my toil.'

194

But I was thinking of a way
   To feed oneself on batter,
And so go on from day to day
   Getting a little fatter.
I shook him well from side to side,
   Until his face was blue:
'Come, tell me how you live,' I cried,
   'And what it is you do!'

He said 'I hunt for haddocks' eyes
   Among the heather bright,
And work them into waistcoat-buttons
   In the silent night.
And these I do not sell for gold
   Or coin of silvery shine,
But for a copper halfpenny,
   And that will purchase nine.

'I sometimes dig for buttered rolls,
   Or set limed twigs for crabs;
I sometimes search the grassy knolls
   For wheels of Hansom-cabs.
And that's the way' (he gave a wink)
   'By which I get my wealth—
And very gladly will I drink
   Your Honour's noble health.'

I heard him then, for I had just
   Completed my design
To keep the Menai bridge from rust
   By boiling it in wine.
I thanked him much for telling me
   The way he got his wealth,
But chiefly for his wish that he
   Might drink my noble health.

And now, if e'er by chance I put
   My fingers into glue,
Or madly squeeze a right-hand foot
   Into a left-hand shoe,
Or if I drop upon my toe
   A very heavy weight,
I weep, for it reminds me so
Of that old man I used to know—
Whose look was mild, whose speech was slow,
Whose hair was whiter than the snow,
Whose face was very like a crow,
With eyes, like cinders, all aglow,
Who seemed distracted with his woe,
Who rocked his body to and fro,
And muttered mumblingly and low,
As if his mouth were full of dough,
Who snorted like a buffalo—
That summer evening long ago
   A-sitting on a gate.

LEWIS CARROLL

HUMPTY DUMPTY'S RECITATION

In winter, when the fields are white,
I sing this song for your delight—

In spring, when woods are getting green,
I'll try and tell you what I mean.

In summer, when the days are long,
Perhaps you'll understand the song:

In autumn, when the leaves are brown,
Take pen and ink, and write it down.

I sent a message to the fish:
I told them 'This is what I wish.'

The little fishes of the sea
They sent an answer back to me.

The little fishes' answer was
'We cannot do it, Sir, because—'

I sent to them again to say
'It will be better to obey.'

The fishes answered with a grin,
'Why, what a temper you are in!'

I told them once, I told them twice:
They would not listen to advice.

I took a kettle large and new,
Fit for the deed I had to do.

My heart went hop, my heart went thump;
I filled the kettle at the pump.

Then some one came to me and said
'The little fishes are in bed.'

I said to him, I said it plain,
'Then you must wake them up again.'

I said it very loud and clear;
I went and shouted in his ear.

But he was very stiff and proud;
He said 'You needn't shout so loud!'

And he was very proud and stiff;
He said 'I'd go and wake them, if—'

I took a corkscrew from the shelf:
I went to wake them up myself.

And when I found the door was locked,
I pulled and pushed and kicked and knocked.

And when I found the door was shut,
I tried to turn the handle, but—

LEWIS CARROLL

THE MAD GARDENER'S SONG

He thought he saw an Elephant,
  That practised on a fife:
He looked again, and found it was
  A letter from his wife.
'At length I realise,' he said,
  'The bitterness of Life!'

He thought he saw a Buffalo
  Upon the chimney-piece:
He looked again, and found it was
  His Sister's Husband's Niece,
'Unless you leave this house,' he said,
  'I'll send for the Police!'

He thought he saw a Rattlesnake
  That questioned him in Greek:
He looked again, and found it was
  The Middle of Next Week.
'The one thing I regret,' he said,
  'Is that it cannot speak!'

He thought he saw a Banker's Clerk
  Descending from the 'bus:
He looked again, and found it was
  A Hippopotamus.
'If this should stay to dine,' he said,
  'There won't be much for us!'

He thought he saw a Kangaroo
   That worked a coffee-mill:
He looked again, and found it was
   A Vegetable-Pill.
'Were I to swallow this,' he said,
   'I should be very ill!'

He thought he saw a Coach-and-Four
   That stood beside his bed:
He looked again, and found it was
   A Bear without a Head.
'Poor thing,' he said, 'poor silly thing!
   It's waiting to be fed!'

He thought he saw an Albatross
   That fluttered round the lamp:
He looked again, and found it was
   A Penny-Postage-Stamp.
'You'd best be getting home,' he said,
   'The nights are very damp!'

He thought he saw a Garden-Door
   That opened with a key:
He looked again, and found it was
   A Double Rule of Three:
'And all its mystery,' he said,
   'Is clear as day to me!'

He thought he saw an Argument
   That proved he was the Pope:
He looked again, and found it was
   A Bar of Mottled Soap.
'A fact so dread,' he faintly said,
   'Extinguishes all hope!'

LEWIS CARROLL

HIAWATHA'S PHOTOGRAPHING

From his shoulder Hiawatha
Took the camera of rosewood,
Made of sliding, folding rosewood;
Neatly put it all together,
In its case it lay compactly,
Folded into nearly nothing;
But he opened out the hinges,
Pushed and pulled the joints and hinges,
Till it looked all squares and oblòngs,
Like a complicated figure
In the second book of Euclid.

    This he perched upon a tripod,
And the family in order
Sat before him for their pictures.
Mystic, awful was the process.

    First a piece of glass he coated
With Collodion, and plunged it
In a bath of Lunar Caustic
Carefully dissolved in water:
There he left it certain minutes.

    Secondly, my Hiawatha
Made with cunning hand a mixture
Of the acid Pyro-gallic,
And of Glacial Acetic,
And of Alcohol and water:
This developed all the picture.

    Finally, he fixed each picture
With a saturate solution
Of a certain salt of Soda—
Chemists call it Hyposulphite.
(Very difficult the name is
For a metre like the present,
But periphrasis has done it.)
    All the family in order

Sat before him for their pictures.
Each in turn, as he was taken,
Volunteered his own suggestions,
His invaluable suggestions.

First the Governor, the Father:
He suggested velvet curtains
Looped about a massy pillar;
And the corner of a table,
Of a rose-wood dining table.
He would hold a scroll of something,
Hold it firmly in his left hand;
He would keep his right hand buried
(Like Napoleon) in his waistcoat;
He would contemplate the distance
With a look of pensive meaning,
As of ducks that die in tempests

Grand, heroic was the notion:
Yet the picture failed entirely:
Failed, because he moved a little,
Moved, because he couldn't help it.

Next, his better half took courage;
She would have her picture taken:
She came dressed beyond description,
Dressed in jewels and in satin
Far too gorgeous for an empress.
Gracefully she sat down sideways,
With a simper scarcely human,
Holding in her hand a nosegay
Rather larger than a cabbage.
All the while that she was taking,
Still the lady chattered, chattered,
Like a monkey in the forest.
'Am I sitting still?' she asked him.
'Is my face enough in profile?
Shall I hold the nosegay higher?
Will it come into the picture?'

And the picture failed completely.
　　Next the Son, the Stunning-Cantab:
He suggested curves of beauty,
Curves pervading all his figure,
Which the eye might follow onward,
Till they centred in the breast-pin,
Centred in the golden breast-pin.
He had learnt it all from Ruskin
(Author of 'The Stones of Venice',
'Seven Lamps of Architecture',
'Modern Painters', and some others);
And perhaps he had not fully
Understood his author's meaning;
But, whatever was the reason,
All was fruitless, as the picture
Ended in an utter failure.
　　Next to him the eldest daughter:
She suggested very little;
Only asked if he would take her
With her look of 'passive beauty'.
　　Her idea of passive beauty
Was a squinting of the left-eye,
Was a drooping of the right-eye,
Was a smile that went up sideways
To the corner of the nostrils.
　　Hiawatha, when she asked him,
Took no notice of the question,
Looked as if he hadn't heard it;
But, when pointedly appealed to,
Smiled in his peculiar manner,
Coughed and said it 'didn't matter',
Bit his lip and changed the subject.
　　Nor in this was he mistaken,
As the picture failed completely.
　　So in turn the other sisters.
Last, the youngest son was taken:

Very rough and thick his hair was,
Very round and red his face was,
Very dusty was his jacket,
Very fidgetty his manner.
And his overbearing sisters
Called him names he disapproved of:
Called him Johnny, 'Daddy's Darling',
Called him Jacky, 'Scrubby School-boy'.
And, so awful was the picture,
In comparison the others
Might be thought to have succeeded,
To have partially succeeded.

Finally my Hiawatha
Tumbled all the tribe together,
'Grouped' is not the right expression,
And, as happy chance would have it,
Did at last obtain a picture
Where the faces all succeeded:
Each came out a perfect likeness.

Then they joined and all abused it,
Unrestrainedly abused it,
As 'the worst and ugliest picture
They could possibly have dreamed of.
Giving one such strange expressions!
Sulkiness, conceit, and meanness!
Really any one would take us
(Any one that did not know us)
For the most unpleasant people!'
(Hiawatha seemed to think so,
Seemed to think it not unlikely.)
All together rang their voices,
Angry, loud, discordant voices,
As of dogs that howl in concert,
As of cats that wail in chorus.

But my Hiawatha's patience,
His politeness and his patience,

Unaccountably had vanished,
And he left that happy party,
Neither did he leave them slowly,
With that calm deliberation,
That intense deliberation
Which photographers aspire to:
But he left them in a hurry,
Left them in a mighty hurry,
Vowing that he would not stand it,
    Hurriedly he packed his boxes,
Hurriedly the porter trundled
On a barrow all his boxes;
Hurriedly he took his ticket,
Hurriedly the train received him:
Thus departed Hiawatha.

LEWIS CARROLL

MY FANCY

I painted her a gushing thing,
    With years about a score;
I little thought to find they were
    At least a dozen more;
My fancy gave her eyes of blue,
    A curly auburn head:
I came to find the blue a green,
    The auburn turned to red.

She boxed my ears this morning,
    They tingled very much;
I own that I could wish her
    A somewhat lighter touch;
And if you ask me how
    Her charms might be improved,
I would not have them added to,
    But just a few removed!

She has the bear's ethereal grace,
   The bland hyena's laugh,
The footstep of the elephant,
   The neck of a giraffe ;
I love her still, believe me,
   Though my heart its passion hides;
'She's all my fancy painted her,'
   But oh! how much besides!

LEWIS CARROLL

THE PARTERRE

I don't know any greatest treat
As sit him in a gay parterre,
And sniff one up the perfume sweet
Of every roses buttoning there.

It only want my charming miss
Who make to blush the self red rose;
Oh! I have envy of to kiss
The end's tip of her splendid nose.

Oh! I have envy of to be
What grass 'neath her pantoffle push,
And too much happy seemeth me
The margaret which her vestige crush.

But I will meet her nose at nose,
And take occasion for her hairs,
And indicate her all my woes,
That she in fine agree my prayers.

I don't know any greatest treat
As sit him in a gay parterre,
With Madame who is too more sweet
Than every roses buttoning there.

E. H. PALMER

THE STORY OF PRINCE AGIB

Strike the concertina's melancholy string!
Blow the spirit-stirring harp like anything!
    Let the piano's martial blast
    Rouse the echos of the past,
For of AGIB, Prince of Tartary, I sing!

Of AGIB, who, amid Tartaric scenes,
Wrote a lot of ballet-music in his teens:
    His gentle spirit rolls
    In the melody of souls—
Which is pretty, but I don't know what it means.

Of AGIB, who could readily, at sight,
Strum a march upon the loud Theodolite.
    He would diligently play
    On the Zoetrope all day,
And blow the gay Pantechnicon all night.

One winter—I am shaky in my dates—
Came two starving Tartar minstrels to his gates;
    Oh, Allah be obeyed,
    How infernally they played!
I remember that they called themselves the 'Oüaits'.

Oh! that day of sorrow, misery and rage,
I shall carry to the Catacombs of Age,
    Photographically lined
    On the tablet of my mind,
When a yesterday has faded from its page!

Alas! PRINCE AGIB went and asked them in;
Gave them beer, and eggs, and sweets, and scent, and tin;
    And when (as snobs would say)
    They had 'put it all away',
He requested them to tune up and begin.

Though its icy horror chill you to the core,
I will tell you what I never told before—
    The consequences true
    Of that awful interview,
For I listened at the keyhole in the door!

They played him a sonata—let me see!
'Medulla oblongata'—key of **G**.
    Then they began to sing
    That extremely lovely thing,
'Scherzando! ma non troppo, ppp.'

He gave them money, more than they could count,
Scent from a most ingenious little fount,
    More beer in little kegs,
    Many dozen hard-boiled eggs,
And goodies to a fabulous amount.

Now follows the dim horror of my tale,
And I feel I'm growing gradually pale;
    For even at this day,
    Though its sting has passed away
When I venture to remember it, I quail!

The elder of the brothers gave a squeal,
All-overish it made me for to feel.
    'O Prince,' he says, says he,
    'If a Prince indeed you be,
I've a mystery I'm going to reveal!

'Oh! listen if you'd shun a horrid death,
To what the gent who's speaking to you saith:
    No "Oüaits" in truth are we,
    As you fancy that we be,
For (ter-remble!) I am ALECK—this is BETH!'

Said AGIB, 'Oh! accursed of your kind,
I have heard that ye are men of evil mind!'
   BETH gave a dreadful shriek—
   But before he'd time to speak
I was mercilessly collared from behind.

In number ten or twelve, or even more,
They fastened me, full length, upon the floor.
   On my face extended flat,
   I was walloped with a cat,
For listening at the keyhole of a door.

Oh! the horror of that agonizing thrill!
(I can feel the place in frosty weather still.)
   For a week from ten to four
   I was fastened to the floor,
While a mercenary wopped me with a will!

They branded me and broke me on a wheel,
And they left me in an hospital to heal;
   And, upon my solemn word,
   I have never, never heard
What those Tartars had determined to reveal.

But that day of sorrow, misery, and rage,
I shall carry to the Catacombs of Age,
   Photographically lined
   On the tablet of my mind,
When a yesterday has faded from its page!

                SIR W. S. GILBERT

THE YARN OF THE 'NANCY BELL'

'Twas on the shores that round our coast
    From Deal to Ramsgate span,
That I found alone on a piece of stone
    An elderly naval man.

His hair was weedy, his beard was long,
    And weedy and long was he,
And I heard this wight on the shore recite,
    In a singular minor key:

'Oh, I am a cook and a captain bold,
    And the mate of the *Nancy* brig,
And a bo'sun tight, and a midshipmite,
    And the crew of the captain's gig.

And he shook his fists and he tore his hair,
    Till I really felt afraid,
For I couldn't help thinking the man had been drinking
    And so I simply said:

'Oh, elderly man, it's little I know
    Of the duties of men of the sea,
But I'll eat my hand if I understand
    How you can possibly be

'At once a cook, and a captain bold,
    And the mate of the *Nancy* brig,
And a bo'sun tight, and a midshipmite,
    And the crew of the captain's gig.'

Then he gave a hitch to his trousers, which
    Is a trick all seamen larn,
And having got rid of a thumping quid,
    He spun this painful yarn:

"'Twas in the good ship *Nancy Bell*
　　That we sailed to the Indian sea,
And there on a reef we come to grief
　　Which has often occurred to me.

'And pretty nigh all o' the crew was drowned
　　(There was seventy-seven o' soul),
And only ten of the *Nancy's* men
　　Said "Here!" to the muster-roll.

'There was me and the cook and the captain bold,
　　And the mate of the *Nancy* brig,
And the bo'sun tight, and a midshipmite,
　　And the crew of the captain's gig.

'For a month we'd neither wittles nor drink,
　　Till a-hungry we did feel,
So we drawed a lot, and accordin' shot
　　The captain for our meal.

'The next lot fell to the *Nancy's* mate,
　　And a delicate dish he made;
Then our appetite with the midshipmite
　　We seven survivors stayed.

'And then we murdered the bo'sun tight,
　　And he much resembled pig;
Then we wittled free, did the cook and me,
　　On the crew of the captain's gig.

'Then only the cook and me was left,
　　And the delicate question, 'Which
Of us two goes to the kettle?' arose
　　And we argued it out as sich.

'For I loved that cook as a brother, I did,
　　And the cook he worshipped me;
But we'd both be blowed if we'd either be stowed
　　In the other chap's hold, you see.

210

'I'll be eat if you dines off me,' says Tom,
  'Yes, that,' says I, 'you'll be,'—
'I'm boiled if I die, my friend,' quoth I,
  And 'Exactly so,' quoth he.

'Says he, "Dear James, to murder me
  Were a foolish thing to do,
For don't you see that you can't cook *me*,
  While I can—and will—cook *you*!"

'So he boils the water, and takes the salt
  And the pepper in portions true
(Which he never forgot), and some chopped shalot,
  And some sage and parsley too.

 "Come here," says he, with a proper pride,
  Which his smiling features tell,
"'Twill soothing be if I let you see,
  How extremely nice you'll smell."

'And he stirred it round and round and round,
  And he sniffed at the foaming froth;
When I ups with his heels, and smothers his squeals
  In the scum of the boiling broth.

'And I eat that cook in a week or less,
  And—as I eating be
The last of his chops, why, I almost drops,
  For a wessel in sight I see!

      *   *   *   *   *

'And I never grin, and I never smile,
  And I never larf nor play,
But I sit and croak, and a single joke
  I have—which is to say:

'Oh, I am a cook and a captain bold,
　And the mate of the *Nancy* brig,
And a bosun tight, *and* a midshipmite,
　And the crew of the captain's gig!'

SIR W. S. GILBERT

GENTLE ALICE BROWN

It was a robber's daughter, and her name was ALICE
　BROWN,
Her father was the terror of a small Italian town;
Her mother was a foolish, weak, but amiable old thing;
But it isn't of her parents that I'm going for to sing.

As ALICE was a-sitting at her window-sill one day
A beautiful young gentleman he chanced to pass that
　way;
She cast her eyes upon him, and he looked so good and
　true,
That she thought, 'I could be happy with a gentleman
　like you!'

And every morning passed her house that cream of
　gentlemen,
She knew she might expect him at a quarter unto ten,
A sorter in the Custom-house, it was his daily road
(The Custom-house was fifteen minutes' walk from her
　abode.)

But ALICE was a pious girl, who knew it wasn't wise
To look at strange young sorters with expressive purple
　eyes;
So she sought the village priest to whom her family
　confessed—
The priest by whom their little sins were carefully
　assessed.

'Oh, holy father,' ALICE said,' 'twould grieve you, would
  it not?
To discover that I was a most disreputable lot!
Of all unhappy sinners, I'm the most unhappy one!'
The padre said, 'Whatever have you been and gone and
  done?'

'I have helped mamma to steal a little kiddy from its
  dad,
I've assisted dear papa in cutting up a little lad.
I've planned a little burglary and forged a little cheque,
And slain a little baby for the coral on its neck!'

The worthy pastor heaved a sigh, and dropped a silent
  tear—
And said, 'You musn't judge yourself too heavily, my
  dear—
It's wrong to murder babies, little corals for to fleece;
But sins like these one expiates at half-a-crown apiece.

'Girls will be girls—you're very young, and flighty in
  your mind;
Old heads upon young shoulders we must not expect to
  find;
We mustn't be too hard upon these little girlish tricks—
Let's see—five crimes at half-a-crown—exactly twelve-
  and-six.'

'Oh, father,' little ALICE cried, 'your kindness makes me
  weep,
You do these little things for me so singularly cheap—
Your thoughtful liberality I never can forget;
But oh, there is another crime I haven't mentioned yet!

'A pleasant-looking gentleman, with pretty purple
  eyes—
I've noticed at my window, as I've sat a-catching flies,

He passes by it every day as certain as can be—
I blush to say I've winked at him, and he has winked at me!

'For shame,' said FATHER PAUL, 'my erring daughter!
    On my word
This is the most distressing news that I have ever heard.
Why, naughty girl, your excellent papa has pledged
    your hand
To a promising young robber, the lieutenant of his band!

'This dreadful piece of news will pain your worthy
    parents so!
They are the most remunerative customers I know;
For many many years they've kept starvation from
    my doors,
I never knew so criminal a family as yours!

'The common country folk in this insipid neighbourhood
Have nothing to confess, they're so ridiculously good;
And if you marry any one respectable at all,
Why, you'll reform, and what will then become of
    FATHER PAUL?'

The worthy priest, he up and drew his cowl upon his
    crown,
And started off in haste to tell the news to ROBBER
    BROWN;
To tell him how his daughter, who was now for
    marriage fit,
Had winked upon a sorter, who reciprocated it.

Good ROBBER BROWN he muffled up his anger pretty
    well,
He said, 'I have a notion, and that notion I will tell;
I will nab this gay young sorter, terrify him into fits,
And get my gentle wife to chop him into little bits.

214

'I've studied human nature, and I know a thing or two;
Though a girl may fondly love a living gent, as many do,
A feeling of disgust upon her senses there will fall
When she looks upon his body chopped particularly
    small.'

He traced that gallant sorter to a still surburban square;
He watched his opportunity and seized him unaware;
He took a life-preserver and he hit him on the head,
And Mrs Brown dissected him before she went to bed.

And pretty little Alice grew more settled in her mind,
She never more was guilty of a weakness of the kind,
Until at length good Robber Brown bestowed her
    pretty hand
On the promising young robber, the lieutenant of his
    band.

SIR W. S. GILBERT

ETIQUETTE

The *Ballyshannon* foundered off the coast of Cariboo,
And down in fathoms many went the captain and the
    crew;
Down went the owners—greedy men whom hope of gain
    allured:
Oh, dry the starting tear, for they were heavily insured.

Besides the captain and the mate, the owners and the
    crew,
The passengers were also drowned excepting only two;
Young Peter Gray, who tasted teas for Baker, Croop,
    and Co.,
And Somers, who from Eastern shores imported indigo.

These passengers, by reason of their clinging to a mast,
Upon a desert island were eventually cast.
They hunted for their meals, as Alexander Selkirk used,
But they could not chat together—they had not been
      introduced.

For Peter Gray, and Somers too, though certainly in
      trade,
Were properly particular about the friends they made;
And somehow thus they settled it without a word of
      mouth—
That Gray should take the northern half, while Somers
      took the south.

On Peter's portion oysters grew—a delicacy rare,
But oysters were a delicacy Peter couldn't bear.
On Somers' side was turtle, on the shingle lying thick
Which Somers couldn't eat, because it always made him
      sick.

Gray gnashed his teeth with envy as he saw a mighty
      store
Of turtle unmolested on his fellow-creature's shore:
The oysters at his feet aside impatiently he shoved,
For turtle and his mother were the only things he loved.

And Somers sighed in sorrow as he settled in the south,
For the thought of Peter's oysters brought the water to
      his mouth.
He longed to lay him down upon the shelly bed, and
      stuff:
He had often eaten oysters, but had never had enough.

How they wished an introduction to each other they
    had had
When on board the *Ballyshannon*! And it drove them
    nearly mad
To think how very friendly with each other they might
    get,
If it wasn't for the arbitrary rule of etiquette!

One day, when out a-hunting for the *mus ridiculus*,
Gray overheard his fellow-man soliloquizing thus:
'I wonder how the playmates of my youth are getting
    on,
M'Connell, S. B. Walters, Paddy Byles, and Robinson?'

These simple words made Peter as delighted as could
    be,
Old Chummies at the Charterhouse were Robinson and
    he!
He walked straight up to Somers, then he turned
    extremely red,
Hesitated, hummed and hawed a bit, then cleared his
    throat and said:

'I beg your pardon—pray forgive me if I seem too bold,
But you have breathed a name I knew familiarly of old.
You spoke aloud of Robinson—I happened to be by—
You know him?' 'Yes, extremely well.' 'Allow me—so
    do I.'

It was enough: they felt they could more sociably get
    on,
For (ah, the magic of the fact!) they each knew
    Robinson!
And Mr Somers' turtle was at Peter's service quite,
And Mr Somers punished Peter's oyster-beds all night.

They soon became like brothers from community of
    wrongs;
They wrote each other little odes and sang each other
    songs;
They told each other anecdotes disparaging their
    wives;
On several occasions, too, they saved each other's
    lives.

They felt quite melancholy when they parted for the
    night,
And got up in the morning soon as ever it was light;
Each other's pleasant company they so relied upon,
And all because it happened that they both knew
    Robinson!

They lived for many years on that inhospitable shore,
And day by day they learned to love each other more
    and more.
At last, to their astonishment, on getting up one day,
They saw a vessel anchored in the offing of the bay!

To Peter an idea occurred. 'Suppose we cross the main?
So good an opportunity may not occur again.'
And Somers thought a minute, then ejaculated, 'Done!
I wonder how my business in the City's getting on?'

'But stay,' said Mr Peter: 'when in England, as you
    know,
I earned a living tasting teas for Baker, Croop, and
    Co.
I may be superseded, my employers think me dead!'
'Then come with me,' said Somers, 'and taste indigo
    instead.'

But all their plans were scattered in a moment when
    they found
The vessel was a convict ship from Portland, outward
    bound!
When a boat came off to fetch them, though they felt it
    very kind
To go on board they firmly but respectfully declined.

As both the happy settlers roared with laughter at the
    joke,
They recognized an unattractive fellow pulling stroke:
'Twas Robinson—a convict, in an unbecoming frock!
Condemned to seven years for misappropriating stock!!!

They laughed no more, for Somers thought he had been
    rather rash
In knowing one whose friend had misappropriated cash;
And Peter thought a foolish tack he must have gone upon,
In making the acquaintance of a friend of Robinson.

At first they didn't quarrel very openly, I've heard;
They nodded when they met, and now and then
    exchanged a word:
The word grew rare, and rarer still the nodding of the
    head,
And when they meet each other now, they cut each
    other dead.

To allocate the island they agreed by word of mouth,
And Peter takes the north again, and Somers takes the
    south:
And Peter has the oysters, which he loathes with horror
    grim,
And Somers has the turtle—turtle disagrees with him.

SIR W. S. GILBERT

FERDINANDO AND ELVIRA

OR, THE GENTLE PIEMAN

PART I

At a pleasant evening party I had taken down to supper
One whom I will call ELVIRA, and we talked of love and
    TUPPER,

MR TUPPER and the poets, very lightly with them
    dealing,
For I've always been distinguished for a strong poetic
    feeling.

Then we let off paper crackers, each of which contained
    a motto,
And she listened while I read them, till her mother told
    her not to.

Then she whispered, 'To the ball-room we had better,
    dear, be walking;
If we stop down here much longer, really people will be
    talking.'

There were noblemen in coronets, and military cousins,
There were captains by the hundred, there were baro-
    nets by dozens.

Yet she heeded not their offers, but dismissed them
    with a blessing;
Then she let down all her back hair which had taken
    long in dressing.

Then she had convulsive sobbings in her agitated
    throttle,
Then she wiped her pretty eyes and smelt her pretty
    smelling-bottle.

So I whispered, 'Dear ELVIRA, say—what can the
    matter be with you?
Does anything you've eaten, darling POPSY, disagree
    with you?'

But spite of all I said, her sobs grew more and more
    distressing,
And she tore her pretty back hair, which had taken long
    in dressing.

Then she gazed upon the carpet, at the ceiling then
    above me,
And she whispered, 'FERDINANDO, do you really, *really*
    love me?'

'Love you?' said I, then I sighed, and then I gazed upon
    her sweetly—
For I think I do this sort of thing particularly neatly—

'Send me to the Arctic regions, or illimitable azure,
On a scientific goose-chase, with my COXWELL or my
    GLAISHER.

'Tell me whither I may hie me, tell me, dear one, that I
    may know—
Is it up the highest Andes? down a horrible volcano?'

But she said, 'It isn't polar bears, or hot volcanic
    grottoes,
Only find out who it is that writes those lovely cracker
    mottoes!'

PART II

'Tell me, HENRY WADSWORTH, ALFRED, POET CLOSE, or
    MISTER TUPPER,
Do you write the bonbon mottoes my ELVIRA pulls at
    supper?'

But HENRY WADSWORTH smiled, and said he had not
    had that honour;
And ALFRED, too, disclaimed the words that told so
    much upon her.

'MISTER MARTIN TUPPER, POET CLOSE, I beg of you
    inform us';
But my question seemed to throw them both into a rage
    enormous.

MISTER CLOSE expressed a wish that he could only get
    anigh to me.
And MISTER MARTIN TUPPER sent the following reply
    to me:—

'A fool is bent upon a twig, but wise men dread a
    bandit.'
Which I think must have been clever, for I didn't under-
    stand it.

Seven weary years I wandered—Patagonia, China,
    Norway,
Till at last I sank exhausted at a pastrycook his
    doorway.

There were fuchsias and geraniums, and daffodils and
    myrtle,
So I entered, and I ordered half a basin of mock turtle.

He was plump and he was chubby, he was smooth and
    he was rosy,
And his little wife was pretty, and particularly cosy.

And he chirped and sang, and skipped about, and
    laughed with laughter hearty—
He was wonderfully active for so very stout a party.

And I said, 'Oh, gentle pieman, why so very, very
  merry?
Is it purity of conscience, or your one-and-seven
  sherry?'

But he answered, 'I'm so happy—no profession could be
  dearer—
If I am not humming "Tra! la! la!" I'm singing, "Tirer,
  lirer!"

'First I go and make the patties, and the puddings and
  the jellies,
Then I make a sugar birdcage, which upon a table swell is;

'Then I polish all the silver, which a supper-table
  lacquers;
Then I write the pretty mottoes which you find inside
  the crackers'—

'Found at last!' I madly shouted.   'Gentle pieman, you
  astound me!'
Then I waved the turtle soup enthusiastically round me.

And I shouted and I danced until he'd quite a crowd
  around him—
And I rushed away, exclaiming, 'I have found him! I
  have found him!'

And I heard the gentle pieman in the road behind me
  trilling,
' "Tira! lira!" stop him, stop him! Tra! la! la! the soup's
  a shilling!'

But until I reached ELVIRA's home, I never, never
  waited,
And ELVIRA to her FERDINAND's irrevocably mated!

SIR W. S. GILBERT

PLAIN LANGUAGE FROM TRUTHFUL JAMES

I reside at Table Mountain, and my name is Truthful
　　James;
I am not up to small deceit, or any sinful games;
And I'll tell in simple language what I know about the
　　row
That broke up our Society upon the Stanislow.

But first I would remark, that it is not a proper plan
For any scientific gent to whale his fellow-man,
And, if a member don't agree with his peculiar whim,
To lay for that same member for to 'put a head' on him.

Now nothing could be finer or more beautiful to see
Than the first six months' proceedings of that same
　　Society,
Till Brown of Calaveras brought a lot of fossil bones
That he found within a tunnel near the tenement of
　　Jones.

Then Brown he read a paper, and he reconstructed
　　there,
From those same bones, an animal that was extremely
　　rare;
And Jones then asked the Chair for a suspension of the
　　rules,
Till he could prove that those same bones was one of his
　　lost mules.

Then Brown he smiled a bitter smile, and said he was
　　at fault,
It seemed he had been trespassing on Jones's family
　　vault;
He was a most sarcastic man, this quiet Mr Brown,
And on several occasions he had cleaned out the town.

Now I hold it is not decent for a scientific gent
To say another is an ass,—at least, to all intent;
Nor should the individual who happens to be meant
Reply by heaving rocks at him to any great extent.

Then Abner Dean of Angel's raised a point of order,
    when
A chunk of old red sandstone took him in the abdomen,
And he smiled a kind of sickly smile, and curled up on
    the floor,
And the subsequent proceedings interested him no more.

For, in less time than I write it, every member did
    engage
In a warfare with the remnants of a palæozoic age;
And the way they heaved those fossils in their anger was
    a sin,
Till the skull of an old mammoth caved the head of
    Thompson in.

And this is all I have to say of these improper games,
For I live at Table Mountain, and my name is Truthful
    James;
And I've told in simple language what I knew about the
    row
That broke up our Society upon the Stanislow.

                              BRET HARTE

FURTHER LANGUAGE FROM
TRUTHFUL JAMES

    Do I sleep? do I dream?
    Do I wonder and doubt?
    Are things what they seem?
    Or is visions about?
    Is our civilization a failure?
    Or is the Caucasian played out?

Which expressions are strong;
Yet would feebly imply
Some account of a wrong—
Not to call it a lie—
As was worked off on William, my pardner,
And the same being W. Nye.

He came down to the Ford
On the very same day
Of that lottery drawed
By those sharps at the Bay;
And he says to me, 'Truthful, how goes it?'
I replied, 'It is far, far from gay;

'For the camp has gone wild
On this lottery game,
And has even beguiled
"Injin Dick" by the same.'
Which said Nye to me, 'Injins is pizen:
Do you know what his number is, James?'

I replied '7, 2,
9, 8, 4, is his hand';
When he started, and drew
Out a list, which he scanned;
Then he softly went for his revolver
With language I cannot command.

Then I said, 'William Nye!'
But he turned upon me,
And the look in his eye
Was quite painful to see;
And he says, 'You mistake; this poor Injin
I protects from such sharps as you be!'

I was shocked and withdrew;
But I grieve to relate,
When he next met my view

Injin Dick was his mate,
And the two around town was a-lying
In a frightfully dissolute state.

Which the war dance they had
Round a tree at the Bend
Was a sight that was sad;
And it seemed that the end
Would not justify the proceedings,
As I quietly remarked to a friend.

For that Injin he fled
The next day to his band;
And we found William spread
Very loose on the strand,
With a peaceful-like smile on his features.
And a dollar greenback in his hand;

Which, the same when rolled out,
We observed with surprise,
That that Injin, no doubt,
Had believed was the prize,—
Them figures in red in the corner,
Which the number of notes specifies.

Was it guile, or a dream?
Is it Nye that I doubt?
Are things what they seem?
Or is visions about?
Is our civilization a failure?
Or is the Caucasian played out?

BRET HARTE

THE HEATHEN CHINEE

Which I wish to remark—
    And my language is plain—
That for ways that are dark
    And for tricks that are vain,
The heathen Chinee is peculiar,
    Which the same I would rise to explain.

Ah Sin was his name;
    And I shall not deny
In regard to the same
    What that name might imply;
But his smile it was pensive and child-like,
    As I frequent remarked to Bill Nye.

It was August the third;
    And quite soft was the skies.
Which it might be inferred
    That Ah Sin was likewise;
Yet he played it that day upon William
    And me in a way I despise.

Which we had a small game,
    And Ah Sin took a hand:
It was Euchre. The same
    He did not understand;
But he smiled as he sat by the table,
    With the smile that was child-like and bland.

Yet the cards they were stocked
    In a way that I grieve,
And my feelings were shocked
    At the state of Nye's sleeve:
Which was stuffed full of aces and bowers,
    And the same with intent to deceive.

228

But the hands that were played
  By that heathen Chinee,
And the points that he made,
  Were quite frightful to see,—
Till at last he put down a right bower,
  Which the same Nye had dealt unto me.

Then I looked up at Nye,
  And he gazed upon me;
And he rose with a sigh,
  And said, 'Can this be?
We are ruined by Chinese cheap labour,'
  And he went for that heathen Chinee.

In the scene that ensued
  I did not take a hand,
But the floor it was strewed
  Like the leaves on the strand
With the cards that Ah Sin had been hiding,
  In the game 'he did not understand'.

In his sleeves, which were long,
  He had twenty-four packs,—
Which was coming it strong,
  Yet I state but the facts;
And we found on his nails, which were taper,
  What is frequent in tapers,—that's wax.

Which is why I remark,
  And my language is plain,
That for ways that are dark,
  And for tricks that are vain,
The heathen Chinee is peculiar—
  Which the same I am free to maintain.

BRET HARTE

HANS BREITMANN'S BARTY

Hans Breitmann gife a barty;
   Dey had biano-blayin',
I felled in lofe mit a Merican frau,
   Her name vas Madilda Yane.
She hat haar as prown ash a pretzel,
   Her eyes vas himmel-plue,
Und vhen dey looket indo mine,
   Dey shplit mine heart in dwo.

Hans Breitmann gife a barty,
   I vent dere you'll pe pound;
I valtzet mit Madilda Yane,
   Und vent shpinnen' round und round
De pootiest Fräulein in de house,
   She vayed 'pout dwo hoondred pound,
Und efery dime she gife a shoomp
   She make de vindows sound.

Hans Breitmann gife a barty,
   I dells you it cost him dear;
Dey rolled in more ash sefen kecks
   Of foost-rate lager beer.
Und vhenefer dey knocks de shpicket in
   De Deutschers gifes a cheer;
I dinks dot so vine a barty
   Nefer coom to a het dis year.

Hans Breitmann gife a barty;
   Dere all vas Souse and Brouse,
Vhen de sooper comed in, de gompany
   Did make demselfs to house;
Dey ate das Brot and Gensy broost,
   De Bratwurst and Braten vine,
Und vash der Abendessen down
   Mit four parrels of Neckarwein.

Hans Breitmann gife a barty;
   Ve all cot troonk ash bigs.
I poot mine mout' to a parrel of beer,
   Und emptied it oop mit a schwigs;
Und den I gissed Madilda Yane,
   Und she shlog me on de kop,
Und de gompany vighted mit daple-lecks
   Dill de coonshtable made oos shtop.

Hans Breitmann gife a barty—
   Vhere ish dot barty now?
Vhere ish de lofely golden cloud
   Dot float on de moundain's prow?
Vhere ish de himmelstrahlende Stern—
   De shtar of de shpirit's light?
All goned afay mit de lager beer—
   Afay in de Ewigkeit!

               C. G. LELAND

THE MODERN HIAWATHA

When he killed the Mudjokivis,
Of the skin he made him mittens,
Made them with the fur side inside,
Made them with the skin side outside,
He, to get the warm side inside,
Put the inside skin side outside;
He, to get the cold side outside,
Put the warm side fur side inside.
That's why he put fur side inside,
Why he put the skin side outside,
Why he turned them inside outside.

               ANON

THE BALLAD OF HIRAM HOVER

Where the Moosatockmaguntic
Pours its waters in the Skuntic,
  Met, along the forest-side,
  Hiram Hover, Huldah Hyde.

She, a maiden fair and dapper,
He, a red-haired, stalwart trapper,
  Hunting beaver, mink, and skunk,
  In the woodlands of Squeedunk.

She, Pentucket's pensive daughter,
Walked beside the Skuntic water,
  Gathering, in her apron wet,
  Snakeroot, mint, and bouncing-bet.

'Why,' he murmured, loath to leave her,
'Gather yarbs for chills and fever,
  When a lovyer, bold and true,
  Only waits to gather you?'

'Go,' she answered, 'I'm not hasty;
I prefer a man more tasty:
  Leastways, one to please me well
  Should not have a beasty smell.'

'Haughty Huldah!' Hiram answered;
'Mind and heart alike are cancered:
  Jest look here! these peltries give
  Cash, wherefrom a pair may live.

'I, you think, am but a vagrant,
Trapping beasts by no means fragrant:
  Yet—I'm sure it's worth a thank—
  I've a handsome sum in bank.'

232

Turned and vanished Hiram Hover;
And, before the year was over,
   Huldah, with the yarbs she sold,
   Bought a cape, against the cold.

Black and thick the furry cape was;
Of a stylish cut the shape was,
   And the girls, in all the town,
   Envied Huldah up and down.

Then, at last, one winter morning,
Hiram came, without a warning:
   'Either,' said he, 'you are blind,
   Huldah, or you've changed your mind.

'Me you snub for trapping varmints,
Yet you take the skins for garments:
   Since you wear the skunk and mink,
   There's no harm in me, I think.'

'Well,' she said, 'we will not quarrel,
Hiram: I accept the moral,
   Now the fashion's so, I guess
   I can't hardly do no less.'

Thus the trouble all was over
Of the love of Hiram Hover;
   Thus he made sweet Huldah Hyde
   Huldah Hover as his bride.

Love employs, with equal favour,
Things of good and equal savour;
   That, which first appeared to part,
   Warmed, at last, the maiden's heart

Under one impartial banner,
Life, the hunter, Love the tanner,
   Draw, from every beast they snare,
   Comfort for a wedded pair!

BAYARD TAYLOR

THE AMERICAN TRAVELLER

To Lake Aghmoogenegamook,
   All in the State of Maine,
A Man from Wittequergaugaum came
   One evening in the rain.

'I am a traveller,' said he,
   'Just started on a tour,
And go to Nomjamskillicock
   Tomorrow morn at four.'

He took a tavern bed that night;
   And, with the morrow's sun,
By way of Sekledobskus went,
   With carpet-bag and gun.

A week passed on; and next we find
   Our native tourist come
To that sequestered village called
   Gcnasagarnagum.

From thence he went to Absequoit,
   And there, quite tired of Maine—
He sought the mountains of Vermont,
   Upon a railroad train.

Dog Hollow, in the Green Mount State,
   Was his first stopping place;
And then Skunk's Misery displayed
   Its sweetness and its grace.

234

By easy stages then he went
   To visit Devil's Den;
And Scramble Hollow, by the way,
   Did come within his ken.

Then *via* Nine Holes and Goose Green
   He travelled through the State;
And to Virginia, finally,
   Was guided by his fate.

Within the Old Dominion's bounds
   He wandered up and down;
Today, at Buzzard Roost ensconced,
   Tomorrow at Hell Town.

At Pole Cat, too, he spent a week,
   Till friends from Bull Ring came,
And made him spend a day with them
   In hunting forest-game.

Then, with his carpet bag in hand,
   To Dog Town next he went,
Though stopping at Free Negro Town,
   Where half a day he spent.

From thence, to Negationburg
   His route of travel lay;
Which having gained, he left the State
   And took a southward way.

North Carolina's friendly soil
   He trod at fall of night,
And, on a bed of softest down,
   He slept at Hell's Delight.

Morn found him on the road again,
   To Lousy Level bound;
At Bull's Tail, and Lick Lizard, too,
   Good provender he found.

The country all about Pinch Gut
    So beautiful did seem
That the beholder thought it like
    A picture in a dream.

But the plantations near Burnt Coat
    Were even finer still,
And made the wondering tourist feel
    A soft delicious thrill.

At Tear Shirt, too, the scenery
    Most charming did appear,
With Snatch It in the distance far,
    And Purgatory near.

But, spite of all these pleasant scenes,
    The tourist stoutly swore
That home is brightest, after all,
    And travel is a bore.

So back he went to Maine straightway:
    A little wife he took;
And now is making nutmegs at
    Moosehicmagunticook.

               ROBERT H. NEWELL

I HAVE NO PAIN

I have no pain, dear mother, now,
    But Oh! I am so dry;
Just fetch your Jim another quart
    To wet the other eye.

               ANON

AFTER DILETTANTE CONCETTI

'Why do you wear your hair like a man,
            Sister Helen?
This week is the third since you began.'
'I'm writing a ballad; be still if you can,
            Little brother.
            (*O Mother Carey, mother!*
What chickens are these between sea and heaven?)'

'But why does your figure appear so lean,
            Sister Helen?
And why do you dress in sage, sage green?'
'Children should never be heard, if seen,
            Little brother.
            (*O Mother Carey, mother!*
What fowls are a-wing in the stormy heaven!)'

'But why is your face so yellowy white,
            Sister Helen?
And why are your skirts so funnily tight?'
'Be quiet, you torment, or how can I write,
            Little Brother?
            (*O Mother Carey, mother!*
How gathers thy train to the sea from the heaven!)'

'And who's Mother Carey, and what is her train,
            Sister Helen?
And why do you call her again and again?'
'You troublesome boy, why that's the refrain,
            Little brother.
            (*O Mother Carey, mother!*
What work is toward in the startled heaven?)'

'And what's a refrain? What a curious word
            Sister Helen!

237

Is the ballad you're writing about a sea-bird?'
'Not at all; why should it be? Don't be absurd,
   Little brother.
    (*O Mother Carey, mother!*
Thy brood flies lower as lowers the heaven.)'

   (*A big brother speaketh:*)

'The refrain you've studied a meaning had
    Sister Helen!
It gave strange force to a weird ballad,
But refrains have become a ridiculous 'fad,'
   Little brother.
    And *Mother Carey, mother,*
Has a bearing on nothing in earth or heaven.

'But the finical fashion has had its day,
    Sister Helen.
And let's try in the style of a different lay
To bid it adieu in poetical way,
   Little brother.
    So, Mother Carey, mother!
Collect your chickens and go to—heaven.'

  (*A pause. Then the big brother singeth, accompany-*
  ing himself in a plaintive wise on the triangle:)

'Look in my face. My name is Used-to-was,
 I am also called Played-out and Done-to-death,
 And It-will-wash-no-more. Awakeneth
Slowly, but sure awakening it has,
The common-sense of man; and I, alas!
 The ballad-burden trick, now known too well,
 Am turned to scorn, and grown contemptible—
A too transparent artifice to pass.

238

What a cheap dodge I am! The cats who dart
  Tin-kettled through the streets in wild surprise
  Assail judicious ears not otherwise;
And yet no critics praise the urchin's 'art',
Who to the wretched creature's caudal part
  Its foolish empty-jingling 'burden' ties.'

H. D. TRAILL

KING ARTHUR GROWING VERY TIRED INDEED

King Arthur, growing very tired indeed
Of wild Tintagel, now that Lancelot
Had gone to Jersey or to Jericho,
And there was nobody to make a rhyme,
And Cornish girls were christened Jennifer,
And the Round Table had grown rickety,
Said unto Merlin (who had been asleep
For a few centuries in Broceliande,
But woke, and had a bath, and felt refreshed):
'What shall I do to pull myself together?'
Quoth Merlin, 'Salad is the very thing,
And you can get it at the "Cheshire Cheese".'
King Arthur went there: *verily,* I believe
That he has dined there every day since then.
Have you not marked the portly gentleman
In his cool corner, with his plate of greens?
The great knight Lancelot prefers the 'Cock',
Where port is excellent (in pints), and waiters
Are portlier than kings, and steaks are tender,
And poets have been known to meditate . . .
Ox-fed orating ominous octastichs.

MORTIMER COLLINS

SARAGOSSA

(In imitation of Thomas Moore)

Pepita, my paragon, bright star of Arragon;
　　Listen, dear, listen; your Cristobal sings.
From my cot that lies buried a short way from Lerida
　　Love and a diligence lent me their wings.
Swift as a falcon I flew to thy balcony.
　　(Is it bronchitis? I can't sing a bar.)
Greet not with merriment Love's first experiment;
　　Listen, Pepita! I've brought my *catarrh*.

Manuel the matador may, like a flat, adore
　　Donna Dolores: I pity his choice,
For they say that her governor lets neither lover nor
　　Anyone else hear the sound of her voice.
Brother Bartolomé (stoutish Apollo) may
　　Sigh for Sabina—you'll pardon this cough?—
And Isabel's votary, Nunez the notary,
　　Vainly—(that sneeze again? Loved one, I'm Off!)

H. S. LEIGH

'TWAS EVER THUS

(In imitation of Thomas Moore)

I never rear'd a young gazelle,
　　(Because, you see, I never tried);
But had it known and loved me well,
　　No doubt the creature would have died.
My rich and aged Uncle John
　　Has known me long and loves me well,
But still persists in living on—
　　I would he were a young gazelle.

H. S. LEIGH

240

BRAHMA

(*In imitation of Emerson*)

If the wild bowler thinks he bowls,
  Or if the batsman thinks he's bowled,
They know not, poor misguided souls,
  They, too, shall perish unconsoled.
I am the batsman and the bat,
  I am the bowler and the ball,
The umpire, the pavilion cat,
  The roller, pitch, and stumps, and all.

ANDREW LANG

RIGID BODY SINGS

Gin a body meet a body
  Flyin' through the air,
Gin a body hit a body,
  Will it fly? and where?
Ilka impact has its measure,
  Ne'er a' ane hae I,
Yet a' the lads they measure me,
  Or, at least, they try.

Gin a body meet a body
  Altogether free,
How they travel afterwards
  We do not always see.
Ilka problem has its method
  By analytics high;
For me, I ken na ane o' them,
  But what the waur am I?

JAMES CLERK MAXWELL

NEPHELIDIA

From the depth of the dreamy decline of the dawn
    through a notable nimbus of nebulous noonshine,
  Pallid and pink as the palm of the flag-flower that
    flickers with fear of the flies as they float,
Are they looks of our lovers that lustrously lean from a
    marvel of mystic miraculous moonshine,
  These that we feel in the blood of our blushes that
    thicken and threaten with throbs through the throat?
Thicken and thrill as a theatre thronged at appeal of an
    actor's appalled agitation.
  Fainter with fear of the fires of the future than pale
    with the promise of pride in the past;
Flushed with the famishing fullness of fever that reddens
    with radiance of rathe recreation,
  Gaunt as the ghastliest of glimpses that gleam through
    the gloom of the gloaming when ghosts go aghast?
Nay, for the nick of the tick of the time is a tremulous
    touch on the temples of terror,
  Strained as the sinews yet strenuous with strife of the
    dead who is dumb as the dust-heaps of death:
Surely no soul is it, sweet as the spasm of erotic emotional
    exquisite error,
  Bathed in the balms of beatified bliss, beatific itself by
    beatitude's breath.
Surely no spirit or sense of a soul that was soft to the
    spirit and soul of our senses
  Sweetens the stress of suspiring suspicion that sobs in
    the semblance and sound of a sigh;
Only this oracle opens Olympian, in mystical moods and
    triangular tenses—
  'Life is the lust of a lamp for the light that is dark till
    the dawn of the day when we die.'
Mild is the mirk and monotonous music of memory,
    melodiously mute as it may be,

While the hope in the heart of a hero is bruised by the
    breach of men's rapiers, resigned to the rod;
Made meek as a mother whose bosom-beats bound with
    the bliss-bringing bulk of a balm-breathing baby.
As they grope through the graveyard of creeds, under
    skies growing green at a groan for the grimness of God.
Blank is the book of his bounty beholden of old, and its
    binding is blacker than bluer:
Out of blue into black is the scheme of the skies, and
    their dews are the wine of the bloodshed of things;
Till the darkling desire of delight shall be free as a fawn
    that is freed from the fangs that pursue her,
Till the heart-beats of hell shall be hushed by a hymn
    from the hunt that has harried the kennel of kings.

A. C. SWINBURNE

AN UNEXPECTED PLEASURE

My heart is like one asked to dine
    Whose evening dress is up the spout;
My heart is like a man would be
    Whose raging tooth is half pulled out.
My heart is like a howling swell
    Who boggles on his upper C;
My heart is madder than all these—
    My wife's mamma has come to tea.

Raise me a bump upon my crown,
    Bang it till green in purple dies;
Feed me on bombs and fulminates,
    And turncocks of a medium size.
Work me a suit in crimson apes
    And sky-blue beetles on the spree;
Because the mother of my wife
    Has come—and means to stay with me.

ANON

OCTOPUS

(In imitation of Swinburne)

Strange beauty, eight-limbed and eight-handed,
    Whence camest to dazzle our eyes?
With thy bosom bespangled and banded
    With the hues of the seas and the skies;
Is thy home European or Asian,
    O mystical monster marine?
Part molluscous and partly crustacean,
    Betwixt and between.

Wast thou born to the sound of sea-trumpets?
    Hast thou eaten and drunk to excess
Of the sponges—thy muffins and crumpets,
    Of the seaweed—thy mustard and cress?
Wast thou nurtured in caverns of coral,
    Remote from reproof or restraint?
Art thou innocent, art thou immoral,
    Sinburnian or Saint?

Lithe limbs, curling free, as a creeper
    That creeps in a desolate place,
To enrol and envelop the sleeper
    In a silent and stealthy embrace,
Cruel beak craning forward to bite us,
    Our juices to drain and to drink,
Or to whelm us in waves of Cocytus,
    Indelible ink!

O breast, that 'twere rapture to writhe on!
    O arms 'twere delicious to feel
Clinging close with the crush of the Python,
    When she maketh her murderous meal!

In thy eight-fold embraces enfolden,
    Let our empty existence escape;
Give us death that is glorious and golden,
    Crushed all out of shape!

Ah! thy red lips, lascivious and luscious,
    With death in their amorous kiss!
Cling round us, and clasp us, and crush us,
    With bitings of agonized bliss;
We are sick with the poison of pleasure,
    Dispense us the potion of pain;
Ope thy mouth to its uttermost measure
    And bite us again!

A. C. HILTON

THE VULTURE AND THE HUSBANDMAN

(*After Lewis Carroll*)

The rain was raining cheerfully,
    As if it had been May;
The Senate-House appeared inside
    Unusually gay;
And this was strange, because it was
    A Viva-Voce day.

The men were sitting sulkily,
    Their paper work was done;
They wanted much to go away
    To ride or row or run;
'It's very rude,' they said, 'to keep
    Us here, and spoil our fun.'

The papers they had finished lay
    In piles of blue and white.

They answered everything they could,
   And wrote with all their might,
But, though they wrote it all by rote,
   They did not write it right.

The Vulture and the Husbandman
   Beside these piles did stand,
They wept like anything to see
   The work they had in hand,
'If this were only finished up,'
   Said they, 'it would be grand!'

'If seven D's or seven C's
   We give to all the crowd,
Do you suppose,' the Vulture said,
   'That we could get them ploughed?'
'I think so,' said the Husbandman,
   'But pray don't talk so loud.'

'O undergraduates, come up,'
   The Vulture did beseech,
'And let us see if you can learn
   As well as we can teach;
We cannot do with more than two
   To have a word with each.'

Two Undergraduates came up,
   And slowly took a seat,
They knit their brows, and bit their thumbs.
   As if they found them sweet,
And this was odd, because you know
   Thumbs are not good to eat.

'The time has come,' the Vulture said,
   'To talk of many things,
Of Accidence and Adjectives,
   And names of Jewish kings,

How many notes a sackbut has,
　　And whether shawms have strings.'

'Please, sir,' the Undergraduates said,
　　Turning a little blue,
'We did not know that was the sort
　　Of thing we had to do.'
'We thank you much,' the Vulture said,
　　'Send up another two.'

Two more came up, and then two more;
　　And more, and more, and more;
And some looked upwards at the roof,
　　Some down upon the floor,
But none were any wiser than
　　The pair that went before.

'I weep for you,' the Vulture said,
　　'I deeply sympathize!'
With sobs and tears he gave them all
　　D's of the largest size,
While at the Husbandman he winked
　　One of his streaming eyes.

'I think,' observed the Husbandman,
　　'We're getting on too quick.
Are we not putting down the D's
　　A little bit too thick?'
The Vulture said with much disgust
　　'Their answers make me sick.'

'Now, Undergraduates,' he cried,
　　'Our fun is nearly done,
Will anybody else come up?'
　　But answer came there none;
And this was scarcely odd, because
　　They'd ploughed them every one!

A. C. HILTON

THE HEATHEN PASS-EE

(In imitation of Bret Harte)

Which I wish to remark,
  And my language is plain,
That for plots that are dark
  And not always in vain,
The heathen Pass-ee is peculiar,
  And the same I would rise to explain.

I would also premise
  That the term of Pass-ee
Most fitly applies,
  As you probably see,
To one whose vocation is passing
  The ' Ordinary B.A. degree.'

Tom Crib was his name.
  And I shall not deny
In regard to the same
  What that name might imply,
But his face it was trustful and childlike,
  And he had the most innocent eye.

Upon April the First
  The Little-Go fell,
And that was the worst
  Of the gentleman's sell,
For he fooled the Examining Body
  In a way I'm reluctant to tell.

The candidates came
  And Tom Crib soon appeared;
It was Euclid. The same
  Was 'the subject he feared,'
But he smiled as he sat by the table
  With a smile that was wary and weird

Yet he did what he could,
   And the papers he showed
Were remarkably good,
   And his countenance glowed
With pride when I met him soon after
   As he walked down the Trumpington Road.

We did not find him out,
   Which I bitterly grieve,
For I've not the least doubt
   That he'd placed up his sleeve
Mr Todhunter's excellent Euclid,
   The same with intent to deceive.

But I shall not forget
   How the next day at two
A stiff paper was set
   By Examiner U . . .
On Euripides' tragedy, Bacchae.
   A subject Tom 'partially knew'.

But the knowledge displayed
   By that heathen Pass-ee,
And the answers he made
   Were quite frightful to see,
For he rapidly floored the whole paper
   By about twenty minutes to three.

Then I looked up at U . . .
   And he gazed upon me.
I observed, 'This won't do.'
   He replied, 'Goodness me!
We are fooled by this artful young person,'
   And he sent for that heathen Pass-ee.

The scene that ensued
   Was disgraceful to view,
For the floor it was strewed
   With a tolerable few
Of the 'tips' that Tom Crib had been hiding
   For the 'subject he partially knew'.

On the cuff of his shirt
   He had managed to get
What we hoped had been dirt,
   But which proved, I regret,
To be notes on the rise of the Drama,
   A question invariably set.

In his various coats
   We proceeded to seek,
Where we found sundry notes
   And—with sorrow I speak—
One of Bohn's publications, so useful
   To the student of Latin or Greek.

In the crown of his cap
   Were the Furies and Fates,
And a delicate map
   Of the Dorian States,
And we found in his palms which were hollow,
   What are frequent in palms,—that is dates.

Which is why I remark,
   And my language is plain,
That for plots that are dark
   And not always in vain,
The heathen Pass-ee is peculiar,
   Which the same I am free to maintain.

A. C. HILTON

POTTED POEMS

(*By Alfred Lord Tennyson, Henry Wadsworth Long-
fellow, John Home and Robert Southey, with the
assistance of Thomas Hood Jr, Stephen Leacock and
others.*)

I

Half a league, half a league, half a league onward,
 Then they rode back, but not, not the six hundred.

II

It was the schooner Hesperus that sailed the wintry sea;
The skipper he blew a whiff from his pipe,
 A frozen corpse was he.

III

My name is Norval. On the Grampian hills
The village smithy stands;
His breast is bare, his matted hair
Was wrecked on the pitiless Goodwin sands,
And by him sported on the green,
His little grandchild, Wilhelmine.

IV

Lady Clara Vere de Vere,
I hardly know what I must say,
But I'm to be Queen of the May, Mother,
I'm to be Queen of the May.

VILLON'S STRAIGHT TIP TO ALL
CROSS COVES

'Tout aux tavernes et aux filles'

Suppose you screeve? or go cheap-jack?
  Or fake the broads? or fig a nag?
Or thimble-rig? or knap a yack?
  Or pitch a snide? or smash a rag?
  Suppose you duff? or nose and lag?
Or get the straight, and land your pot?
  How do you melt the multy swag?
Booze and the blowens cop the lot.

Fiddle, or fence, or mace, or mack;
  Or moskeneer, or flash the drag;
Dead-lurk a crib, or do a crack;
  Pad with a slang, or chuck a fag;
  Bonnet, or tout, or mump and gag;
Rattle the tats, or mark the spot;
  You cannot bank a single stag;
Booze and the blowens cop the lot.

Suppose you try a different tack,
  And on the square you flash your flag?
At penny-a-lining make your whack,
  Or with the mummers mug and gag?
  For nix, for nix the dibbs you bag!
At any graft, no matter what,
  Your merry goblins soon stravag:
Booze and the blowens cop the lot.

  It's up the spout and Charley Wag
With wipes and tickers and what not
  Until the squeezer nips your scrag,
Booze and the blowens cop the lot.

                              W. E. HENLEY

252

PROVERBIAL PHILOSOPHY:
OF READING

Read not Milton, for he is dry; nor Shakespeare, for he
    wrote of common life:
Nor Scott, for his romances, though fascinating, are yet
    intelligible:
Nor Thackeray, for he is a Hogarth, a photographer who
    flattereth not:
Nor Kingsley, for he shall teach thee that thou shouldest
    not dream, but do.
Read incessantly thy Burke; that Burke who, nobler
    than he of old,
Treateth of the Peer and Peeress, the truly Sublime and
    Beautiful:
Likewise study the 'creations' of 'the Prince of modern
    Romance';
Sigh over Leonard the Martyr, and smile on Pelham the
    puppy:
Learn how 'love is the dram-drinking of existence';
And how we 'invoke, in the Gadara of our still closets,
The beautiful ghost of the Ideal, with the simple wand
    of the pen.'
Listen how Maltravers and the orphan 'forgot all but
    love,'
And how Devereux's family chaplain 'made and unmade
    kings':
How Eugene Aram, though a thief, a liar, and a
    murderer,
Yet, being intellectual, was amongst the noblest of
    mankind.
So shalt thou live in a world peopled with heroes and
    master-spirits;
And if thou canst not realize the Ideal, thou shalt at
    least idealize the Real.

C. S. CALVERLEY

BEER

In those old days which poets say were golden—
    (Perhaps they laid the gilding on themselves:
And, if they did, I'm all the more beholden
    To those brown dwellers in my dusty shelves,
Who talk to me 'in language quaint and olden'
    Of gods and demigods and fauns and elves,
Pan with his pipes, and Bacchus with his leopards,
And staid young goddesses who flirt with shepherds:)

In those old days, the Nymph called Etiquette
    (Appalling thought to dwell on) was not born.
They had their May, but no Mayfair as yet,
    No fashions varying as the hues of morn.
Just as they pleased they dressed and drank and ate,
    Sang hymns to Ceres (their John Barleycorn)
And danced unchaperoned, and laughed unchecked,
And were no doubt extremely incorrect.

Yet do I think their theory was pleasant:
    And oft, I own, my 'wayward fancy roams'
Back to those times, so different from the present;
    When no one smoked cigars, nor gave At-homes,
Nor smote a billiard-ball, nor winged a pheasant,
    Nor 'did' their hair by means of long-tailed combs,
Nor migrated to Brighton once a year,
Nor—most astonishing of all—drank Beer.

No, they did not drink Beer, 'which brings me to'
    (As Gilpin said) 'the middle of my song.'
Not that 'the middle' is precisely true,
    Or else I should not tax your patience long:
If I had said 'beginning' it might do;
    But I have a dislike to quoting wrong:
I was unlucky—sinned against, not sinning—
When Cowper wrote down 'middle' for 'beginning'.

So to proceed. That abstinence from Malt
  Has always struck me as extremely curious.
The Greek mind must have had some vital fault,
  That they should stick to liquors so injurious—
(Wine, water, tempered p'raps with Attic salt)—
  And not at once invent that mild, luxurious,
And artful beverage, Beer. How the digestion
Got on without it, is a startling question.

Had they digestions? and an actual body
  Such as dyspepsia might make attacks on?
Were they abstract ideas—(like Tom Noddy
  And Mr Briggs)—or men, like Jones and Jackson?
Then nectar—was that beer, or whisky-toddy?
  Some say the Gaelic mixture, *I* the Saxon:
I think a strict adherence to the latter
Might make some Scots less pigheaded, and fatter.

Besides, Bon Gaultier definitely shows
  That the real beverage for feasting gods on
Is a soft compound, grateful to the nose
  And also to the palate, known as ' Hodgson'.
I know a man—a tailor's son—who rose
  To be a peer: and this I would lay odds on,
(Though in his memoirs it may not appear,)
That that man owed his rise to copious Beer.

O Beer! O Hodgson, Guinness, Allsopp, Bass!
  Names that should be on every infant's tongue!
Shall days and months and years and centuries pass,
  And still your merits be unrecked, unsung?
Oh! I have gazed into my foaming glass,
  And wished that lyre could yet again be strung
Which once rang prophet-like through Greece, and
    taught her
Misguided sons that 'the best drink was water'.

How would he now recant that wild opinion,
　　And sing—as would that I could sing—of you!
I was not born (alas!) the 'Muses' minion,'
　　I'm not poetical, not even blue:
And he, we know, but strives with waxen pinion,
　　Whoe'er he is that entertains the view
Of emulating Pindar, and will be
Sponsor at last to some now nameless sea.

Oh! when the green slopes of Arcadia burned
　　With all the lustre of the dying day,
And on Cithaeron's brow the reaper turned,
　　(Humming, of course, in his delightful way,
How Lycidas was dead, and how concerned
　　The Nymphs were when they saw his lifeless clay;
And how rock told to rock the dreadful story
That poor young Lycidas was gone to glory:)

What would that lone and labouring soul have given,
　　At that soft moment, for a pewter pot!
How had the mists that dimmed his eye been riven,
　　And Lycidas and sorrow all forgot!
If his own grandmother had died unshriven,
　　In two short seconds he'd have recked it not;
Such power hath Beer. The heart which Grief hath
　　canker'd
Hath one unfailing remedy—the Tankard.

Coffee is good, and so no doubt is cocoa;
　　Tea did for Johnson and the Chinamen;
When 'Dulce est desipere in loco'
　　Was written, real Falernian winged the pen.
When a rapt audience has encored 'Fra Poco'
　　Or 'Casta Diva', I have heard that then
The Prima Donna, smiling herself out,
Recruits her flagging powers with bottled stout.

But what is coffee, but a noxious berry,
   Born to keep used-up Londoners awake?
What is Falernian, what is Port or Sherry,
   But vile concoctions to make dull heads ache?
Nay stout itself—(though good with oysters, very)—
   Is not a thing your reading man should take.
He that would shine, and petrify his tutor,
Should drink draught Allsopp in its 'native pewter'.

But hark! a sound is stealing on my ear—
   A soft and silvery sound—I know it well.
Its tinkling tells me that a time is near
   Precious to me—it is the Dinner Bell.
O blessed Bell! Thou bringest beef and beer,
   Thou bringest good things more than tongue may
      tell:
Seared is, of course, my heart—but unsubdued
Is, and shall be, my appetite for food.

I go. Untaught and feeble is my pen:
   But on one statement I may safely venture:
That few of our most highly gifted men
   Have more appreciation of the trencher.
I go. One pound of British beef, and then
   What Mr Swiveller called a 'modest quencher';
That home-returning, I may 'soothly say',
'Fate cannot touch me: I have dined to-day.'

C. S. CALVERLEY

ODE TO TOBACCO

Thou who, when fears attack,
Bidst them avaunt, and Black
Care, at the horseman's back
 Perching, unseatest;
Sweet when the morn is gray;
Sweet, when they've cleared away
Lunch; and at close of day
 Possibly sweetest:

I have a liking old
For thee, though manifold
Stories, I know, are told,
 Not to thy credit;
How one (or two at most)
Drops make a cat a ghost—
Useless, except to roast—
 Doctors have said it:

How they who use fusees
All grow by slow degrees
Brainless as chimpanzees,
 Meagre as lizards;
Go mad, and beat their wives;
Plunge (after shocking lives)
Razors and carving knives
 Into their gizzards.

Confound such knavish tricks!
Yet know I five or six
Smokers who freely mix
Still with their neighbours;
Jones—(who, I'm glad to say
Asked leave of Mrs J——)
Daily absorbs a clay
 After his labours.

258

Cats may have had their goose
Cooked by tobacco-juice;
Still why deny its use
    Thoughtfully taken?
We're not as tabbies are:
Smith, take a fresh cigar!
Jones, the tobacco-jar!
    Here's to thee, Bacon!

C. S. CALVERLEY

LINES ON HEARING THE ORGAN

Grinder, who serenely grindest
    At my door the Hundredth Psalm,
Till thou ultimately findest
    Pence in thy unwashen palm:

Grinder, jocund-hearted Grinder,
    Near whom Barbary's nimble son,
Poised with skill upon his hinder
    Paws, accepts the proffered bun:

Dearly do I love thy grinding;
    Joy to meet thee on thy road
Where thou prowlest through the blinding
    Dust with that stupendous load,

'Neath the baleful star of Sirius,
    When the postmen slowlier jog,
And the ox becomes delirious,
    And the muzzle decks the dog.

Tell me by what art thou bindest
    On thy feet those ancient shoon:
Tell me, Grinder, if thou grindest
    Always, always out of tune.

259

Tell me if, as thou art buckling
   On thy straps with eager claws,
Thou forecastest, inly chuckling,
   All the rage that thou wilt cause.

Tell me if at all thou mindest
   When folks flee, as if on wings,
From thee as at ease thou grindest:
   Tell me fifty thousand things.

Grinder, gentle-hearted Grinder!
   Ruffians who led evil lives,
Soothed by thy sweet strains, are kinder
   To their bullocks and their wives:

Children, when they see thy supple
   Form approach, are out like shots;
Half-a-bar sets several couple
   Waltzing in convenient spots;

Not with clumsy Jacks or Georges:
   Unprofaned by grasp of man
Maidens speed those simple orgies,
   Betsey Jane with Betsey Ann.

As they love thee in St Giles's
   Thou art loved in Grosvenor Square:
None of those engaging smiles is
   Unreciprocated there.

Often, ere yet thou hast hammer'd
   Through thy four delicious airs,
Coins are flung thee by enamour'd
   Housemaids upon area stairs:

E'en the ambrosial-whisker'd flunkey
   Eyes thy boots and thine unkempt
Beard and melancholy monkey
   More in pity than contempt.

Far from England, in the sunny
   South, where Anio leaps in foam,
Thou wast rear'd, till lack of money
   Drew thee from thy vineclad home:

And thy mate, the sinewy Jocko,
   From Brazil or Afric came,
Land of simoom and sirocco—
   And he seems extremely tame.

There he quaff'd the undefilèd
   Spring, or hung with apelike glee,
By his teeth or tail or eyelid,
   To the slippery mango-tree:

There he woo'd and won a dusky
   Bride, of instincts like his own;
Talk'd of love till he was husky
   In a tongue to us unknown:

Side by side 'twas theirs to ravage
   The potato ground, or cut
Down the unsuspecting savage
   With the well-aim'd cocoa-nut:—

Till the miscreant Stranger tore him
   Screaming from his blue-faced fair;
And they flung strange raiment o'er him,
   Raiment which he could not bear:

Sever'd from the pure embraces
   Of his children and his spouse,
He must ride fantastic races
   Mounted on reluctant sows:

But the heart of wistful Jocko
   Still was with his ancient flame
In the nutgroves of Morocco;
   Or if not it's all the same.

Grinder, winsome grinsome Grinder!
  They who see thee and whose soul
Melts not at thy charms, are blinder
  Than a trebly-bandaged mole:

They to whom thy curt (yet clever)
  Talk, thy music and thine ape,
Seem not to be joys for ever,
  Are but brutes in human shape.

'Tis not that thy mien is stately,
  'Tis not that thy tones are soft;
'Tis not that I care so greatly
  For the same thing played so oft:

But I've heard mankind abuse thee;
  And perhaps it's rather strange,
But I thought that I would choose thee
  For encomium, as a change.

C. S. CALVERLEY

BALLAD

The auld wife sat at her ivied door,
  (*Butter and eggs and a pound of cheese*)
A thing she had frequently done before;
  And her spectacles lay on her apron'd knees.

The piper he piped on the hill-top high,
  (*Butter and eggs and a pound of cheese*)
Till the cow said 'I die,' and the goose ask'd 'Why?'
  And the dog said nothing, but search'd for fleas.

The farmer he strode through the square farmyard;
  (*Butter and eggs and a pound of cheese*)
His last brew of ale was a trifle hard—
  The connexion of which with the plot one sees.

The farmer's daughter hath frank blue eyes;
  (*Butter and eggs and a pound of cheese*)
She hears the rooks caw in the windy skies,
    As she sits at her lattice and shells her peas.

The farmer's daughter hath ripe red lips;
  (*Butter and eggs and a pound of cheese*)
If you try to approach her, away she skips
    Over tables and chairs with apparent ease.

The farmer's daughter hath soft brown hair;
  (*Butter and eggs and a pound of cheese*)
And I met with a ballad, I can't say where,
    Which wholly consisted of lines like these.

PART II

She sat with her hands 'neath her dimpled cheeks,
  (*Butter and eggs and a pound of cheese*)
And spake not a word. While a lady speaks
    There is hope, but she didn't even sneeze.

She sat, with her hands 'neath her crimson cheeks;
  (*Butter and eggs and a pound of cheese*)
She gave up mending her father's breeks,
    And let the cat roll in her new chemise.

She sat, with her hands 'neath her burning cheeks;
  (*Butter and eggs and a pound of cheese*)
And gazed at the piper for thirteen weeks;
    Then she follow'd him out o'er the misty leas.

Her sheep follow'd her, as their tails did them.
  (*Butter and eggs and a pound of cheese*)
And this song is consider'd a perfect gem,
    And as to the meaning, it's what you please.

                                    C. S. CALVERLEY

LOVERS, AND A REFLECTION

In moss-prankt dells which the sunbeams flatter
  (And heaven it knoweth what that may mean:
Meaning, however, is no great matter)
  Where woods are a-tremble, with rifts atween;

Thro' God's own heather we wonn'd together,
  I and my Willie (O love my love):
I need hardly remark it was glorious weather,
  And flitterbats waver'd alow, above:

Boats were curtseying, rising, bowing,
  (Boats in that climate are so polite),
And sands were a ribbon of green endowing,
  And O the sundazzle on bark and bight!

Thro' the rare red heather we danced together,
  (O love my Willie!) and smelt for flowers:
I must mention again it was gorgeous weather,
  Rhymes are so scarce in this world of ours:—

By rises that flush'd with their purple favours,
  Thro' becks that brattled o'er grasses sheen,
We walked and waded, we two young shavers,
  Thanking our stars we were both so green.

We journeyed in parallels, I and Willie,
  In fortunate parallels! Butterflies,
Hid in weltering shadows of daffodilly
  Or marjoram, kept making peacock eyes:

Songbirds darted about, some inky
  As coal, some snowy (I ween) as curds;
Or rosy as pinks, or as roses pinky—
  They reck of no eerie To-come, those birds!

But they skim over bents which the millstream washes,
  Or hang in the lift 'neath a white cloud's hem;
They need no parasols, no goloshes;
  And good Mrs Trimmer she feedeth them.

Then we thrid God's cowslips (as erst His heather)
  That endowed the wan grass with their golden blooms
And snapt—(it was perfectly charming weather)—
  Our fingers at Fate and her goddess-glooms:

And Willie 'gan sing (O, his notes were fluty;
  Wafts fluttered them out to the white-wing'd sea)—
Something made up of rhymes that have done much
      duty,
  Rhymes (better to put it) of 'ancientry':

Bowers of flowers encounter'd showers
  In William's carol—(O love my Willie!)
Then he bade sorrow borrow from blithe to-morrow
  I quite forget what—say a daffodilly:

A nest in a hollow, 'with buds to follow,
  I think occurred next in his nimble strain;
And clay that was 'kneaden' of course in Eden—
  A rhyme most novel, I do maintain:

Mists, bones, the singer himself, love-stories,
  And all least furlable things got 'furled';
Not with any design to conceal their 'glories',
  But simply and solely to rhyme with 'world'.

        *   *   *   *

O if billows and pillows and hours and flowers,
  And all the brave rhymes of an elder day,

Could be furled together, this genial weather,
   And carted, or carried on ' wafts ' away,
Nor ever again trotted out—ah me!
How much fewer volumes of verse there'd be!

C. S. CALVERLEY

COMPANIONS

A TALE OF A GRANDFATHER

(By the Author of 'Dewy Memories' etc.)

I know not of what we ponder'd
   Or made pretty pretence to talk,
As, her hand within mine, we wander'd
   Tow'rd the pool by the limetree walk,
While the dew fell in showers from the passion flowers
   And the blush-rose bent on her stalk.

I cannot recall her figure:
   Was it regal as Juno's own?
Or only a trifle bigger
   Than the elves who surround the throne
Of the Faëry Queen, and are seen, I ween,
   By mortals in dreams alone?

What her eyes were like, I know not:
   Perhaps they were blurr'd with tears;
And perhaps in your skies there glow not
   (On the contrary) clearer spheres.
No! as to her eyes I am just as wise
   As you or the cat, my dears.

Her teeth, I presume, were 'pearly':
   But which was she, brunette or blonde?
Her hair, was it quaintly curly,

266

Or as straight as a beadle's wand?
That I fail'd to remark;—it was rather dark
And shadowy round the pond.

Then the hand that reposed so snugly
In mine—was it plump or spare?
Was the countenance fair or ugly?
Nay, children, you have me there!
My eyes were p'raps blurr'd; and besides I'd heard
That it's horribly rude to stare.

And I—was I brusque and surly?
Or oppressively bland and fond?
Was I partial to rising early?
Or why did we twain abscond,
All breakfastless too, from the public view
To prowl by a misty pond?

What pass'd, what was felt or spoken—
Whether anything pass'd at all—
And whether the heart was broken
That beat under that shelt'ring shawl—
(If shawl she had on, which I doubt)—has gone,
Yes, gone from me past recall.

Was I haply the lady's suitor?
Or her uncle? I can't make out—
Ask your governess, dears, or tutor.
For myself, I'm in hopeless doubt
As to why we were there, who on earth we were,
And what this is all about.

C. S. CALVERLEY

THE COCK AND THE BULL

You see this pebble-stone? It's a thing I bought
Of a bit of a chit of a boy i' the mid o' the day—
I like to dock the smaller parts-o'-speech,
As we curtail the already cur-tail'd cur
(You catch the paronomasia, play 'po' words?)
Did, rather, i' the pre-Landseerian days.
Well, to my muttons. I purchased the concern,
And clapt it i' my poke, having given for same
By way o' chop, swop, barter or exchange—
'Chop' was my snickering dandiprat's own term—
One shilling and fourpence, current coin o' the realm.
O-n-e one and f-o-u-r four
Pence, one and fourpence—you are with me, sir?—
What hour it skills not: ten or eleven o' the clock,
One day (and what a roaring day it was
Go shop or sight-see—bar a spit o' rain!)
In February, eighteen sixty nine,
Alexandrina Victoria, Fidei
Hm—hm—how runs the jargon? being on throne.

Such, sir, are all the facts, succinctly put,
The basis or substratum—what you will—
Of the impending eighty thousand lines.
'Not much in 'em either,' quoth perhaps simple Hodge.
But there's a superstructure. Wait a bit.

Mark first the rationale of the thing:
Hear logic rivel and levigate the deed.
That shilling—and for matter o' that, the pence—
I had o' course upo' me—wi' me say—
(*Mecum*'s the Latin, make a note o' that)
When I popp'd pen i' stand, scratch'd ear, wiped snout,
(Let everybody wipe his own himself)
Sniff'd—tch!—at snuffbox; tumbled up, he-hced,

268

Haw-haw'd (not hee-haw'd, that's another guess thing:)
Then fumbled at, and stumbled out of, door,
I shoved the timber ope wi' my omoplat;
And *in vestibulo*, i' the lobby to-wit,
(Iacobi Facciolati's rendering, sir,)
Donn'd galligaskins, antigropeloes,
And so forth; and, complete with hat and gloves,
One on and one a-dangle i' my hand,
And ombrifuge (Lord love you!), case o' rain,
I flopp'd forth, 'sbuddikins! on my own ten toes,
(I do assure you there be ten of them),
And went clump-clumping up hill and down dale
To find myself o' the sudden i' front o' the boy.
Put case I hadn't 'em on me, could I ha' bought
This sort-o'-kind-o'-what-you-might-call toy,
This pebble-thing, o' the boy-thing? Q.E.D.
That's proven without aid from mumping Pope,
Sleek porporate or bloated Cardinal.
(Isn't it, old Fatchaps? You're in Euclid now.)
So, having the shilling—having i' fact a lot—
And pence and halfpence, ever so many o' them,
I purchased, as I think I said before,
The pebble (*lapis, lapidis, -di, -dem, -de*—
What nouns 'crease short i' the genitive, Fatchaps, eh?)
O' the boy, a bare-legg'd beggarly son of a gun,
For one-and-fourpence. Here we are again.

Now Law steps in, bigwigg'd, voluminous-jaw'd,
Investigates and re-investigates.
Was the transaction illegal? Law shakes head.
Perpend, sir, all the bearings of the case.

At first the coin was mine, the chattel his.
But now (by virtue of the said exchange
And barter) *vice versa* all the coin,
Per juris operationem, vests

I' the boy and his assigns till ding o' doom;
(*In sæcula sæculo-o-o-orum;*
I think I hear the Abate mouth out that.)
To have and hold the same to him and them . . .
Confer some idiot on Conveyancing.
Whereas the pebble and every part thereof,
And all that appertaineth thereunto,
Quodcunque pertinet ad eam rem,
(I fancy, sir, my Latin's rather pat)
Or shall, will, may, might, can, could, would or should,
(*Subaudi cætera*—clap we to the close—
For what's the good of law in a case o' the kind)
Is mine to all intents and purposes.
This settled, I resume the thread o' the tale.

   Now for a touch o' the vendor's quality.
He says a gen'lman bought a pebble of him,
(This pebble i' sooth, sir, which I hold i' my hand)—
And paid for't, *like* a gen'lman, on the nail.
'Did I o'ercharge him a ha'penny? Devil a bit.
Fiddlepin's end! Get out, you blazing ass!
Gabble o' the goose. Don't bugaboo-baby *me!*
Go double or quits? Yah! tittup! what's the odds?'
—There's the transaction view'd i' the vendor's light.

   Next ask that dumpled hag, stood snuffling by,
With her three frowsy blowsy brats o' babes,
The scum o' the kennel, cream o' the filth-heap—Faugh!
Aie, aie, aie, aie! ὀτοτοτοτοτοῖ,
('Stead which we blurt out Hoighty toighty now)—
And the baker and candlestickmaker, and Jack and Gill,
Blear'd Goody this and queasy Gaffer that.
Ask the schoolmaster. Take schoolmaster first

   He saw a gentleman purchase of a lad
A stone, and pay for it *rite*, on the square,

And carry it off *per saltum*, jauntily,
Propria quæ maribus, gentleman's property now
(Agreeably to the law explain'd above),
In proprium usum, for his private ends.
The boy he chuck'd a brown i' the air, and bit
I' the face the shilling: heaved a thumping stone
At a lean hen that ran cluck clucking by,
(And hit her, dead as nail i' post o' door,)
Then *abiit*—what's the Ciceronian phrase?—
Excessit, evasit, erupit—off slogs boy
Off like bird, *avi similis*—(you observed
The dative? Pretty i' the Mantuan!)—*Anglice*
Off in three flea skips. *Hactenus*, so far,
So good, *tam bene. Bene, satis, male*—,
Where was I with my trope 'bout one in a quag?
I did once hitch the syntax into verse:
Verbum personale, a verb personal,
Concordat—ay, 'agrees', old Fatchaps—*cum*
Nominativo, with its nominative,
Genere, i' point o' gender, *numero*,
O' number, *et persona*, and person. *Ut*,
Instance: *Sol ruit*, down flops sun, *et* and,
Montes umbrantur, out flounce mountains. Pah!
Excuse me, sir, I think I'm going mad.
You see the trick on't though, and can yourself
Continue the discourse *ad libitum*.
It takes up about eighty thousand lines,
A thing imagination boggles at:
And might, odds-bobs, sir! in judicious hands,
Extend from here to Mesopotamy.

C. S. CALVERLEY

A GIRTONIAN FUNERAL

(The ACADEMY reports that the students of Girton College have
dissolved their 'Browning Society', and expended its remaining
funds, two shillings and twopence, upon chocolate creams.)

Let us begin and portion out these sweets,
　　　　Sitting together.
Leave we our deep debates, our sage conceits,—
　　　　Wherefore? and whether?
Thus with a fine that fits the work begun
　　　　Our labours crowning,
For we, in sooth, our duty well have done
　　　　By Robert Browning.
Have we not wrought at essay and critique,
　　　　Scorning supine ease?
Wrestled with clauses crabbed as Bito's Greek,
　　　　Baffling as Chinese?
Out the Inn Album's mystic heart we took,
　　　　Lucid of soul, and
Threaded the mazes of the Ring and Book;
　　　　Cleared up Childe Roland.
We settled Fifine's business—let her be—
　　　　(Strangest of lasses;)
Watched by the hour some thick-veiled truth to see
　　　　Where Pippa passes.
(Though, dare we own, secure in victor's gains,
　　　　Ample to shield us?
Red Cotton Night-cap Country for our pains
　　　　Little would yield us.)
What then to do? Our culture-feast drag out
　　　　E'en to satiety?
Oft such the fate that findeth, nothing doubt,
　　　　Such a Society.
Oh, the dull meetings! Some one yawns an *aye*,
　　　　One gapes again a *yea*,

272

We girls determined not to yawn, but buy
    Chocolate Ménier.
Fry's creams are cheap, but Cadbury's excel,
    (Quick, Maud, for none wait)
Nay, now, 'tis Ménier bears away the bell,
    Sold by the ton-weight.
So, with unburdened brains and spirits light,
    Blithe did we troop hence,
All our funds voted for this closing rite,—
    Just two-and-two-pence.
Do—make in scorn, old Crœsus, proud and glum,
    Peaked eyebrow lift eye;
Put case one stick's a halfpenny; work the sum;
    Full two and fifty.
Off with the twine! who scans each smooth brown slab
    Yet not supposeth
What soft, sweet, cold, pure whiteness, bound in drab,
    Tooth's bite discloseth?
Are they not grand? Why (you may think it odd)
    Some power alchemic
Turns, as we munch, to Zeus-assenting nod
    Sneers Academic.
Till, when one cries, "Ware hours that fleet like clouds,
    Time, deft escaper!'
We answer bold: 'Leave Time to Dons and Dowds;
    (Grace, pass the paper)
Say, boots it aught to evermore affect
    Raptures high-flying?
Though *we* choose chocolate, will the world suspect
    Gen us undying?'

                       ANON

ANDREW M'CRIE

(*In imitation of Edgar Allan Poe*)

It was many and many a year ago,
    In a city by the sea,
That a man there lived whom I happened to know
    By the name of Andrew M'Crie;
And this man he slept in other room
    But ground and had meals with me.

I was an ass and he was an ass,
    In this city by the sea;
But we ground in a way that was more than a grind,
    I and Andrew M'Crie;
In a way that the idle semi-s next door
    Declared was shameful to see.

And this was the reason that, one dark night,
    In this city by the sea,
A stone flew in at the window, hitting
    The milk-jug and Andrew M'Crie.
And once some low-bred tertians came,
    And bore him away from me,
And shoved him into a private house
    Where the people were having tea.

Professors, not half so well up in their work.
    Went envying him and me—
Yes!—that was the reason, I always thought
    (And Andrew agreed with me),
Why they ploughed us both at the end of the year
    Chilling and killing poor Andrew M'Crie.

But his ghost is more terrible far than the ghosts
    Of many more famous than he—

274

Of many more gory than he—
And neither visits to foreign coasts,
  Nor tonics, can ever set free
Two well-known Profs from the haunting wraith
  Of the injured Andrew M'Crie.

For at night, as they dream, they frequently scream,
  'Have mercy, Mr M'Crie!'
And at morn they will rise with bloodshot eyes,
  And the very first thing they will see,
When they dare to descend to their coffee and rolls,
Sitting down on the scuttle, the scuttle of coals,
  With a volume of notes on its knee,
  Is the spectre of Andrew M'Crie.

ROBERT MURRAY

THE CRIMES OF LIZZIE BORDEN

Lizzie Borden with an axe,
Hit her father forty whacks,
When she saw what she had done,
She hit her mother forty-one.

ANON

I USED TO LOVE MY GARDEN

I used to love my garden
  But now my love is dead
For I found a bachelor's button
  In black-eyed Susan's bed.

C. P. SAWYER

VILLANELLE

(How to compose a *villanelle*, which is said to require 'an elaborate amount of care in production, which those who read only would hardly suspect existed'.)

It's all a trick, quite easy when you know it,
As easy as reciting ABC;
You need not be an atom of a poet.

If you've a grain of wit, and want to show it,
Writing a *villanelle*—take this from me—
It's ail a trick, quite easy when you know it

You start a pair of rimes, and then you 'go it'
With rapid-running pen and fancy free;
You need not be an atom of a poet.

Take any thought, write round it or below it,
Above or near it, as it liketh thee;
It's all a trick, quite easy when you know it.

Pursue your task, till, like a shrub, you grow it,
Up to the standard size it ought to be;
You need not be an atom of a poet.

Clear it of weeds, and water it, and hoe it,
Then watch it blossom with triumphant glee.
It's all a trick, quite easy when you know it;
You need not be an atom of a poet.

W. W. SKEAT

POACHING *IN EXCELSIS*

('Two men were fined £120 apiece for poaching a white rhino-
ceros.'—*South African Press*.)

I've poached a pickle paitricks when the leaves were
    turnin' sere,
I've poached a twa-three hares an' grouse, an' mebbe
    whiles a deer,
But ou, it seems an unco thing, an' jist a wee mysterious
Hoo any mortal could contrive tae poach a rhinocerious.

I've crackit wi' the keeper, pockets packed wi' pheasants'
    eggs,
An' a ten-pun' saumon hangin' doun in baith my trouser
    legs,
But eh, I doot effects wud be a wee thing deleterious
Gin ye shuld stow intil yer breeks a brace o' rhinocerious.

I mind hoo me an' Wullie shot a Royal in Braemar,
An' brocht him doun tae Athol by the licht o' mune an'
    star.
An' eh, Sirs! but the canny beast contrived tae fash an'
    weary us—
Yet staigs maun be but bairn's play beside a rhinocerious.

I thocht I kent o' poachin' jist as muckle's ither men,
But there is still a twa-three things I doot I dinna ken;
An' noo I cannot rest, my brain is growin' that deleerious
Tae win awa' tae Africa an' poach a rhinocerious.

G. K. MENZIES

BALLIOL RHYMES

I

First come I, my name is Jowett,
There's no knowledge but I know it.
I am Master of this College,
What I don't know isn't knowledge.

II

My name is George Nathaniel Curzon,
I am a most superior person.
My hair is soft, my face is sleek,
I dine at Blenheim twice a week.

III

I am the Dean of Christ Church, sir,
This is my wife—look well at her.
She is the Broad: I am the High:
We are the University.

ANON

THE RAIN

The rain it raineth every day,
    Upon the just and unjust fellow,
But more upon the just, because
    The unjust hath the just's umbrella.

ANON

IN MEMORIAM

Willie had a purple monkey climbing on a yellow
    stick,
And when he had sucked the paint all off it made him
    deadly sick;
And in his latest hours he clasped that monkey in his
    hand,
And bade good-bye to earth and went into a better
    land.

Oh no more he'll shoot his sister with his little wooden
    gun;
And no more he'll twist the pussy's tail and make her
    yowl for fun.
The Pussy's tail now stands out straight; the gun is
    laid aside;
The monkey doesn't jump around since little Willie
    died.

MAX ADELER

SACRED TO THE MEMORY OF MARIA (TO SAY NOTHING OF JANE AND MARTHA) SPARKS

Stranger, pause and drop a tear,
For Susan Sparks lies buried here:
Mingled in some perplexing manner,
With Jane, Maria, and portions of Hannah.

MAX ADELER

THE PESSIMIST

Nothing to do but work,
  Nothing to eat but food,
Nothing to wear but clothes,
  To keep one from going nude.

Nothing to breathe but air,
  Quick as a flash 'tis gone;
Nowhere to fall but off,
  Nowhere to stand but on.

Nothing to comb but hair,
  Nowhere to sleep but in bed,
Nothing to weep but tears,
  Nothing to bury but dead.

Nothing to sing but songs,
  Ah, well, alas! alack!
Nowhere to go but out,
  Nowhere to come but back.

Nothing to see but sights,
  Nothing to quench but thirst,
Nothing to have but what we've got,
  Thus through life we are cursed.

Nothing to strike but a gait;
  Everything moves that goes.
Nothing at all but common sense
  Can ever withstand these woes.

BEN KING

MALUM OPUS

Prope ripam fluvii solus
A senex silently sat;
Super capitum ecce his wig,
Et wig super, ecce his hat.

Blew Zephyrus alte, acerbus,
Dum elderly gentleman sat;
Et a capite took up quite torve
Et in rivum projecit his hat.

Tunc soft maledixit the old man,
Tunc stooped from the bank where he sat
Et cum scipio poked in the water,
Conatus servare his hat.

Blew Zephyrus alte, acerbus,
The moment it saw him at that;
Et whisked his novum scratch wig,
In flumen, along with his hat.

Ab imo pectore damnavit
In coeruleus eye dolor sat;
Tunc despairingly threw in his cane
Nare cum his wig and his hat.

L'envoi

Contra bonos mores, don't swear,
It is wicked, you know (verbum sat),
Si this tale habet no other moral,
Mehercle! You're gratus to that!

J. A. MORGAN

A FALSE GALLOP OF ANALOGIES

'The Chavender, or Chub'—Izaak Walton

There is a fine stuffed chavender,
  A chavender or chub,
That decks the rural pavender,
  The pavender or pub,
Wherein I eat my gravender,
  My gravender or grub.

How good the honest gravender!
  How snug the rustic pavender!
From sheets as sweet as lavender,
  As lavender, or lub,
I jump into my tavender,
  My tavender, or tub.

Alas! for town and clavender,
  For business and club!
They call me from my pavender
To-night; ay, there's the ravender
  Ay, there comes in the rub!
To leave each blooming shravender,
  Each Spring-bedizened shrub,
And meet the horsey savender,
  The very forward sub,
At dinner at the clavender,
And then at billiards dravender,
  At billiards roundly drub
The self-sufficient cavender,
  The not ill-meaning cub,
Who me a bear will davender,
  A bear unfairly dub,

282

Because I sometimes snavender,
　　Not too severely snub
His setting right the clavender,
　　His teaching all the club!

Farewell to peaceful pavender,
　　My river-dreaming pub,
To bed as sweet as lavender,
To homely, wholesome gravender,
And you, inspiring chavender,
　　Stuff'd chavender, or chub.

W. ST LEGER

THE CHILD IS FATHER TO THE MAN

'The child is father to the man.'
How can he be? The words are wild.
Suck any sense from that who can:
'The child is father to the man.'
No; what the poet did write ran,
'The man is father to the child.'
'The child is father to the man!'
How *can* he be? The words are wild.

GERARD MANLEY HOPKINS

CRAZY ARITHMETIC

4 in 2 goes twice as fast,
　　If 2 and 4 change places;
But how can 2 and 3 make four,
　　If 3 and 2 make faces?

D'ARCY THOMPSON

283

THE AMERICAN INDIAN

There once were some people called Sioux
Who spent all their time making shioux
Which they coloured in various hioux;
   Don't think that they made them to ioux
   Oh! no, they just sold them for bioux.

ANON

A STRIKE AMONG THE POETS

In his chamber, weak and dying,
   While the Norman Baron lay,
Loud, without, his men were crying,
   'Shorter hours and better pay.'

Know you why the ploughman, fretting,
   Homeward plods his weary way
Ere his time? He's after getting
   Shorter hours and better pay.

See! the *Hesperus* is swinging
   Idle in the wintry bay,
And the skipper's daughter's singing,
   'Shorter hours and better pay.'

Where's the minstrel boy? I've found him
   Joining in the labour fray
With his placards slung around him,
   'Shorter hours and better pay.'

Oh, young Lochinvar is coming;
   Though his hair is getting grey,
Yet I'm glad to hear him humming,
   'Shorter hours and better pay.'

284

E'en the boy upon the burning
   Deck has got a word to say,
Something rather cross concerning
   Shorter hours and better pay.

Lives of great men all remind us
   We can make as much as they,
Work no more, until they find us
   Shorter hours and better pay.

Hail to thee, blithe spirit! (Shelley)
   Wilt thou be a blackleg? Nay.
Soaring, sing above the mêlée,
   'Shorter hours and better pay.'

ANON

A SONNET

Two voices are there: one is of the deep;
It learns the storm-cloud's thunderous melody,
Now roars, now murmurs with the changing sea,
Now bird-like pipes, now closes soft in sleep;
And one is of an old half-witted sheep
Which bleats articulate monotony,
And indicates that two and one are three,
That grass is green, lakes damp, and mountains steep:
And, Wordsworth, both are thine: at certain times
Forth from the heart of thy melodious rhymes,
The form and pressure of high thoughts will burst:
At other times—good Lord! I'd rather be
Quite unacquainted with the ABC
Than write such hopeless rubbish as thy worst.

J. K. STEPHEN

THE LAST RIDE TOGETHER

(*After Browning*)

(*From Her point of view*)

When I had firmly answered 'No',
And he allowed that that was so,
I really thought I should be free
For good and all from Mr B.,
    And that he would soberly acquiesce:
I said that it would be discreet
That for a while we should not meet;
I promised I would always feel
A kindly interest in his weal;
I thanked him for his amorous zeal;
    In short, I said all I could but 'yes'.

I said what I'm accustomed to,
I acted as I always do;
I promised he should find in me
A friend,—a sister, if that might be:
    But he was still dissatisfied:
He certainly was most polite;
He said exactly what was right,
He acted very properly,
Except indeed for this, that he
Insisted on inviting me
    To come with him for 'one more last ride'.

A little while in doubt I stood:
A ride, no doubt, would do me good:
I had a habit and a hat
Extremely well worth looking at:
    The weather was distinctly fine:
My horse too wanted exercise,
And time, when one is riding, flies:

Besides it really seemed, you see,
The only way of ridding me
Of pertinacious Mr B.:
  So my head I graciously incline.

I won't say much of what happened next:
I own I was extremely vexed:
Indeed I should have been aghast
If anyone had seen what passed:
  But nobody need ever know
That, as I leaned forward to stir the fire,
He advanced before I could well retire,
And I suddenly felt, to my great alarm,
The grasp of a warm unlicensed arm,
An embrace in which I found no charm;
  I was awfully glad when he let me go.

Then we began to ride: my steed
Was rather fresh, too fresh indeed,
And at first I thought of little, save
The way to escape an early grave,
  As the dust rose up on either side.
My stern companion jogged along
On a brown old cob both broad and strong:
He looked as he does when he's writing verse,
Or endeavouring not to swear and curse,
Or wondering where he has left his purse,
  Indeed it was a sombre ride.

I spoke of the weather to Mr B.:
But he neither listened nor spoke to me;
I praised his horse, and I smiled the smile
Which was wont to move him once on a while;
  I said I was wearing his favourite flowers:
But I wasted my words on the desert air,
For he rode with a fixed and gloomy stare:

I wonder what he was thinking about:
As I don't read verse, I shan't find out:
It was something subtle and deep, no doubt,
  A theme to detain a man for hours.

Ah! there was the corner where Mr S.
So nearly induced me to whisper 'yes':
And here it was that the next but one
Proposed on horseback, or would have done,
  Had his horse not most opportunely shied;
Which perhaps was due to the unseen flick
He received from my whip: 'twas a scurvy trick,
But I never could do with that young man:
I hope his present young woman can.
Well, I must say, never, since time began,
  Did I go for a duller or longer ride.

He never smiles and he never speaks:
He might go on like this for weeks:
He rolls a slightly frenzied eye
Towards the blue and burning sky,
  And the cob bounds on with tireless stride.
If we aren't at home for lunch at two
I don't know what Papa will do;
But I know full well he will say to me
'I never approved of Mr B.:
It's the very devil that you and he
  Ride, ride together, for ever ride.'

                              J. K. STEPHEN

TO R. K. (1891)

As long as I dwell on some stupendous
And tremendous (Heaven defend us!)
Monstr'-inform'-ingens-horrendous
Demoniaco-seraphic
Penman's latest piece of graphic.

BROWNING

Will there never come a season
Which shall rid us from the curse
Of a prose that knows no reason
And an unmelodious verse:
When the world shall cease to wonder
At the genius of an Ass,
And a boy's eccentric blunder
Shall not bring success to pass;

When mankind shall be delivered
From the clash of magazines,
And the inkstands shall be shivered
Into countless smithereens:
When there stands a muzzled stripling,
Mute, beside a muzzled bore:
When the Rudyards cease from Kipling
And the Haggards Ride no more?

J. K. STEPHEN

ON THE TRIUMPH OF RATIONALISM

When Reason's ray shines over all
And puts the Saints to rout,
Then Peter's holiness will pall
And Paul's will peter out.

CANON AINGER

289

O GOD! O MONTREAL!

Stowed away in a Montreal lumber room
The Discobolus standeth and turneth his face to the
      wall;
Dusty, cobweb-covered, maimed and set at naught,
Beauty lieth in an attic and no man regardeth:
                    O God! O Montreal!

Beautiful by night and day, beautiful in summer and
      winter,
Whole or maimed, always and alike beautiful—
He preacheth gospel of grace to the skins of owls
And to one who seasoneth the skins of Canadian owls;
                    O God! O Montreal!

When I saw him I was wroth and I said, 'O Discobolus!
Beautiful Discobolus, a Prince both among Gods and
      men,
What doest thou here, how camest thou hither, Disco
      bolus,
Preaching gospel in vain to the skins of owls?'
                    O God! O Montreal!

And I turned to the man of skins and said unto him, 'O
      thou man of skins,
Wherefore hast thou done thus to shame the beauty of
      the Discobolus?'
But the Lord had hardened the heart of the man of
      skins,
And he answered, 'My brother-in-law is haberdasher to
      Mr Spurgeon.'
                    O God! O Montreal!

'The Discobolus is put here because he is vulgar,
He has neither vest nor pants with which to cover his
    limbs;
I, Sir, am a person of most respectable connections—
My brother-in-law is haberdasher to Mr Spurgeon.'
              O God! O Montreal!

Then I said, 'O brother-in-law to Mr Spurgeon's haber-
    dasher,
Who seasonest also the skins of Canadian owls,
Thou callest trousers 'pants', whereas I call them
    'trousers',
Therefore, thou art in hell-fire and may the Lord pity
    thee!'
              O God! O Montreal!

'Preferrest thou the gospel of Montreal to the gospel of
    Hellas,
The gospel of thy connection with Mr Spurgeon's
    haberdashery to the gospel of the Discobolus?'
Yet none the less blasphemed he beauty saying, 'The
    Discobolus hath no gospel,
But my brother-in-law is haberdasher to Mr Spurgeon.'
              O God! O Montreal!

                    SAMUEL BUTLER

BOSTON

I come from the city of Boston,
The home of the bean and the cod,
Where the Cabots speak only to Lowells,
And the Lowells speak only to God.

              JOHN COLLINS BOSSIDY

A CODE OF MORALS

Lest you should think this story true
I merely mention I
Evolved it lately. 'Tis a most
Unmitigated misstatement.

Now Jones had left his new-wed bride to keep his house
    in order,
And hied away to the Hurrum Hills above the Afghan
    border,
To sit on a rock with a heliograph; but ere he left he
    taught
His wife the working of the Code that sets the miles at
    naught.

And Love had made him very sage, as Nature made her
    fair;
So Cupid and Apollo linked, *per* heliograph, the pair.
At dawn, across the Hurrum Hills, he flashed her
    counsel wise—
At e'en, the dying sunset bore her husband's homilies.

He warned her 'gainst seductive youths in scarlet clad
    and gold,
As much as 'gainst the blandishments paternal of the old;
But kept his gravest warnings for (hereby the ditty
    hangs)
That snowy-haired Lothario, Lieutenant-General Bangs.

'Twas General Bangs, with Aide and Staff, that
    tittupped on the way,
When they beheld a heliograph tempestuously at play.
They thought of Border risings, and of stations sacked
    and burnt—
So stopped to take the message down—and this is what
    they learnt —

Dash dot dot, dot, dot dash, dot dash dot' twice. The
    General swore.
'Was ever General Officer addressed as 'dear' before?
' 'My love,' i' faith! 'My Duck,' Gadzooks! 'My darling
    popsy-wop!'
'Spirit of great Lord Wolseley, *who* is on that mountain-
    top?'

The artless Aide-de-camp was mute; the gilded Staff
    were still,
As, dumb with pent-up mirth, they booked that mess-
    age from the hill;
For clear as summer lightning-flare, the husband's
    warning ran:—
'Don't dance or ride with General Bangs—a most
    immoral man.'

(At dawn, across the Hurrum Hills, he flashed her
    counsel wise—
But, howsoever Love be blind, the world at large hath
    eyes.)
With damnatory dot and dash he heliographed his wife
Some interesting details of the General's private life.

The artless Aide-de-camp was mute; the shining Staff
    were still,
And red and ever redder grew the General's shaven gill.
And this is what he said at last (his feelings matter not):—
'I think we've tapped a private line. Hi! Threes about
    there! Trot!'

All honour unto Bangs, for ne'er did Jones thereafter know
By word or act official who read off that helio;
But the tale is on the Frontier, and from Michni to
    Mool*tan*
They know the worthy General as 'that most immoral
    man'.

                    RUDYARD KIPLING

THE ANONYMOUS LIMERICK

I

There was an old man of Cape Race
Whose mind was a perfect disgrace;
    He thought Marie Corelli
    Lived long before Shelley,
And imagined that Wells was a place.

II

There was an old man of Boulogne
Who sang a most topical song.
    It wasn't the words
    Which frightened the birds,
But the horrible double entendre.

III

There was an old party of Lyme
Who married three wives at one time.
    When asked: 'Why the third?'
    He replied: 'One's absurd,
And bigamy, sir, is a crime.'

IV

There was a young lady of Riga
Who went for a ride on a tiger:
    They returned from the ride
    With the lady inside
And a smile on the face of the tiger.

V

There was a young lady of Spain
Who was dreadfully sick in a train,
    Not once, but again,
    And again and again,
And again and again and again.

VI

A wonderful bird is the pelican,
His mouth can hold more than his belican,
 He can take in his beak
 Enough food for a week—
I'm damned if I know how the helican.

VII

There was a young man of Quebec
Who was frozen in snow to his neck,
 When asked, 'Are you friz?'
 He replied, 'Yes, I is,
But we don't call this cold in Quebec.'

VIII

There was a young curate of Salisbury
Whose manners were quite halisbury-scalisbury:
 He ran about Hampshire
 Without any pampshire
Till his bishop compelled him to walisbury.

IX

There was a young man of St Bees
Who was stung on the arm by a wasp;
 When they said, 'Does it hurt?'
 He replied, 'No it doesn't:
'It's a good job it wasn't a hornet.'

X

There was a young man of Japan
Whose limericks never would scan;
 When they said it was so,
 He replied, 'Yes, I know,
But I always try to get as many words into the
  last line as ever I possibly can.'

295

MOTOR BUS

What is this that roareth thus?
Can it be a Motor Bus?
Yes, the smell and hideous hum
Indicat Motorem Bum!
Implet in the Corn and High
Terror me Motoris Bi:
Bo Motori clamitabo
Ne Motore caedar a Bo—
Dative be or Ablative
So thou only let us live:
Whither shall thy victims flee?
Spare us, spare us, Motor Be!
Thus I sang: and still anigh
Came in hordes Motores Bi,
Et complebat omne forum
Copia Motorum Borum.
How shall wretches live like us
Cincti Bis Motoribus?
Domine, defende nos
Contra hos Motores Bos!

A. D. GODLEY

INFANT INNOCENCE

The Grizzly Bear is huge and wild;
He has devoured the infant child.
The infant child is not aware
He has been eaten by the bear.

A. E. HOUSMAN

ABSOLUTE AND ABITOFHELL

(Being a Satire in the Manner of Mr John Dryden upon a newly-issu'd Work entitl'd Foundations)

In former Times, when Israel's ancient Creed
Took Root so widely that it ran to Seed;
When Saints were more accounted of than Soap,
And MEN in happy Blindness serv'd the POPE:
Uxorious JEROBOAM, waxen bold,
Tore the Ten Tribes from DAVID's falt'ring Hold,
And, spurning Threats from Salem's Vatican,
Set gaiter'd Calves in Bethel and in Dan.
So, Freedom reign'd: so, Priests, dismay'd by naught,
Thought what they pleas'd, and mention'd what they
    thought.
Three hundred Years, and still the Land was free'd,
And Bishops still, and Judges disagreed,
Till men began for some Account to call,
What we believ'd, or why believ'd at all?
The thing was canvass'd, and it seem'd past doubt
Much we adher'd to we could do without;
First, ADAM fell; then NOAH's Ark was drown'd,
And SAMSON under close inspection bound;
For DANIEL's Blood the Critick Lions roar'd,
And trembling Hands threw JONAH overboard.
    Lux Mundi came, and here we found indeed
A Maximum and Minimum of Creed:
But still the Criticks, bent on MATTHEW's Fall,
And setting PETER by the Ears with PAUL,
Brought unaccustom'd Doctrines oversea
Suggesting rather, *Caeli Tenebrae.*
So, while our Ark let in, through Seams ill-join'd
And gaping Timbers, *Bilge* of ev'ry Kind,
Ran to and fro, and like a Drunkard shook,
Seven of the Younger Men compos'd a *Book.*

297

Seven Men, in Views and Learning near ally'd,
Whom *Forms* alone and *Dogmas* did divide,
Their Differences sunk, in Conclave met,
And each his Seal (with Reservations) set:
Each in his Turn subscrib'd the fateful Scroll,
And stamp'd his *Nihil Constat* on the whole.

Sing, Heavenly MUSE, from high Olympus bowing,
Their Names, their Training, and their Welt-
    anschauung.
Say, why did Magdala,[1] renown'd in Ships,
Withhold the Tribute of *his* dauntless Lips,
Who, setting out the Gospel Truths t'explain,
Thought all that was not German, not germane:
Whose queasy Stomach, while it tried in vain
Recorded Miracles to entertain,
Eschewing LUKE, JOHN, MATTHEW, and the rest,
Read MARK, but could not inwardly digest?
Why did Neapolis,[2] aloof like ASHER,
Withhold—the Name is in the Book of Jasher—
Where, 'mid the Thunders of a boisterous Quad,
He ponders on the Raison d'Être of God?
Not such the Arms, not such the vain Defence,
That rallied to thy Standard, Common Sense.

First, from the Public Schools—*Lernaean* Bog—
No paltry Bulwark, stood the Form of OG.[3]
A man so broad, to some he seem'd to be
Not one, but all Mankind in Effigy:
Who, brisk in Term, a Whirlwind in the Long,
Did everything by turns, and nothing wrong,

[1] The Reverend Mr J. M. Thompson, Dean of Divinity at the College of St Mary Magdalen in Oxford.

[2] The Reverend Dr Hastings Rashdall, S.T.D., Fellow of the College of St Mary of Winton, in Oxford.

[3] The Reverend Mr William Temple, sometime Head Master of Repton School; since Incumbent of the Church of St James, Picca-dilly, in Westminster.

Bill'd at each Lecture-hall from Thames to Tyne
As Thinker, Usher, Statesman, or Divine.
Born in the Purple, swift he chose the Light,
And Lambeth mark'd him for a Nazirite:
Discerning *Balliol* snatch'd him in his teens,
And mourn'd him, early forfeited to *Queen's*.
His name suffic'd to leave th' insidious tome
A household word in every English Home:
No academick Treatise, high and dry,
Canvass'd in Walks round Mesopotamy,
Or where in Common Room, when days are short,
Soulless Professors gulp disgusted Port.
'Not from the few, the learned, and the pale'
—So ran his message—'we expect our Sale;
Man in the Street, our Publication con—
What matter, if the Street be Ashkelon?'
    In Weight not less, but more advanc'd in Height,
Gigantic ELIPHAZ[1] next hove in Sight:
Who 'mid the Prophets' Sons his Trade did ply
In teaching Wells to bless and magnify.
The Pomegranate upon his Helm display'd
His prebendarial Dignity betray'd:
Magdalen to *Univ.* gave him, and from there
He rapidly achiev'd a wider sphere;
Gray Hairs alone he wanted, but for that
Ripe for the Apron and the shovel Hat.
Those other Six, in punier arms array'd,
Crouch'd in his Shadow, and were not afraid.
    Yet something marr'd that order'd Symmetry:
Say, what did STRATO[2] in their company?

---

[1] The Reverend R. G. Parsons, S.T.B., sometime Fellow of University College in Oxford; since Rector of Wells Seminary, in the County of Somerset.

[2] The Reverend Mr B. H. Streeter, Fellow of Queen's College in Oxford, and Canon of Hereford.

Who, like a Leaven, gave his Tone to all,
'Mid prophet Bands an unsuspected Saul.
For he, discerning with nice arguings
'Twixt non-essential and essential Things,
Himself believing, could no reason see
Why any other should believe, but he
(Himself believing, as believing went
In that wild Heyday of th' Establishment,
When suave Politeness, temp'ring bigot Zeal,
Corrected 'I believe', to 'One does feel.')
He wish'd the *Bilge* away, yet did not seek
To man the *Pumps*, or plug the treach'rous Leak:
Would let into our Ark the veriest Crow,
That had the measliest Olive-branch to show.
Who has not known how pleasant 'tis to sigh,
'Others, thank God, are less correct than I?'
  From such Conclusion (so men said) averse,
A Balaam, blessing what he dared not curse,
A Scaeva, raising Powers he could not quell,
Dragging their Coat-tails, followed ABDIEL.[1]
In Height magnificent, in Depth profound,
Bless'd with more Sense than some, than all more sound,
Gifted as if with Tongues, were there but wit
Among his Audience to interpret it:
Still, like a clumsy Falconer, he'd untie
Tradition's Hood from Reason's piercing Eye,
And then complain, because she soar'd too high.
So labour'd he, in Devorguilla's Pile,
Jowett's and Manning's views to reconcile:
Beneath his Rule (I quote from Dryden's Rhyme)
'The Sons of Belial had a glorious Time,'
And, when he shook his Fist and talk'd of Eve,
Like Devils trembled, but did not believe.

[1] The Reverend Mr N. E. Talbot, Fellow of Balliol College in Oxford.

With sunnier Faith, with more unclouded Brow,
Brilliant ARCTURUS[1] did the Fates endow:
Who cried, as joyfully he bound his Sheaves,
'What I believe is what the Church believes':
Yet some might find it matter for Research,
Whether the Church taught him, or he the Church.
Corpus had trained him Reason's Truth to doubt,
And Keble added Faith, to do without.
What matter, whether two and two be four,
So long as none account them to be more?
What difference, whether black be black or white,
If no officious Hand turn on the Light?
Whether our Fact be Fact, no Man can know,
But, Heav'n preserve us, we will treat it so.

Yet, lest some envious Critick might complain
The BIBLE had been jettisoned as vain,
Pellucid JABBOK[2] show'd us, how much more
The Bible meant to us than e'er before.
Twelve *Prophets* our unlearn'd forefathers knew,
We are scarce satisfy'd with twenty-two:
A single *Psalmist* was enough for them,
Our List of Authors rivals A. and M.:
They were content MARK, MATTHEW, LUKE and JOHN
Should bless th' old-fashion'd Beds they lay upon:
But we, for ev'ry one of theirs, have two,
And trust the Watchfulness of blessed Q.

The last, EPIGONUS,[3] but not the least,
Levite by Birth, yet not by Calling Priest,
Woo'd coy Philosophy, reluctant Maid,
To bring her troubl'd Sister timely aid.

[1] The Reverend Mr A. E. Rawlinson, Student of Christ Church in Oxford.
[2] The Reverend Mr Richard Brook, Fellow of Merton College in Oxford.
[3] W. Moberley, Esquire, Fellow of Lincoln College in Oxford.

His Views on Punishment what need to tell?
Poor, proctor'd Victims lately knew them well,
His pregnant Logick fill'd their only Want,
Temp'ring EZEKIEL with a Dash of KANT.
 Hail, dauntless Mariners, that far outstrip
Previous Attempts to undergird the Ship!
To you this Rhyme, now falt'ring to its End,
Is dedicated by an humble Friend,
Praying that Providence this Wind may use
To puff your Sales, and to confound your Views.

R. A. KNOX

THE WISHES OF AN ELDERLY MAN

(*At a garden-party, June 1914*)

I wish I loved the Human Race;
I wish I loved its silly face;
I wish I liked the way it walks;
I wish I liked the way it talks;
And when I'm introduced to one
I wish I thought *What Jolly Fun!*

WALTER RALEIGH

THE BETTER WAY

If you desire to paralyze
Your enemy, don't 'd—n his eyes';
From futile blasphemy desist:
Send him to Blank the oculist.

WALTER LEAF

A LUNCHEON

*In the summer of 1923 when the Prince of Wales was
about to pay his annual visit to the Duchy of Cornwall,
someone at Court suggested that he should, on his way,
visit Mr Thomas Hardy*

Lift latch, step in, be welcome, Sir,
Albeit to see you I'm unglad
And your face is fraught with a deathly shyness
Bleaching what pink it may have had.
Come in, come in, Your Royal Highness.

Beautiful weather?—Sir, that's true,
Though the farmers are casting rueful looks
At tilth and pasture's dearth of spryness.—
Yes, Sir, I've written several books.—
A little more chicken, Your Royal Highness?

Lift latch, step out, your car is there,
To bear you hence from this antient vale.
We are both of us aged by our strange brief nighness,
But each of us lives to tell the tale.
Farewell, farewell, Your Royal Highness.

MAX BEERBOHM

A REFUSAL

Said the grave dean of Westminster:
Mine is the best minster
Seen in Great Britain,
As many have written:
So therefore I cannot
Rule here if I ban not
Such liberty-taking
As movements for making
Its grayness environ
The memory of Byron,

303

Which some are demanding
Who think them of standing,
But in my own viewing
Require some subduing
For tendering suggestions
On Abbey-wall questions
That must interfere here
With my proper sphere here,
And bring to disaster
This fane and its master,
Whose dict is but Christian
Though nicknamed Philistian.

A lax Christian charity—
No mental clarity
Ruling its movements
For fabric improvements—
Demands admonition
And strict supervision
When bent on enshrining
Rapscallions, and signing
Their names on God's stonework,
As if like His own work
Were their lucubrations:
And passed is my patience
That such a creed-scorner
(Not mentioning horner)
Should claim Poet's Corner.

'Tis urged that some sinners
Are here for worms' dinners
Already in person;
That he could not worsen
The walls by a name mere
With men of such fame here.
Yet nay; they but leaven
The others in heaven

In just due proportion,
While more mean distortion.
'Twill next be expected
That I get erected
To Shelley a tablet
In some niche or gablet.
Then—what makes my skin burn,
Yea, forehead to chin burn—
That I ensconce Swinburne!

THOMAS HARDY

ANTICHRIST, OR THE REUNION OF CHRISTENDOM: AN ODE

('A Bill which has shocked the conscience of every Christian community in Europe.'—Mr F. E. Smith, on the Welsh Disestablishment Bill.)

Are they clinging to their crosses,
    F. E. Smith,
Where the Breton boat-fleet tosses,
    Are they, Smith?
Do they, fasting, trembling, bleeding,
    Wait the news from this our city?
Groaning 'That's the Second Reading!'
    Hissing 'There is still Committee!'
If the voice of Cecil falters,
    If McKenna's point has pith,
Do they tremble for their altars?
    Do they, Smith?

Russian peasants round their pope
    Huddled, Smith,
Hear about it all, I hope,
    Don't they, Smith?

In the mountain hamlets clothing
    Peaks beyond Caucasian pales,
Where Establishment means nothing
    And they never heard of Wales,
Do they read it all in Hansard
    With a crib to read it with—
'Welsh Tithes: Dr Clifford Answered.'
        Really, Smith?

In the lands where Christians were,
        F. E. Smith,
In the little lands laid bare,
        Smith, O Smith!
Where the Turkish bands are busy,
    And the Tory name is blessed
Since they hailed the cross of Dizzy
    On the banners from the West!
Men don't think it half so hard if
    Islam burns their kin and kith,
Since a curate lives in Cardiff
        Saved by Smith.

It would greatly, I must own,
        Soothe me, Smith,
If you left this theme alone,
        Holy Smith!
For your legal cause or civil
    You fight well and get your fee;
For your God or dream or devil
    You will answer, not to me.
Talk about the pews and steeples
    And the Cash that goes therewith!
But the souls of Christian peoples . . .
        Chuck it, Smith!

G. K. CHESTERTON

WINE AND WATER

Old Noah he had an ostrich farm and fowls on the
    largest scale,
He ate his egg with a ladle in an egg-cup big as a pail,
And the soup he took was Elephant Soup and the fish he
    took was Whale,
But they all were small to the cellar he took when he set
    out to sail,
And Noah he often said to his wife when he sat down
    to dine,
'I don't care where the water goes if it doesn't get into
    the wine.'

The cataract of the cliff of heaven fell blinding off the
    brink
As if it would wash the stars away as suds go down a
    sink,
The seven heavens came roaring down for the throats of
    hell to drink,
And Noah he cocked his eye and said, 'It looks like rain,
    I think,
The water has drowned the Matterhorn as deep as a
    Mendip mine,
But I don't care where the water goes if it doesn't get
    into the wine.'

But Noah he sinned, and we have sinned; on tipsy feet
    we trod,
Till a great big black teetotaller was sent to us for a
    rod,
And you can't get wine at a P.S.A., or chapel, or
    Eisteddfod,
For the Curse of Water has come again because of the
    wrath of God,

And water is on the Bishop's board and the Higher
    Thinker's shrine,
But I don't care where the water goes if it doesn't get
    into the wine.

                  G. K. CHESTERTON

THE SONG AGAINST GROCERS

God made the wicked Grocer
For a mystery and a sign,
That men might shun the awful shops
And go to inns to dine;
Where the bacon's on the rafter
And the wine is in the wood,
And God that made good laughter
Has seen that they are good.

The evil-hearted Grocer
Would call his mother 'Ma'am',
And bow at her and bob at her,
Her aged soul to damn,
And rub his horrid hands and ask
What article was next,
Though *mortis in articulo*
Should be her proper text.

His props are not his children,
But pert lads underpaid,
Who call out 'Cash!' and bang about
To work his wicked trade;
He keeps a lady in a cage
Most cruelly all day,
And makes her count and calls her 'Miss'
Until she fades away.

The righteous minds of innkeepers
Induce them now and then
To crack a bottle with a friend
Or treat unmoneyed men,
But who hath seen the Grocer
Treat housemaids to his teas
Or crack a bottle of fish-sauce
Or stand a man a cheese?

He sells us sands of Araby
As sugar for cash down;
He sweeps his shop and sells the dust
The purest salt in town,
He crams with cans of poisoned meat
Poor subjects of the King,
And when they die by thousands
Why, he laughs like anything.

The wicked Grocer groces
In spirits and in wine,
Not frankly and in fellowship
As men in inns do dine;
But packed with soap and sardines
And carried off by grooms,
For to be snatched by Duchesses
And drunk in dressing-rooms.

The hell-instructed Grocer
Has a temple made of tin,
And the ruin of good innkeepers
Is loudly urged therein;
But now the sands are running out
From sugar of a sort,
The Grocer trembles; for his time,
Just like his weight, is short.

G. K. CHESTERTON

SONGS OF EDUCATION:

III. FOR THE CRÊCHE

(Form 8277059, Sub-Section K)

I remember my mother, the day that we met,
A thing I shall never entirely forget;
And I toy with the fancy that, young as I am,
I should know her again if we met in a tram.
    But mother is happy in turning a crank
    That increases the balance at somebody's bank;
    And I feel satisfaction that mother is free
    From the sinister task of attending to me.

They have brightened our room, that is spacious and
      cool,
With diagrams used in the Idiot School,
And Books for the Blind that will teach us to see;
But mother is happy, for mother is free.
    For mother is dancing up forty-eight floors,
    For love of the Leeds International Stores,
    And the flame of that faith might perhaps have
      grown cold,
    With the care of a baby of seven weeks old.

For mother is happy in greasing a wheel
For somebody else, who is cornering Steel;
And though our one meeting was not very long,
She took the occasion to sing me this song:
    'O, hush thee, my baby, the time will soon come
    When thy sleep will be broken with hooting and hum;
    There are handles want turning and turning all day,
    And knobs to be pressed in the usual way;

'O, hush thee, my baby, take rest while I croon,
For Progress comes early, and Freedom too soon.'

G. K. CHESTERTON

LINES TO A DON

Remote and ineffectual Don
That dared attack my Chesterton,
With that poor weapon, half-impelled,
Unlearnt, unsteady, hardly held,
Unworthy for a tilt with men—
Your quavering and corroded pen;
Don poor at Bed and worse at Table,
Don pinched, Don starved, Don miserable
Don stuttering, Don with roving eyes,
Don nervous, Don of crudities;
Don clerical, Don ordinary,
Don self-absorbed and solitary;
Don here-and-there, Don epileptic;
Don puffed and empty, Don dyspeptic;
Don middle-class, Don sycophantic,
Don dull, Don brutish, Don pedantic;
Don hypocritical, Don bad,
Don furtive, Don three-quarters mad;
Don (since a man must make an end),
Don that shall never be my friend.

.   .   .   .

Don different from those regal Dons!
With hearts of gold and lungs of bronze,
Who shout and bang and roar and bawl
The Absolute across the hall,
Or sail in amply bellying gown
Enormous through the Sacred Town,
Bearing from College to their homes
Deep cargoes of gigantic tomes;
Dons admirable! Dons of Might!
Uprising on my inward sight
Compact of ancient tales, and port
And sleep—and learning of a sort.

311

Dons English, worthy of the land;
Dons rooted; Dons that understand.
Good Dons perpetual that remain
A landmark, walling in the plain—
The horizon of my memories—
Like large and comfortable trees.

.   .   .   .

Don very much apart from these,
Thou scapegoat Don, thou Don devoted,
Don to thine own damnation quoted,
Perplexed to find thy trivial name
Reared in my verse to lasting shame.
Don dreadful, rasping Don and wearing,
Repulsive Don—Don past all bearing.
Don of the cold and doubtful breath,
Don despicable, Don of death;
Don nasty, skimpy, silent, level;
Don evil; Don that serves the devil.
Don ugly—that makes fifty lines.
There is a Canon which confines
A Rhymed Octosyllabic Curse
If written in Iambic Verse
To fifty lines. I never cut;
I far prefer to end it—but
Believe me I shall soon return.
My fires are banked, but still they burn
To write some more about the Don
That dared attack my Chesterton.

HILAIRE BELLOC

ON HIS BOOKS

When I am dead, I hope it may be said:
'His sins were scarlet, but his books were read.'

HILAIRE BELLOC

GODOLPHIN HORNE

WHO WAS CURSED WITH THE SIN OF PRIDE, AND BECAME A BOOT-BLACK

Godolphin Horne was Nobly Born;
He held the Human Race in Scorn,
And lived with all his Sisters where
His Father lived, in Berkeley Square.
And oh! the Lad was Deathly Proud!

He never shook your Hand or Bowed,
But merely smirked and nodded thus:
How perfectly ridiculous!
Alas! That such Affected Tricks
Should flourish in a Child of Six!
(For such was Young Godolphin's age).
Just then, the Court required a Page,
Whereat the Lord High Chamberlain
(The Kindest and the Best of Men),
He went good-naturedly and took
A Perfectly Enormous Book
Called *People Qualified to Be*
Attendant on His Majesty,
And murmured, as he scanned the list
(To see that no one should be missed),
'There's William Coutts has got the Flu,
And Billy Higgs would never do,
And Guy de Vere is far too young,
And . . . wasn't D'Alton's Father hung?
And as for Alexander Byng!— . . .
I think I know the kind of thing,
A Churchman, cleanly, nobly born,
Come let us say Godolphin Horne?'
But hardly had he said the word
When Murmurs of Dissent were heard.

The King of Iceland's Eldest Son
Said, 'Thank you! I am taking none!'
The Aged Duchess of Athlone
Remarked, in her sub-acid tone,
'I doubt if He is what we need!'
With which the Bishops all agreed;
And even Lady Mary Flood
(*So* Kind, and oh! so *really* good)
Said, 'No! He wouldn't do at all,
He'd make us feel a lot too small.'
The Chamberlain said, '. . . Well, well, well!
No doubt you're right. . . . One cannot tell!'
He took his Gold and Diamond Pen
And scratched Godolphin out again.
So now Godolphin is the Boy
Who blacks the Boots at the Savoy.

HILAIRE BELLOC

LORD FINCHLEY

Lord Finchley tried to mend the Electric Light
Himself. It struck him dead: And serve him right!
It is the business of the wealthy man
To give employment to the artisan.

HILAIRE BELLOC

FATIGUE

I'm tired of Love: I'm still more tired of Rhyme.
But Money gives me pleasure all the time.

HILAIRE BELLOC

LORD LUNDY

WHO WAS TOO FREELY MOVED TO TEARS AND THEREBY RUINED HIS POLITICAL CAREER

Lord Lundy from his earliest years
Was far too freely moved to Tears.
For instance, if his Mother said,
'Lundy! It's time to go to Bed!'
He bellowed like a Little Turk.
Or if his father, Lord Dunquerque
Said, 'Hi!' in a Commanding Tone,
'Hi, Lundy! Leave the Cat alone!'
Lord Lundy, letting go its tail,
Would raise so terrible a wail
As moved his Grandpapa the Duke
To utter the severe rebuke:
'When I, Sir! was a little Boy,
An Animal was not a Toy!'

His father's Elder Sister, who
Was married to a Parvenoo,
Confided to Her Husband, 'Drat!
The Miserable, Peevish Brat!
Why don't they drown the Little Beast?'
Suggestions which, to say the least,
Are not what we expect to hear
From Daughters of an English Peer.
His Grandmama, his Mother's Mother,
Who had some dignity or other,
The Garter, or no matter what,
I can't remember all the Lot!
Said, 'Oh! that I were Brisk and Spry
To give him that for which to cry!'
(An empty wish, alas! for she
Was Blind and nearly ninety-three.)

The Dear Old Butler thought—but there!
I really neither know nor care
For what the Dear Old Butler thought!
In my opinion Butlers ought
To know their place, and not to play
The Old Retainer night and day.
I'm getting tired and so are you,
Let's cut the Poem into two!

Second Canto

It happened to Lord Lundy then,
As happens to so many men:
Towards the age of twenty-six,
They shoved him into politics;
In which profession he commanded
The income that his rank demanded
In turn as Secretary for
India, the Colonies, and War.
But very soon his friends began
To doubt if he were quite the man:
Thus, if a member rose to say
(As members do from day to day),
'Arising out of that reply . . .!'
Lord Lundy would begin to cry.
A Hint at harmless little jobs.
Would shake him with convulsive sobs.

While as for Revelations, these
Would simply bring him to his knees,
And leave him whimpering like a child
It drove his Colleagues raving wild!
They let him sink from Post to Post,
From fifteen hundred at the most
To eight, and barely six—and then
To be Curator of Big Ben! . .

316

And finally there came a Threat
To oust him from the Cabinet!

The Duke—his aged grandsire—bore
The shame till he could bear no more.
He rallied his declining powers,
Summoned the youth to Brackley Towers,
And bitterly addressed him thus—
'Sir! you have disappointed us!
We had intended you to be
The next Prime Minister but three:
The stocks were sold; the Press was squared;
The Middle Class was quite prepared.
But as it is! . . . My language fails!
Go out and govern New South Wales!'

    .   .   .   .

The Aged Patriot groaned and died:
And gracious! how Lord Lundy cried!

HILAIRE BELLOC

ON LADY POLTAGRUE, A PUBLIC PERIL

The Devil, having nothing else to do,
Went off to tempt My Lady Poltagrue.
My Lady, tempted by a private whim,
To his extreme annoyance, tempted him.

HILAIRE BELLOC

ON A GENERAL ELECTION

The accursèd power which stands on Privilege
(And goes with Women, and Champagne and Bridge)
Broke—and Democracy resumed her reign:
(Which goes with Bridge, and Women and Champagne).

HILAIRE BELLOC

THE PURPLE COW

I never saw a Purple Cow,
  I never hope to see one;
But I can tell you, anyhow,
  I'd rather see than be one.

GELETT BURGESS

SEQUEL TO THE PURPLE COW

Ah, Yes! I wrote the 'Purple Cow'—
I'm Sorry, now, I wrote it!
But I can Tell you Anyhow,
I'll Kill you if you Quote it.

GELETT BURGESS

A CASE

As I was going up the stair
I met a man who wasn't there.
He wasn't there again today—
I wish to God he'd go away!

ANON

COMMUTERS

Commuter—one who spends his life
In riding to and from his wife;
A man who shaves and takes a train
And then rides back to shave again.

E. B. WHITE

BIOGRAPHY FOR BEGINNE

SIR CHRISTOPHER WREN

Sir Christopher Wren
Said, 'I am going to dine with some men.
If anybody calls
Say I am designing St Paul's.'

GEORGE III

George the Third
Ought never to have occurred.
One can only wonder
At so grotesque a blunder.

ADAM SMITH

Adam Smith
Was disowned by all his kith,
But he was backed through thick and thin
By all his kin.

SIR HUMPHRY DAVY

Sir Humphry Davy
Abominated gravy.
He lived in the odium
Of having discovered Sodium.

J. S. MILL

John Stuart Mill,
By a mighty effort of will,
Overcame his natural bonhomie
And wrote 'Principles of Political Economy'.

E. C. BENTLEY

BALLADE OF LIQUID REFRESHMENT

Last night we started with some dry vermouth;
  Some ancient sherry with a golden glow;
Then many flagons of the soul of fruit
  Such as Burgundian vineyards only grow;
  A bottle each of port was not *de trop*;
And then old brandy till the east was pink
  —But talking makes me hoarse as any crow.
Excuse me while I go and have a drink.

Some talk of Alexander: some impute
  Absorbency to Mirabeau-Tonneau;
Some say that General Grant and King Canute,
  Falstaff and Pitt and Edgar Allan Poe,
  Prince Charlie, Carteret, Hans Breitmann—so
The list goes on—they say that these could clink
  The can, and take their liquor—*A propos!*
Excuse me while I go and have a drink.

Spirit of all that lives, from God to brute,
  Spirit of love and life, of sun and snow,
Spirit of leaf and limb, of race and root,
  How wonderfully art thou prison'd! Lo!
  I quaff the cup, I feel the magic flow,
And Superman succeeds to Missing Link,
  (I say, 'I quaff'; but am I quaffing? No!
Excuse me while I go and have a drink.)

Envoi

Hullo there, Prince! Is that you down below
Kicking and frying by the brimstone brink?
  Well, well! It had to come some time, you know.
Excuse me while I go and have a drink.

E. C. BENTLEY

RUTHLESS RHYMES

OPPORTUNITY

When Mrs Gorm (Aunt Eloïse)
Was stung to death by savage bees,
Her husband (Prebendary Gorm)
Put on his veil, and took the swarm.
He's publishing a book next May
On 'How to Make Bee-keeping Pay'.

MR JONES

'There's been an accident,' they said,
'Your servant's cut in half; he's dead!'
'Indeed!' said Mr Jones, 'and please,
Send me the half that's got my keys.'

L'ENFANT GLACÉ

When Baby's cries grew hard to bear,
I popped him in the Frigidaire.
I never would have done so if
I'd known that he'd be frozen stiff.
My wife said: 'George, I'm so unhappé
Our darling's now completely *frappé!*'

WASTE

I had written to Aunt Maud,
Who was on a trip abroad,
When I heard she'd died of cramp
Just too late to save the stamp.

LORD GORBALS

Once, as old Lord Gorbals motored
    Round his moors near John o' Groats,
He collided with a goatherd
    And a herd of forty goats.
By the time his car got through
They were all defunct but two.

Roughly he addressed the goatherd:
    'Dash my whiskers and my corns!
Can't you teach your goats, you dotard,
    That they ought to sound their horns?
Look, my A.A. badge is bent!
I've a mind to raise your rent!'

BILLY

Billy, in one of his nice new sashes,
    Fell in the fire and was burned to ashes;
Now, although the room grows chilly,
    I haven't the heart to poke poor Billy.

NECESSITY

Late last night I killed my wife,
    Stretched her on the parquet flooring;
I was loath to take her life,
    But I *had* to stop her snoring!

HARRY GRAHAM

POETICAL ECONOMY

What hours I spent of precious time,
 What pints of ink I used to waste,
Attempting to secure a rhyme
 To suit the public taste,
Until I found a simple plan
Which makes the lamest lyric scan!

When I've a syllable *de trop*,
 I cut it off, without apol.:
This verbal sacrifice, I know,
 May irritate the schol.;
But all must praise my dev'lish cunn.
Who realise that Time is Mon.

My sense remains as clear as cryst.,
 My style as pure as any Duch.
Who does not boast a bar sinist.
 Upon her fam. escutch.;
And I can treat with scornful pit.
The sneers of ev'ry captious crit.

I gladly publish to the pop.
 A scheme of which I make no myst.,
And beg my fellow scribes to cop.
 This-labour-saving syst.
I offer it to the consid.
Of ev'ry thoughtful individ.

The author, working like a beav.,
 His readers' pleasure could redoub.
Did he but now and then abbrev.
 The work he gives his pub.
(This view I most partic. suggest
To A. C. Bens. and G. K. Chest.)

If Mr Caine rewrote *The Scape.*,
  And Miss Correll condensed *Barabb.*,
What could they save in foolscap pape.
  Did they but cult. the hab.
Which teaches people to suppress
All syllables that are unnec.!

If playwrights would but thus dimin.:
  The length of time each drama takes,
(*The Second Mrs Tanq.* by Pin.
  Or even *Ham.*, by Shakes.)
We could maintain a watchful att.
When at a Mat. on Wed. or Sat.

Have done, ye bards, with dull monot.!
  Foll. my examp., O, Stephen Phill.,
O, Owen Seam., O, William Wat.,
  O, Ella Wheeler Wil.,
And share with me the grave respons.
Of writing this amazing nons.!

HARRY GRAHAM

ERE YOU WERE QUEEN OF SHEBA

When we were a soft amoeba, in ages past and gone,
Ere you were Queen of Sheba, or I King Solomon,
Alone and undivided, we lived a life of sloth,
Whatever you did, I did; one dinner served for both.
Anon came separation, by fission and divorce,
A lonely pseudopodium I wandered on my course.

SIR ARTHUR SHIPLEY

THE COMMON CORMORANT

The common cormorant or shag
Lays eggs inside a paper bag
The reason you will see no doubt
It is to keep the lightning out.
But what these unobservant birds
Have never noticed is that herds
Of wandering bears may come with buns
And steal the bags to hold the crumbs.

CHRISTOPHER ISHERWOOD

THE RABBIT

The rabbit has a charming face:
Its private life is a disgrace.
I really dare not name to you
The awful things that rabbits do;
Things that your paper never prints—
You only mention them in hints.
They have such lost, degraded souls
No wonder they inhabit holes;
When such depravity is found
It only can live underground.

ANON

THE HORSE

I know two things about the horse,
And one of them is rather coarse.

NAOMI ROYDE SMITH

TO BE OR NOT TO BE

I sometimes think I'd rather crow
And be a rooster than to roost
And be a crow. But I dunno.

A rooster he can roost also,
Which don't seem fair when crows can't crow.
Which may help some. Still I dunno.

Crows should be glad of one thing, though:
Nobody thinks of eating crow,
While roosters they are good enough
For anyone unless they're tough.

There are lots of tough old roosters though,
And anyway a crow can't crow,
So mebby roosters stand more show.
It looks that way. But I dunno.

ANON

TONY O

Over the bleak and barren snow
A voice there came a-calling:
'Where are you going to, Tony O!
Where are you going this morning?'

'I am going where there are rivers of wine,
The mountains bread and honey;
There Kings and Queens do mind the swine,
And the poor have all the money.'

COLIN FRANCIS

THE INTELLECTUAL LIMERICK

DETERMINISM

There was a young man who said, 'Damn!'
It appears to me now that I am
Just a being that moves
In predestinate grooves,
Not a taxi or bus, but a tram.

ANON

MATERIALISM

There was a professor of Beaulieu
Who said mind was matter or ὕλη;
This contempt for the εἶδος,
Though common at Cnidos,
Distressed the New Forest unduly.

C. E. M. JOAD

IDEALISM

There once was a man who said, 'God
Must think it exceedingly odd
If he finds that this tree
Continues to be
When there's no one about in the Quad.'

RONALD KNOX

A REPLY

Dear Sir, Your astonishment's odd,
I am always about in the Quad;
And that's why this tree
Will continue to be,
Since observed by Yours faithfully, GOD.

ANON

RELATIVITY

There was a young lady named Bright,
Who travelled much faster than light,
    She started one day
    In the relative way,
And returned on the previous night.

ANON

MENDELIAN THEORY

There was a young woman called Starkie,
Who had an affair with a darky.
    The result of her sins
    Was quadruplets, not twins—
One black, and one white, and two khaki.

ANON

MIND AND MATTER

There was a faith-healer of Deal,
Who said, 'Although pain isn't real,
    If I sit on a pin
    And it punctures my skin,
I dislike what I fancy I feel.'

ANON

ULTIMATE REALITY

There was an old man in a trunk,
Who inquired of his wife, 'Am I drunk?'
    She replied with regret,
    'I'm afraid so, my pet.'
And he answered, 'It's just as I thunk.'

OGDEN NASH

THE CURSE

*(To a sister of an enemy of the author's who disapproved
of 'The Playboy')*

Lord, confound this surly sister,
Blight her brow with blotch and blister,
Cramp her larynx, lung and liver,
In her guts a galling give her.

Let her live to earn her dinners
In Mountjoy with seedy sinners:
Lord, this judgment quickly bring,
And I'm your servant, J. M. Synge.

J. M. SYNGE

THE LAKE ISLE

O God, O Venus, O Mercury, patron of thieves,
Give me in due time, I beseech you, a little tobacco-shop,
With the little bright boxes
            piled up neatly upon the shelves
And the loose fragrant cavendish
            and the shag,
And the bright Virginia
            loose under the bright glass cases,
And a pair of scales not too greasy,
And the whores dropping in for a word or two in passing,
For a flip word, and to tidy their hair a bit.

O God, O Venus, O Mercury, patron of thieves,
Lend me a little tobacco-shop,
            or install me in any profession
Save this damn'd profession of writing,
            where one needs one's brains all the time.

EZRA POUND

329

ANCIENT MUSIC

Winter is icummen in,
Lhude sing Goddamm,
Raineth drop and staineth slop,
And how the wind doth ramm!
     Sing: Goddamm.
Skiddeth bus and sloppeth us,
An ague hath my ham.
Freezeth river, turneth liver,
     Damn you, sing: Goddamm.
Goddamm, Goddamm, 'tis why I am, Goddamm,
     So 'gainst the winter's balm.
Sing goddamm, damm, sing Goddamm,
Sing goddamm, sing goddamm, DAMM.

        EZRA POUND

A GLASS OF BEER

The lanky hank of a she in the inn over there
Nearly killed me for asking the loan of a glass of beer;
May the devil grip the whey-faced slut by the hair,
And beat bad manners out of her skin for a year.

That parboiled ape, with the toughest jaw you will see
On virtue's path, and a voice that would rasp the dead,
Came roaring and raging the minute she looked at me,
And threw me out of the house on the back of my head!

If I asked her master he'd give me a cask a day;
But she, with the beer at hand, not a gill would arrange!
May she marry a ghost and bear him a kitten, and may
The High King of Glory permit her to get the mange.

    JAMES STEPHENS (*From the Irish*)

TWO POEMS

(*After A. E. Housman*)

1

What, still alive at twenty-two,
A clean upstanding chap like you?
Sure, if your throat 'tis hard to slit,
Slit your girl's, and swing for it.

Like enough, you won't be glad,
When they come to hang you, lad:
But bacon's not the only thing
That's cured by hanging from a string.

So, when the spilt ink of the night
Spreads o'er the blotting pad of light,
Lads whose job is still to do
Shall whet their knives, and think of you.

2

'Tis Summer Time on Bredon,
    And now the farmers swear;
The cattle rise and listen
    In valleys far and near,
    And blush at what they hear.

But when the mists in autumn
    On Bredon tops are thick,
The happy hymns of farmers
    Go up from fold and rick,
    The cattle then are sick.

HUGH KINGSMILL

cheerio my deario

(by archy the cockroach)

well boss i met
mehitabel the cat
trying to dig a
frozen lamb chop
out of a snow
drift the other day

a heluva comedown
that is for me archy
she says a few
brief centuries
ago one of old
king
tut
ankh
amens favorite
queens and today
the village scavenger
but wotthehell
archy wotthehell
it s cheerio
my deario that
pulls a lady through

see here mehitabel
i said i thought
you told me that
it was cleopatra
you used to be
before you
transmigrated into
the carcase of a cat

332

where do you get
this tut
ankh
amen stuff
question mark

i was several
ladies my little
insect says she
being cleopatra was
only an incident
in my career
and i was always getting
the rough end of it
always being
misunderstood by some
strait laced
prune faced bunch
of prissy mouthed
sisters of uncharity
the things that
have been said
about me archy
exclamation point

and all simply
because i was a
live dame
the palaces i have
been kicked out of
in my time
exclamation point

but wotthehell
little archy wot
thehell

333

it s cheerio
my deario
that pulls a
lady through
exclamation point

framed archy always
framed that is the
story of all my lives
no chance for a dame
with the anvil chorus
if she shows a little
motion it seems to
me only yesterday
that the luxor local
number one of
the ladies axe
association got me in
dutch with king tut and
he slipped me the
sarcophagus always my
luck yesterday an empress
and today too
emaciated to interest
a vivisectionist but
toujours gai archy
toujours gai and always
a lady in spite of hell
and transmigration
once a queen
archy
period

one of her
feet was frozen
but on the other three

she began to caper and
dance singing it s
cheerio my deario
that pulls a lady
through her morals may
have been mislaid somewhere
in the centuries boss but
l admire her spirit
                    archy
                                DON MARQUIS

the old trouper

i ran onto mehitabel again
last evening
she is inhabiting
a decayed trunk
which lies in an alley
in greenwich village
in company with the
most villainous tom cat
i have ever seen
but there is nothing.
wrong about the association
archy she told me
it is merely a plutonic
attachment
and the thing can be
believed for the tom
looks like one of pluto s demons
it is a theatre trunk
archy mehitabel told me
and tom is an old theatre cat
he has given his life
to the theatre
he claims that richard
335

mansfield once
kicked him out of the way
and then cried because
he had done it and
petted him
and at another time
he says in a case
of emergency
he played a bloodhound
in a production of
uncle tom s cabin
the stage is not what it
used to be tom says
he puts his front paw
on his breast and says
they don t have it any more
they don t have it here
the old troupers are gone
there s nobody can troupe
any more
they are all amateurs nowadays
they haven t got it
here
there are only
five or six of us oldtime
troupers left
this generation does not know
what stage presence is
personality is what they lack
personality
where would they get
the training my old friends
got in the stock companies
i knew mr booth very well
says tom
and a law should be passed

preventing anybody else
from ever playing
in any play he ever
played in
there was a trouper for you
i used to sit on his knee
and purr when i was
a kitten he used to tell me
how much he valued my opinion
finish is what they lack
finish
and they haven t got it
here
and again he laid his paw
on his breast
i remember mr daly very
well too
i was with mr daly s company
for several years
there was art for you
there was team work
there was direction
they knew the theatre
and they all had it
here
for two years mr daly
would not ring up the curtain
unless i was in the
prompter s box
they are amateurs nowadays
rank amateurs all of them
for two seasons i played
the dog in joseph
jefferson s rip van winkle
it is true i never came
on the stage

but he knew i was just off
and it helped him
i would like to see
one of your modern
theatre cats
act a dog so well
that it would convince
a trouper like jo jefferson
but they haven t got it
nowadays
they haven t got it
here
jo jefferson had it he had it
here
i come of a long line
of theatre cats
my grandfather
was with forrest
he had it he was a real trouper
my grandfather said
he had a voice
that used to shake
the ferryboats
on the north river
once he lost his beard
and my grandfather
dropped from the
fly gallery and landed
under his chin
and played his beard
for the rest of the act
you don t see any theatre
cats that could do that
nowadays
they haven t got it they
haven t got it

here
once i played the owl
in modjeska s production
of macbeth
i sat above the castle gate
in the murder scene
and made my yellow
eyes shine through the dusk
like an owl s eyes
modjeska was a real
trouper she knew how to pick
her support i would like
to see any of these modern
theatre cats play the owl s eyes
to modjeska s lady macbeth
but they haven t got it nowadays
they haven t got it
here

mehitabel he says
both our professions
are being ruined
by amateurs
                    archy

                    DON MARQUIS

WHO DRAGS THE FIERY ARTIST
DOWN?

Who drags the fiery artist down?
Who keeps the pioneer in town?
Who hates to let the seaman roam?
It is the wife, it is the home.

                    CLARENCE DAY

THE BREWER'S MAN

Have I a wife? Bedam I have!
    But we was badly mated:
I hit her a great clout one night,
    And now we're separated.

And mornin's, going to my work,
    I meets her on the quay:
'Good mornin' to ye, ma'am,' says I;
    'To hell with ye,' says she.

L. A. G. STRONG

A MEMORY

When I was as high as that
I saw a poet in his hat.
I think the poet must have smiled
At such a solemn gazing child.

Now wasn't it a funny thing
To get a sight of J. M. Synge,
And notice nothing but his hat?
Yet life is often queer like that.

L. A. G. STRONG

A SHOT AT RANDOM

(*In imitation of Longfellow*)

I shot an arrow into the air:
I don't know how it fell, or where;
But, strangely enough, at my journey's end,
I found it again in the neck of a friend.

D. B. W. LEWIS

340

ON A STATUE OF SIR ARTHUR
SULLIVAN

(*A bronze figure of Grief leaning against the high pedestal*)

Sorrowing nymph, oh why display
Your beauty in such disarray?
Is it decent, is it just
To so conventional a bust?

G. ROSTREVOR HAMILTON

DON'S HOLIDAY

Professor Robinson each summer beats
The fishing record of the world—such feats
As one would hardly credit from a lesser
Person than a history professor.

G. ROSTREVOR HAMILTON

ON A DISTANT PROSPECT OF AN
ABSCONDING BOOKMAKER

Alas! what boots it that my noble steed,
Chosen so carefully, the field outran?
I did not reckon, bookie, on *your* speed:
The proper study of mankind is man.

G. ROSTREVOR HAMILTON

EMINENT COSMOLOGISTS

Nature, and Nature's laws, lay hid in night,
God said, *Let Newton be!* and all was light.

ALEXANDER POPE

It did not last: the Devil howling *Ho*,
Let Einstein be, restored the status quo.

J. C. SQUIRE

341

NOBODY LOSES ALL THE TIME

nobody loses all the time

i had an uncle named
Sol who was a born failure and
nearly everybody said he should have gone
into vaudeville perhaps because my Uncle Sol could
sing McCann He Was A Diver on Xmas Eve like Hell
    Itself which
may or may not account for the fact that my Uncle

Sol indulged in that possibly most inexcusable
of all to use a highfalootin phrase
luxuries that is or to
wit farming and be
it needlessly
added

my Uncle Sol's farm
failed because the chickens
ate the vegetables so
my Uncle Sol had a
chicken farm till the
skunks ate the chickens when

my Uncle Sol
had a skunk farm but
the skunks caught cold and
died and so
my Uncle Sol imitated the
skunks in a subtle manner

or by drowning himself in the watertank
but somebody who'd given my Uncle Sol a Victor
Victrola and records while he lived presented to

him upon the auspicious occasion of his decease a
scrumptious not to mention splendiferous funeral with
tall boys in black gloves and flowers and everything and

i remember we all cried like the Missouri
when my Uncle Sol's coffin lurched because
somebody pressed a button
(and down went
my Uncle
Sol

and started a worm farm)

E. E. CUMMINGS

A POEM INTENDED TO INCITE THE
UTMOST DEPRESSION

Cervantes, Dostoievsky, Poe,
Drained the dregs and lees of woe;
Gogol, Beethoven and Keats
Got but meagre share of sweets.
Milton, Homer, Dante had
Reason to be more than sad;
Caesar and Napoleon
Saw the blood upon their sun;
Martyr, hermit, saint and priest
Lingered long at Sorrow's feast:
Paid with pyre and perishing
For every feather in each wing;—
Well, if such as these could be
So foredoomed to misery,
And Fate despise her own elect—
What the deuce do you expect?

SAMUEL HOFFENSTEIN

343

ODIHAM

Put his head
and anxious face
out of a car.
Seemed to have said
Yell's the name
of this place;
seven, three, four.

Man addressed
tried to evince
interest,
as often before
and often since.
Said the name
of where they were
was Odiham.
Delighted, sir.

Fat, pale chap
seemed dissatisfied;
snatched a map
from those inside.
Engine tried
as much as it could
to drown the voices
with throbbing noises.
Man understood
him to say:
We know the way
to the south of France;
but Brodenham
is not in Hants;
we almost came
this way instead

344

He said: I said
Odiham.
Odium: hatred.
Odi: I hate.
ham: ham.
A ridiculous name
in that point of view.

He said: Are you
then a Jew?

He said: No.

He said: Oh;
I thought I'd like to know;
but I can't wait.

JOHN GRAY

PREMATURE EPITAPHS

JACOB EPSTEIN

From life's grim nightmare he is now released
Who saw in every face the lurking beast.
'A loss to Art', say friends both proud and loyal,
'A loss', say others, 'to the Café Royal'.

LLOYD GEORGE

Count not his broken pledges as a crime:
He MEANT them, HOW he meant them—at the time.

ANON

THE HARDSHIP OF ACCOUNTING

Never ask of money spent
Where the spender thinks it went.
Nobody was ever meant
To remember or invent
What he did with every cent.

ROBERT FROST

NOT ALL THERE

I turned to speak to God
About the world's despair;
But to make bad matters worse
I found God wasn't there.

God turned to speak to me
(Don't anybody laugh);
God found I wasn't there—
At least not over half.

ROBERT FROST

AN IMPORTER

Mrs Someone's been to Asia.
What she brought back would amaze ye.
Bamboos, ivories, jades and lacquers,
Devil-scaring firecrackers,
Recipes for tea with butter,
Sacred rigmaroles to mutter,
Subterfuge for saving faces,
A developed taste in vases,
Arguments too stale to mention
'Gainst American invention—
Most of all the mass production

346

Destined to prove our destruction.
What are telephones, skyscrapers,
Safety razors, Sunday papers
But the silliest evasion
Of the truths we owe an Asian?
But the best of her exhibit
Was a prayer machine from Tibet
That by brook power in the garden
Kept repeating Pardon, pardon;
And as picturesque machinery
Beat a sundial in the scenery—
The most primitive of engines
Mass producing with a vengeance.
Teach those Asians mass production?
Teach your grandmother egg suction.

ROBERT FROST

THE PERSIAN VERSION

Truth-loving Persians do not dwell upon
The trivial skirmish fought near Marathon.
As for the Greek theatrical tradition
Which represents that summer's expedition
Not as a mere reconnaissance in force
By three brigades of foot and one of horse
(Their left flank covered by some obsolete
Light craft detached from the main Persian fleet)
But as a grandiose, ill-starred attempt
To conquer Greece—they treat it with contempt;
And only incidentally refute
Major Greek claims, by stressing what repute
The Persian monarch and the Persian nation
Won by this salutary demonstration:
Despite a strong defence and adverse weather
All arms combined magnificently together.

ROBERT GRAVES

PHILATELIST ROYAL

The Philatelist Royal
Was always too loyal
To say what he honestly
Thought of Philately.

Must it rank as a Science?
Then he had more reliance
(As he told the press wittily),
On Royal Philately
Than on all your geologies
All your psychologies,
Bacteriologies,
Physics and such.
It was honester, much,
Free of mere speculations
And doubtful equations
So therefore more true
From a pure science view
Than other school courses;
For Nature's blind forces
Here alone, they must own,
Played no meddlesome part.
It was better than Art:
It enforced education,
It strengthened the nation
In the arts of mensuration
And colour-discrimination,
In cleanliness, in hope,
In use of the microscope,
In mercantile transactions
In a love of abstractions,
In geography and history.
It was a noble mystery.

348

So he told them again
That Philately's reign,
So mild and humane,
Would surely last longer
Would surely prove stronger
Than the Glory of Greece,
Than the Grandeur of Rome.
It brought goodwill and peace
Wherever it found a home.
It was more democratic,
More full, more ecstatic,
Than the Bible, the Bottle,
The Complete Works of Aristotle,
And worthierer and betterer
And etceterier and etcetera.

The Philatelist Royal
Was always too loyal
To say what he honestly
Thought of Philately.

ROBERT GRAVES

FRAGMENT FROM THE ELIZABETHANS

PARACELSUS (*entering hurriedly*):
I am become a frightful Bloody murtherer:
Meeting my grandam in the buttery hatch,
I hackt, forsooth, and hewed her jauntilie,
And cast her reeking fragments on the air.
(*Exit, pursued by a Cow.*)

W. BRIDGES-ADAMS

ON SOME SOUTH AFRICAN NOVELISTS

You praise the firm restraint with which they write—
I'm with you there, of course:
They use the snaffle and the curb all right,
But where's the bloody horse?

ROY CAMPBELL

HEADLINE HISTORY

Grave Charge in Mayfair Bathroom Case;
Roman Remains for Middle West;
Golfing Bishop Calls for Prayers;
How Murdered Bride was Dressed;

Boxer Insures his Joie-de-Vivre;
Duchess Denies that Vamps are Vain;
Do Women make Good Wives?
Giant Airship over Spain;

Soprano Sings for Forty Hours;
Cocktail Bar on Mooring Mast;
'Noise, more Noise!' Poet's Last Words;
Compulsory Wireless Bill is Passed;

Alleged Last Trump Blown Yesterday;
Traffic Drowns Call to Quick and Dead;
Cup Tie Crowd sees Heavens Ope;
'Not End of World,' says Well-Known Red.

WILLIAM PLOMER

UP TO DATE

Christ, wha'd ha'e been Chief Rabbi gin he lik't,
Wi publicans and sinners did foregether,
But, losh! the publicans noo are Pharisees,
And I'm no shair o' maist the sinners either.

HUGH MACDIARMID

MACAVITY: THE MYSTERY CAT

Macavity's a Mystery Cat: he's called the Hidden Paw—
For he's the master criminal who can defy the Law.
He's the bafflement of Scotland Yard, the Flying
    Squad's despair:
For when they reach the scene of crime—*Macavity's
    not there!*

Macavity, Macavity, there's no one like Macavity,
He's broken every human law, he breaks the law of
    gravity.
His powers of levitation would make a fakir stare,
And when you reach the scene of crime—*Macavity's
    not there!*
You may seek him in the basement, you may look up in
    the air—
But I tell you once and once again, *Macavity's not there!*

Macavity's a ginger cat, he's very tall and thin;
You would know him if you saw him, for his eyes are
    sunken in.
His brow is deeply lined with thought, his head is highly
    domed;
His coat is dusty from neglect, his whiskers are uncombed.
He sways his head from side to side, with movements
    like a snake;
And when you think he's half asleep, he's always wide
    awake.

Macavity, Macavity, there's no one like Macavity,
For he's a fiend in feline shape, a monster of depravity.
You may meet him in a by-street, you may see him in
    the square—
But when a crime's discovered, then *Macavity's not
    there!*

He's outwardly respectable. (They say he cheats at cards.)
And his footprints are not found in any file of Scotland
    Yard's.
And when the larder's looted, or the jewel-case is rifled,
Or when the milk is missing, or another Peke's been
    stifled,
Or the greenhouse glass is broken, and the trellis past
    repair—
Ay, there's the wonder of the thing! *Macavity's not
    there!*

And when the Foreign Office find a Treaty's gone astray,
Or the Admiralty lose some plans and drawings by the
    way,
There may be a scrap of paper in the hall or on the stair—
But it's useless to investigate—*Macavity's not there!*
And when the loss has been disclosed, the Secret Service
    say:
'It *must* have been Macavity!'—but he's a mile away.
You'll be sure to find him resting, or a-licking of his
    thumbs,
Or engaged in doing complicated long division sums.

Macavity, Macavity, there's no one like Macavity,
There never was a Cat of such deceitfulness and suavity.
He always has an alibi, and one or two to spare:
At whatever time the deed took place—MACAVITY
    WASN'T THERE!
And they say that all the Cats whose wicked deeds are
    widely known
(I might mention Mungojerrie, I might mention
    Griddlebone)
Are nothing more than agents for the Cat who all the
    time
Just controls their operations: the Napoleon of Crime.

T. S. ELIOT

SKIMBLESHANKS: THE RAILWAY CAT

There's a whisper down the line at 11.39
When the Night Mail's ready to depart,
Saying 'Skimble where is Skimble has he gone to hunt
    the thimble?
We must find him or the train can't start.'
All the guards and all the porters and the stationmaster's
    daughters
They are searching high and low,
Saying 'Skimble where is Skimble for unless he's very
    nimble
Then the Night Mail just can't go.'
At 11.42 then the signal's nearly due
And the passengers are frantic to a man—
Then Skimble will appear and he'll saunter to the rear:
He's been busy in the luggage van!
       He gives one flash of his glass-green eyes
         And the signal goes 'All Clear!'
       And we're off at last for the northern part
         Of the Northern Hemisphere!

You may say that by and large it is Skimble who's in
    charge
Of the Sleeping Car Express.
From the driver and the guards to the bagmen playing
    cards
He will supervise them all, more or less.
Down the corridor he paces and examines all the faces
Of the travellers in the First and in the Third;
He establishes control by a regular patrol
And he'd know at once if anything occurred.
He will watch you without winking and he sees what
    you are thinking
And it's certain that he doesn't approve

Of hilarity and riot, so the folk are very quiet
When Skimble is about and on the move.
> You can play no pranks with Skimbleshanks!
> He's a Cat that cannot be ignored;
> So nothing goes wrong on the Northern Mail
> When Skimbleshanks is aboard.

Oh it's very pleasant when you have found your little den
With your name written up on the door.
And the berth is very neat with a newly folded sheet
And there's not a speck of dust on the floor.
There is every sort of light—you can make it dark or
> bright;
There's a handle that you turn to make a breeze.
There's a funny little basin you're supposed to wash
> your face in
And a crank to shut the window if you sneeze.
Then the guard looks in politely and will ask you very
> brightly
'Do you like your morning tea weak or strong?'
But Skimble's just behind him and was ready to remind
> him,
For Skimble won't let anything go wrong.
> And when you creep into your cosy berth
> And pull up the counterpane,
> You ought to reflect that it's very nice
> To know that you won't be bothered by mice—
> You can leave all that to the Railway Cat,
> The Cat of the Railway Train!

In the watches of the night he is always fresh and
> bright;
Every now and then he has a cup of tea
With perhaps a drop of Scotch while he's keeping on the
> watch,
Only stopping here and there to catch a flea.

You were fast asleep at Crewe and so you never knew
That he was walking up and down the station;
You were sleeping all the while he was busy at Carlisle,
Where he greets the stationmaster with elation.
But you saw him at Dumfries, where he speaks to the police
If there's anything they ought to know about:
When you get to Gallowgate there you do not have to
    wait—
For Skimbleshanks will help you to get out!
      He gives you a wave of his long brown tail
        Which says: 'I'll see you again!
      You'll meet without fail on the Midnight Mail
        The Cat of the Railway Train.'

T. S. ELIOT

JUST A SMACK AT AUDEN

Waiting for the end, boys, waiting for the end.
What is there to be or do?
What's become of me or you?
Are we kind or are we true?
Sitting two and two, boys, waiting for the end.

Shall I build a tower, boys, knowing it will rend
Crack upon the hour, boys, waiting for the end?
Shall I pluck a flower, boys, shall I save or spend?
All turns sour, boys, waiting for the end.

Shall I send a wire, boys? Where is there to send?
All are under fire, boys, waiting for the end.
Shall I turn a sire, boys? Shall I choose a friend?
The fat is in the pyre, boys, waiting for the end.

Shall I make it clear, boys, for all to apprehend,
Those that will not hear, boys, waiting for the end,
Knowing it is near, boys, trying to pretend,
Sitting in cold fear, boys, waiting for the end?

Shall we send a cable, boys, accurately penned,
Knowing we are able, boys, waiting for the end,
Via the Tower of Babel, boys? Christ will not ascend.
He's hiding in his stable, boys, waiting for the end.

Shall we blow a bubble, boys, glittering to distend,
Hiding from our trouble, boys, waiting for the end?
When you build on rubble, boys, Nature will append
Double and re-double, boys, waiting for the end.

Shall we make a tale, boys, that things are sure to mend,
Playing bluff and hale, boys, waiting for the end?
It will be born stale, boys, stinking to offend,
Dying ere it fail, boys, waiting for the end.

Shall we go all wild, boys, waste and make them lend,
Playing at the child, boys, waiting for the end?
It has all been filed, boys, history has a trend,
Each of us enisled, boys, waiting for the end.

What was said by Marx, boys, what did he perpend?
No good being sparks, boys, waiting for the end.
Treason of the clerks, boys, curtains that descend,
Lights becoming darks, boys, waiting for the end.

Waiting for the end, boys, waiting for the end.
Not a chance of blend, boys, things have got to tend.
Think of those who vend, boys, think of how we wend,
Waiting for the end, boys, waiting for the end.

WILLIAM EMPSON

CHARD WHITLOW

(*Mr Eliot's Sunday Evening Postscript*)

As we get older we do not get any younger.
Seasons return, and to-day I am fifty-five,
And this time last year I was fifty-four,
And this time next year I shall be sixty-two.
And I cannot say I should like (to speak for myself)
To see my time over again—if you can call it time:
Fidgeting uneasily under a draughty stair,
Or counting sleepless nights in the crowded tube.

There are certain precautions—though none of them
        very reliable—
Against the blast from bombs and the flying splinter,
But not against the blast from heaven, *vento dei venti*,
The wind within a wind unable to speak for wind;
And the frigid burnings of purgatory will not be touched
By any emollient.
                        I think you will find this put,
Better than I could ever hope to express it,
In the words of Kharma: 'It is, we believe,
Idle to hope that the simple stirrup-pump
Will extinguish hell.'
                        Oh, listeners,
And you especially who have turned off the wireless,
And sit in Stoke or Basingstoke listening appreciatively
        to the silence,
(Which is also the silence of hell) pray, not for your
        skins, but your souls.

And pray for me also under the draughty stair.
As we get older we do not get any younger.

And pray for Kharma under the holy mountain.

HENRY REED

357

FIRST FAMILIES MOVE OVER!

Carry me back to Ole Virginny,
And there I'll meet a lot of people from New York,
There the Ole Marsa of the Hounds is from Smithtown
    or Peapack or Millbrook,
And the mocking bird makes music in the sunshine
    accompanied by the rattling shaker and the
    popping cork.

All up and down the old plantation
Socialites are riding hell-for-leather like witches and
    warlocks,
And there is only one thing that keeps the squirearchy
    from being a genuine reproduction,
Which is that the peasantry's hair is kinky so they
    haven't any forelocks so they can't tug their
    forelocks.

In the evening by the bright light you can hear those
    darkies singing,
How the white folks do enjoy it and call the attention
    of their friends from Piping Rock to the natural
    musical talent of the dusky proletariat.
You can hear these banjos ringing because the hands
    have been ordered to exchange their saxophones
    for banjos,
And they wish they were singing Lookie lookie lookie,
    here comes Cookie, but their instructions are to
    sing Swing Low Sweet Chariot.

Oh what is more beautiful and more Southern than a
    Southern beauty from Philadelphia or Rumson,
And indeed where was Southern beauty before the
    advent of Rubinstein and Elizabeth Arden?
And what is more gracious than a hostess calling you
    you-all in the singular and plural
    indiscriminately,

And what has more local colour than a lovely girl in
    jodhpurs telling you about her gyarrden?

Oh the long happy days spent huntin' or shootin' or
    fishin',
Or in any other sport provided it's lackin' in g's!
Oh the long 'happy evenings spent sniffing jasmine and
    poring over the shiny new family Bible,
And figuring out that after all this is really your
    home because great grandmother Wilkins was a
    Filkins and the Filkinses were related by marriage
    to the Randolphs or the Lees!

So please somebody carry me back to Ole Virginny,
Where gentlemen are gentlemen and a lady is known
    by the product she endorses,
Where the atmosphere is as Southern as an
    advertisement for a medium-priced rye whiskey,
And where the Virginians from Virginia have to ride
    automobiles because the Virginians from Long
    Island are the only ones who can afford to ride
    horses.

OGDEN NASH

HA! ORIGINAL SIN!

Vanity, vanity, all is vanity
That's any fun at all for humanity.
Food is vanity, so is drink,
And undergarments of gossamer pink.
P. G. Wodehouse and long vacations,
Going abroad, and rich relations,
The kind of engagements you want to keep,
A hundred honours, and twelve hours' sleep.
Vanities all—Oh Worra, worra!
Rooted in Sodom and Gomorrah.

Vanity, vanity, all is vanity
That's any fun at all for humanity.
That is the gist of the prophet's case,
From Bishop Cannon to Canon Chase.
The prophets chant and the prophets chatter,
But somehow it never seems to matter,
For the world hangs on to its ancient sanity
And orders another round of vanity.
Then Hey! for Gomorrah! and Nonny! for Sodom!
Marie! the Chanel model for Modom!

OGDEN NASH

CALLING SPRING VII-MMMC

As an old traveller, I am indebted to paper-bound
    thrillers,
Because you travel faster from Cleveland to Terre
    Haute when you travel with a lapful of victims
    and killers.
I am by now an authority on thumbprints and
    fingerprints and even kneeprints,
But there is one mystery I have never been able to
    solve in certain of my invaluable reprints.
I am happily agog over their funerals, which are
    always satisfactorily followed by exhumerals,
But I can't understand why so many of them carry
    their copyright lines in Roman numerals.
I am just as learned as can be,
But if I want to find out when a book was first
    published, I have to move my lips and count on
    my fingers to translate Copyright MCMXXXIII
    into Copyright 1933.
I have a horrid suspicion
That something lies behind the publisher's display of
    erudition.

360

I may be oversensitive to clues,
But I detect a desire to obfuscate and confuse.
Do they think that because a customer cannot
      translate MCMXXXIII into 1933 because he is
      not a classical scholar,
He will therefore assume the book to have been first
      published yesterday and will therefore sooner
      lay down his XXV cents or I/IV of a dollar?
Or do they, straying equally far from the straight and
      narrow,
Think that the scholarly will snatch it because the
      Roman copyright line misleads him to believe it
      the work of Q. Horatius Flaccus or P. Virgilius
      Maro?
Because anybody can make a mistake when dealing
      with MCMs and XLVs and things, even Jupiter,
      ruler of gods and men;
All the time he was going around with IO he
      pronounced it Ten.

OGDEN NASH

SONG OF THE OPEN ROAD

I think that I shall never see
A billboard lovely as a tree.
Indeed, unless the billboards fall
I'll never see a tree at all.

OGDEN NASH

REMINISCENT REFLECTION

When I consider how my life is spent,
I hardly ever repent.

OGDEN NASH

IN WESTMINSTER ABBEY

Let me take this other glove off
   As the *vox humana* swells,
And the beauteous fields of Eden
   Bask beneath the Abbey bells.
Here, where England's statesmen lie,
Listen to a lady's cry.

Gracious Lord, oh bomb the Germans.
   Spare their women for Thy Sake.
And if that is not too easy
   We will pardon Thy Mistake.
But, gracious Lord, whate'er shall be,
Don't let anyone bomb me.

Keep our Empire undismembered
   Guide our Forces by Thy Hand.
Gallant blacks from far Jamaica,
   Honduras and Togoland;
Protect them Lord in all their fights,
And, even more, protect the whites.

Think of what our Nation stands for,
   Books from Boots' and country lanes,
Free speech, free passes, class distinction,
   Democracy and proper drains.
Lord, put beneath Thy special care
One-eighty-nine Cadogan Square.

Although dear Lord I am a sinner,
   I have done no major crime;
Now I'll come to Evening Service
   Whensoever I have the time.
So, Lord, reserve for me a crown,
And do not let my shares go down.

I will labour for Thy Kingdom,
  Help our lads to win the war,
Send white feathers to the cowards
  Join the Women's Army Corps,
Then wash the Steps around Thy Throne
In the Eternal Safety Zone.

Now I feel a little better,
  What a treat to hear Thy Word,
Where the bones of leading statesmen,
  Have so often been interr'd.
And now, dear Lord, I cannot wait
Because I have a luncheon date.

JOHN BETJEMAN

BETJEMAN, 1984

I saw him in the Airstrip Gardens
  (Fahrenheit at 451)
Feeding automative orchids
  With a little plastic bun,
While above his brickwork cranium
  Burned the trapped and troubled sun.

'Where is Piper? Where is Pontefract?
  (Devil take my boiling pate!)
Where is Pam? and where's Myfanwy?
  Don't remind me of the date!
Can it be that I am *really*
  Knocking on for 78?

'In my splendid State Apartment
  Underneath a secret lock
Finger now forbidden treasures
  (Pray for me St Enodoc!):
T.V. plate and concrete lamp-post
  And a single nylon sock.

'Take your ease, pale-haired admirer,
    As I, half the century saner,
Pour a vintage Mazawattee
    Through the Marks and Spencer strainer
In a *genuine* British Railways
    (Luton made) cardboard container.

'Though they say my verse-compulsion
    Lacks an interstellar drive,
Reading Beverley and Daphne
    Keeps *my* sense of words alive.
Lord, but *how* much beauty was there
    Back in 1955!'

CHARLES CAUSLEY

PARTIAL COMFORT

Whose love is given over-well
Shall look on Helen's face in hell,
Whilst they whose love is thin and wise
May view John Knox in Paradise.

DOROTHY PARKER

THEOLOGICAL LIMERICK

There was a young man of Mauritius
Who said 'I'm becoming suspicious.
    It was God let us in
    For Original Sin—
If so, the whole system is vicious'.

T. LINDSAY

SHORTER AUDENS

When Statesmen gravely say 'We must be realistic',
The chances are they're weak and, therefore,
      pacifistic,
But when they speak of Principles, look out: perhaps
Their generals are already poring over maps.

Why are the public buildings so high? How come you
      don't know?
Why, that's because the spirits of the public are so
      low.

EPITAPH FOR THE UNKNOWN SOLDIER

To save your world, you asked this man to die:
Would this man, could he see you now, ask why?

PARABLE

The watch upon my wrist
Would soon forget that I exist,
If it were not reminded
By days when I forget to wind it.

SIR RIDER HAGGARD

Sir Rider Haggard,
Was completely staggered
When his bride-to-be
Announced 'I AM SHE!'

                    W. H. AUDEN

EPITAPH

Stavro's dead. A truant vine
Grows out of him at either end
Like muscles through the trunk and spine
For wine was Stavro's closest friend.

Up through the barrel of the chest
To scatter on his polished dome
A vine-leaf from the poet's crown.
The pint-pot was his only home.

Out of this confusing paste
The best of us are only made,
Sleep and sloth and wine were his
Who drank and drank and never paid.

Beauty vomit truth and waste
Somehow joined to give him grace
Who clasped the sky's blue demijohn
Drunk, in a drowning man's embrace.

Silenus of these olive-groves
He broached a wine-dark universe
And tasted on the crater's brim
Mother lover hearth and nurse.

The vulgar grape his earthly task:
Wine was a cradle, muse and guide,
Till body like some leather flask
Matured a laughing sun inside.

His bounty was life's usufruct:
Such lips to lay at nature's breast
With earth below and sky above,
Till tapsters lay us all to rest.

Stained tablecloths for epitaphs!
Set us full glasses nose to nose!
Good drunkards, pledge him with your laughs
Before the city's taverns close.

LAWRENCE DURRELL

366

BALLAD OF THE OEDIPUS COMPLEX

From Travancore to Tripoli
I trailed the great Imago,
Wherever Freud has followed me
I felt Mama and Pa go.

(The engine loves the driver
And the driver loves his mate,
The mattress strokes the pillow
And the pencil pokes the slate).

I tried to strangle it one day
While sitting in the Lido
But it got up and tickled me
And now I'm all Libido.

My friends spoke to the Censor
And the censor warned the Id
But though they tried to hush things up
They neither of them did.

(The barman loves his potion
And the admiral his barge,
The frogman loves the ocean
And the soldier his discharge).

(The critic loves urbanity
The plumber loves his tool.
The preacher all humanity
The poet loves the fool).

If seven psychoanalysts
On seven different days
Condemned my coloured garters
Or my neo-Grecian stays,

I'd catch a magic constable
And lock him behind bars
To be a warning to all men
Who have mamas and pas.

LAWRENCE DURRELL

COPTIC POEM

A Coptic deputation, going to Ethiopia,
Disappeared up one morning like the ghost in Aubrey

'With a Sweet Odour and a Melodious Twang'.
Who saw them go with their Melodious Odour?

I, said the arrow, the aboriginal arrow,
I saw them go, Coptic and Mellifluous,

Fuzzy-wig, kink-haired, with cocoa-butter shining,
With stoles on poles, sackbuts and silver salvers

Walking the desert ways howling and shining:
A Coptic congregation, red blue and yellow,

With Saints on parchment and stove-pipe hats,
All disappeared up like the ghost in Aubrey

Leaving only a smell of cooking and singing,
Rancid goat-butter and the piss of cats.

LAWRENCE DURRELL

TRIALS OF A TOURIST

It is three o'clock in the morning.
I am in a hurry.
I will have some fried fish.
It does not smell nice.
Bring some coffee now—and some wine.
Where is the toilet? There is a mistake in the bill.
You have charged me too much.
I have left my glasses, my watch and my ring, in the
    toilet.
Bring them.

368

Porter, here is my luggage.
I have only a suitcase and a bag.
I shall take this myself.
Be very careful with that.
Look out! The lock is broken.
Don't forget that.
I have lost my keys.
Help me to close this.
How much do I owe you? I did not know I had to
    pay.
Find me a non-smoking compartment, a corner seat,
    facing the engine.
Put the case on the rack.
Someone has taken my seat.
Can you help me to open the window.
Where is the toilet?
I have left my ticket, my gloves and my glasses in the
    toilet.
Can they be sent on?
Stop! I want to get off again. I have got into the
    wrong train.

Who is speaking?
Wrong number!
I don't understand you.
Do you speak English?
I am an Englishwoman. Does no-one here speak
    English?
Wait. I am looking for a phrase in my book.

My bag has been stolen.
That man is following me everywhere.
Go away. Leave me alone.
I shall call a policeman.

You are mistaken. I didn't do it.
It has nothing to do with me. I have done nothing.

Let me pass. I have paid you enough.
Where is the British Consulate?
Beware!

Bring me some cottonwool.
I think there is a mistake in your calculations.
I do not feel well.
Ring a doctor.

Can you give me something for diarrhoea?
I have a pain. Here.
I have pains all over.
I can't eat.
I do not sleep.
I think I have a temperature.
I have caught a cold.
I have been burnt by the sun.
My skin is smarting. Have you nothing to soothe it?
My nose is bleeding.
I feel giddy.
I keep vomiting.
I have been stung by sea-urchins.
I have been bitten by a dog.
I think I have food-poisoning.
You are hurting me.
I shall stay in bed.
Bring me some brandy—please.
Help!
Fire!
Thief!

ANNE TIBBLE

AFTERNOONS WITH BAEDEKER

ITALIAN

In yonder marble hero's shade
Aunt Drusilla used to sit
With her memories of the Slade
And her water-colour kit.

There, E.V. Lucas lay, well-thumbed, beside her,
Buckling a little in the foreign sun,
While round that dim *Risorgimento* rider
(Claiming some long-forgotten vict'ry won)
The circling pigeons' flight grew ever wider,
Fainter the echos of the midday gun.

Across the square a monsignore
Late for his siesta goes:
The prison scene from *Trovatore*
Dies on a dozen radios.

ENGLISH

In 1910 a royal princess
Contracted measles here;
Last spring a pregnant stewardess
Was found beneath the pier;
Her throat, according to the Press,
Was slit from ear to ear.

In all the years that passed between
These two distressing dates
Our only tragedy has been
The raising of the rates,
Though once a flying-bomb was seen
Far out across the straits.

Heard on this coast, the music of the spheres
Would sound like something from *The Gondoliers.*

FRENCH

I shall not linger in that draughty square
Attracted by the art-nouveau hotel
Nor ring in vain the concierge's bell
And then, engulfed by a profound despair
That finds its echoes in the passing trains,
Sit drinking in the café, wondering why,
Maddened by love, a butcher at Versailles
On Tuesday evening made to jump his brains.
Nor shall I visit the Flamboyant church,
Three stars in Michelin, yet by some strange fluke
Left unrestored by Viollet-le-Duc,
To carry out some long-desired research.
Too well I know the power to get one down
Exerted by this grey and shuttered town.

OSBERT LANCASTER

HEALTH AND FITNESS

Bruised by the masseur's final whack,
The patient lay without a sound;
Then, coming to, he hit him back.
Now masseur's in the cold, cold ground.

J. B. MORTON

SOME FRENCHMEN

Monsieur Etienne de Silhouette
    Was slim and uniformly black;
His profile was superb, and yet
    He vanished when he turned his back.

Humane and gaunt, precise and tall
    Was Docteur J. I. Guillotin;
He had one tooth, diagonal
    And loose, which, when it fell, spelled *fin*.

372

André Marie Ampere, a spark,
  Would visit other people's homes
And gobble volts until the dark
  Was lit by his resisting ohms.

Another type, Daguerre (Louis),
  In silver salts would soak his head,
Expose himself to light, and be
  Developed just in time for bed.

JOHN UPDIKE

FROM A CHEERFUL ALPHABET

APPLE
Since Time began, such alphabets begin
With Apple, source of Knowledge and of Sin.
My child, take heart: the fruit that undid Man
Brought out as well the best in Paul Cézanne.

COG
Not for him the darkly planned
  Ambiguities of flesh.
His maker gave him one command:
  Mesh.

JACK
A card, a toy, a hoist,
a flag, a stay, a fruit,
a sailor, John, a pot,
a rabbit, knife, and boot;
o'lantern, in-the-box
or -pulpit, Ketch, a daw,
a-dandy, of-all-trades,
anapes, an ass, a straw.

MIRROR

When you look	kool uoy nehW
into a mirror	rorrim a otni
it is not	ton si ti
yourself you see,	,ees uoy flesruoy
but a kind	dnik a tub
of apish error	rorre hsipa fo
posed in fearful	lufraef ni desop
symmetry.	.yrtemmys

VACUUM CLEANER

This humming broom, with more aplomb
Than tracts by A. Camus,
Refutes the ancient axiom
That Nothing has no use.

JOHN UPDIKE

BEOWULF

So, bored with dragons, he lay down to sleep,
Locking for good his massive hoard of words
(Discuss and illustrate), forgetting now
The hope of heathens, muddled thoughts on fate.

Councils would have to get along without him:
The peerless prince had taken his last bribe
(*Lif is Læne*); useless now the byrnie
Hard and hand-locked, fit for a baseball catcher.

Only with Grendel was he man-to-man;
Grendel's dam was his only sort of woman
(Weak conjugation). After they were gone
How could he stand the bench-din, the yelp-word?

Someone has told us this man was a hero.
Must we then reproduce his paradigms,
Trace out his rambling regress to his forbears
(An instance of Old English harking-back)?

KINGSLEY AMIS

374

LINES
inspired by the controversy on the value or otherwise of Old English studies

Our Norman betters
Taught English letters
To bathe in the fresh
Warm springs of the south
So turn your backs on
Anglo-Saxon
The þ in the flesh,
The æ in the mouth.

ANTHONY BURGESS

THOUGHTS ABOUT THE PERSON FROM PORLOCK

Coleridge received the Person from Porlock
And ever after called him a curse,
Then why did he hurry to let him in?
He could have hid in the house.

It was not right of Coleridge in fact it was wrong
(But often we all do wrong)
As the truth is I think he was already stuck
With Kubla Khan.

He was weeping and wailing: I am finished, finished,
I shall never write another word of it,
When along comes the Person from Porlock
And takes the blame for it.

It was not right, it was wrong,
But often we all do wrong.

May we enquire the name of the Person from Porlock?
Why, Porson, didn't you know?
He lived at the bottom of Porlock Hill
So had a long way to go,

He wasn't much in the social sense
Though his grandmother was a Warlock,
One of the Rutlandshire ones I fancy
And nothing to do with Porlock,

And he lived at the bottom of a hill as I said
And had a cat named Flo,
And had a cat named Flo.

I long for the Person from Porlock
To bring my thoughts to an end,
I am growing impatient to see him,
I think of him as a friend,

Often I look out of the window
Often I run to the gate
I think, he will come this evening,
I think it is rather late.

I am hungry to be interrupted
For ever and ever amen
O Person from Porlock come quickly
And bring my thoughts to an end.

STEVIE SMITH

I LOVE . . . .

I love the English country scene
But sometimes think there's too much Hooker's green,
Especially in August, when the flowers that might
     have lent a
Lightness, don't; being gamboge or magenta.

STEVIE SMITH

SOME ARE BORN

Some are born to peace and joy
And some are born to sorrow
But only for a day as we
Shall not be here tomorrow.

STEVIE SMITH

NAMES

A, a noble failure, turns his critical wits on B,
Who has sold out to Fleet Street, Wardour Street,
Bouverie Street and Kingsway, whose name is on
Posters and television screens and a number of lips.

B, an ignoble success, patronises A (good work in the
Provinces, lots of children, rarely answers B's long
Witty letters. . .), whose name is occasionally seen at
The foot of a stringent review in a non-paying organ.

Meanwhile the rest of the alphabet smile to themselves,
Who never write anything, who only work five days a
Week, eight hours a day, who are assured of a pension,
Whose names are on monthly cheques, who have
    succeeded.

D. J. ENRIGHT

2001: THE TENNYSON/HARDY POEM

When I am old and long turned gray
And enjoy the aura of being eighty,
I may see the dawn of that critical day
When my lightest verse will seem quite weighty.
I shall live somewhere far away,
Where the illiterate birds are nesting.
To pilgrim admirers my wife will say:
        Ewart is resting.

Instead of the heedless sensual play
And the youthful eyes of love and brightness
I shall see critics who kneel and pray
In homage—I shan't dispute their rightness—
And Supplements keen to seem okay
Will flatter me with fulsome pieces.
Scholars will put it another way:
        Ewart's a thesis.

When the aching back and the bleary eye
And the dimness and the rationed drinking,
The cold unease of the earth and sky,
Leave me no pleasures except thinking
I shall be warmed (but what will be 'I'?)
With the awe inspired by what's Jurassic,
And people will say, before I die:
        Ewart's a classic.

Soon comes the day when the stream runs dry
And the boat runs back as the tide is turning,
The voice once strong no more than a sigh
By the hearth where the fire is scarcely burning.
Stiff in my chair like a children's guy,
Simply because I have no seniors
The literati will raise the cry:
        Ewart's a genius!

GAVIN EWART

LAST LAUCH

The Minister said it wad dee,
the cypress bush I plantit.
But the bush grew til a tree,
naething dauntit.

Hit's growin, stark and heich,
derk and straucht and sinister,
kirkyairdie-like and dreich.
But whaur's the Minister?

DOUGLAS YOUNG

A CONSUMER'S REPORT

The name of the product I tested is *Life*,
I have completed the form you sent me
And understand that my answers are confidential.

I had it as a gift,
I didn't feel much while using it,
in fact I think I'd have liked to be more excited.
It seemed gentle on the hands
But left an embarrassing deposit behind.
It was not economical
And I have used much more than I thought
(I suppose I have about half left
but it's difficult to tell)—
although the instructions are fairly large
there are so many of them
I don't know which to follow, especially
as they seem to contradict each other.
I'm not sure such a thing
should be put in the way of children—
It's difficult to think of a purpose
for it. One of my friends says
it's just to keep its maker in a job.
Also the price is much too high.
Things are piling up so fast,
after all, the world got by
for a thousand million years
without this, do we need it now?
(Incidentally, please ask your man
to stop calling me 'the respondent',
I don't like the sound of it).
There seems to be a lot of different labels,
sizes and colours should be uniform,
the shape is awkward, it's waterproof
but not heat resistant, it doesn't keep
yet it's very difficult to get rid of:

whenever they make it cheaper they seem
to put less in—if you say you don't
want it, then it's delivered anyway.
I'd agree it's a popular product,
it's got into the language; people
even say they're on the side of it.
Personally I think it's overdone,
a small thing people are ready
to behave badly about. I think
we should take it for granted. If its
experts are called philosophers or market
researchers or historians, we shouldn't
care. We are the consumers and the last
law makers. So, finally, I'd buy it.
But the question of a 'best buy'
I'd like to leave until I get
The competitive product you said you'd send.

PETER PORTER

CANEDOLIA

an off-concrete scotch fantasia

Oa! hoy! awe! ba! mey!

who saw?
rhu saw rum. garve saw smoo. nigg saw tain. lairg saw
lagg. rigg saw eigg. largs saw haggs. tongue saw luss.
mull saw yell. stoer saw strone. drem saw muck. gask
saw noss. unst saw cults. echt saw banff. weem saw
wick. trool saw twatt.

how far?
from largo to lunga from joppa to skibo from ratho to
shona from ulva to minto from tinto to tolsta from
soutra to marsco from braco to barra from alva to stobo
from fogo to fada from gigha to gogo from kelso to
stroma from hirta to spango.

380

what is it like there?
och it's freuchie, it's faifley, it's wamphray, it's frandy,
it's sliddery.

what do you do?
we foindle and fungle, we bonkle and meigle and max-
poffle. we scotstarvit, armit, wormit and even whifflet.
we play at crossstobs, leuchars, gorbals and finfan. we
scavaig, and there's aye a bit of tilquhilly. if it's wet,
treshnish and mishnish.

what is the best of the country?
blinkbonny! airgold! thundergay!

and the worst?
scrishven, shiskine, scrabster, and snizort.

listen! what's that?
catacol and wauchope, never heed them.

tell us about last night
well, we had a wee ferintosh and we lay on the quiraing.
it was pure strontian!

but who was there?
petermoidart and craigenkenneth and cambusputtock
and ecclemuchty and corrihulish and balladolly and
altnacanny and clauchanvrechan and stronachlochan
and auchenlachar and tighnacrankie and tilliebruaich
and killieharra and invervannach and achnatudlem and
machrishellach and inchtamurchan and auchterfechan
and kinlochculter and ardnawhallie and invershuggle

and what was the toast?
schiehallion! schiehallion! schiehallion!

EDWIN MORGAN

THE COMPUTER'S
FIRST CHRISTMAS CARD

jollymerry
hollyberry
jollyberry
merryholly
happyjolly
jollyjelly
jellybelly
bellymerry
hollyheppy
jollyMolly
marryJerry
merryHarry
hoppyBarry
heppyJarry
boppyheppy
berryjorry
jorryjolly
moppyjelly
Mollymerry
Jerryjolly
bellyboppy
jorryhoppy
hollymoppy
Barrymerry
Jarryhappy
happyboppy
boppyjolly
jollymerry
merrymerry
merrymerry
merryChris

                    ammerryasa
                    Chrismerry
                    asMERRYCHR
                    YSANTHEMUM

                              EDWIN MORGAN

              RHYMING PROPHECY
              FOR A NEW YEAR

        written for 1956 but still all-too serviceable

Fog and snow for New Year's greeting, ban on all
    domestic heating,
Russia leave a UNO meeting, threat of war in Middle
    East.
Feb. Australian Test team chosen, everything but
    wages frozen,
Eggs at two pounds ten a dozen, all war criminals
    released.

March—a scream for science teachers, eighteen horses
    fall at Bechers,
Oxford sink in Chiswick Reach as Cambridge win in
    record time.
April Budget, banks stop lending, Chancellor remains
    unbending,
'Money is not made for spending', hire purchase made
    a crime.

Summer—one long string of crises, catastrophic rise in
    prices.
Thousands die from poisoned ices, crops destroyed by
    storm and pests.
Bread and meat go back on ration, fearful smash at
    Croydon station,
Living up to expectation, England lose the first four
    Tests.

                    383

Autumn Budget doubles taxes, U.S.A. and Soviet
    Axis,
Export wanes and Import waxes, Oval triumph—
    Rain. No Play.
Cabinet re-shuffle places, strictly on an Old Boy basis,
Same old names and same old faces; M.P.'s strike for
    higher pay.

LEONARD COOPER

REFLECTIONS ON ICE-BREAKING

        Candy
        Is dandy
        But liquor
        Is quicker.

OGDEN NASH

Index of First Lines

(The Useful Couplets on p. 71, the Occasional Lapses on pp. 159–162, and the Potted Poems on p. 251, are not indexed)

Index of Authors
Parodied or Imitated

It is not always possible to say that the parodist had one particular poem in mind. Bayard Taylor's *Ballad of Hiram Hover*, for example, echoes *The Maids of Attitash* as well as *The Bridal of Pennacook*; and in *Lovers, and a Reflection* Calverley mingles the styles of Jean Ingelow and William Morris. Sometimes the poem parodied is itself a parody: thus Canning's *Elderly Gentleman*, of which J. A. Morgan's *Malum Opus* is a partial translation, is a parody of Nicholas Rowe. At other times, the comic writer borrows and distorts a theme without imitating the manner of the original. The *Story of Prince Agib* certainly owes something to the *Persian Eclogues*, but scarcely enough to make one call it a parody. The references given below are meant to help the reader to find his way about the book: they are not intended to be dogmatic assertions.